THE
TELEVISION
SERIES

D1425643

Jimmy Perry
and David Croft

Published in our
centenary year
∽ **2004** ∽

THE
TELEVISION
SERIES

series editors

SARAH CARDWELL
JONATHAN BIGNELL

SIMON MORGAN-RUSSELL

Jimmy Perry and David Croft

Manchester University Press

MANCHESTER AND NEW YORK

distributed exclusively in the USA by Palgrave

Published by Manchester University Press
Oxford Road, Manchester M13 9NR, UK
and Room 400, 175 Fifth Avenue, New York, NY 10010, USA
www.manchesteruniversitypress.co.uk

Distributed exclusively in the USA by
Palgrave, 175 Fifth Avenue, New York, NY 10010, USA

Distributed exclusively in Canada by
UBC Press, University of British Columbia, 2029 West Mall,
Vancouver, BC, Canada V6T 1Z2

British Library Cataloguing-in-Publication Data
A catalogue record for this book is available from the British Library

Library of Congress Cataloging-in-Publication Data applied for

ISBN 0 7190 6555 0 *hardback*
  0 7190 6556 9 *paperback*

First published 2004

13 12 11 10 09 08 07 06 05 04   10 9 8 7 6 5 4 3 2 1

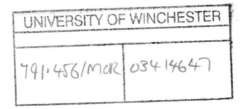
Typeset in Scala with Meta display
by Koinonia, Manchester
Printed in Great Britain
by Bell & Bain Limited, Glasgow

Contents

List of illustrations

General editors' preface

Television is part of our everyday experience, and is one of the most significant features of our cultural lives today. Yet its practitioners and its artistic and cultural achievements remain relatively unacknowledged. The books in this series aim to remedy this by addressing the work of major television writers and creators. Each volume provides an authoritative and accessible guide to a particular practitioner's body of work, and assesses his or her contribution to television over the years. Many of the volumes draw on original sources, such as specially conducted interviews and archive material, and all of them list relevant bibliographic sources and provide full details of the programmes discussed. The author of each book makes a case for the importance of the work considered therein, and the series includes books on neglected or overlooked practitioners alongside well-known ones.

In comparison with some related disciplines, Television Studies scholarship is still relatively young, and the series aims to contribute to establishing the subject as a vigorous and evolving field. This series provides resources for critical thinking about television. Whilst maintaining a clear focus on the writers, on the creators and on the programmes themselves, the books in this series also take account of key critical concepts and theories in Television Studies. Each book is written from a particular critical or theoretical perspective, with reference to pertinent issues, and the approaches included in the series are varied and sometimes dissenting. Each author explicitly outlines the reasons for his or her particular focus, methodology or perspective. Readers are invited to think critically about the subject matter and approach covered in each book.

Although the series is addressed primarily to students and scholars of television, the books will also appeal to the many people who are interested in how television programmes have been commissioned, made and enjoyed. Since television has been so much a part of personal and public life in the twentieth and twenty-first centuries, we hope that the series will engage with, and sometimes challenge, a broad and diverse readership.

Sarah Cardwell
Jonathan Bignell

Preface

The date, according to Mark Lewisohn's *Radio Times Guide to TV Comedy*, was 21 March 1973, two weeks shy of my seventh birthday. My parents were 'having their alterations done' and we had moved into my grandparents' house further along the same street. I remember very clearly settling down on the floor in front of the television to watch the first episode of a new situation comedy on BBC 1, with all the members of my family present, and hearing for the first time the now distinctive chorus of till-ringing, lift-operating and parcel-thumping that is the signature tune of *Are You Being Served?* It seems odd to me that I should have such a clear memory of the circumstances surrounding this event and yet no recollection of any of the episode's details; a minimum of research turns up the fact that the episode was called 'Dear Sexy Knickers' – surely a distinctively scandalous topic for a six-year-old boy. Twenty years later, and a continent apart, I was interviewed for an academic job at a university to teach early British literature. At some point during the process a senior faculty member specialising in the British Romantic poets made a lofty pronouncement about the work of William Wordsworth and then, tipping me a wink, he added 'And I am unanimous in that!' I laughed to indicate that I got the joke. I also got the job.

I don't suppose that these anecdotes would stand much sustained critical analysis, but they do suggest some interesting points about the roles that sitcom can play in our lives. Even if we are not writers, critics, students or diehard fans of situation comedy, it can, nevertheless, work its way into our experience as much as any other cultural stimulus. Like many other British families of the 1970s, my family turned on the television for children's programming and turned it off when we went to bed; this is not to suggest we were a family (or nation) of slavish 'telly addicts' necessarily, but to recognise that television represented a continuous narrative in many British households, often playing in the background of domestic events, and woven inextricably with the other discourses that structure our lives. I'm not old enough to remember the Kennedy assassination, but I recall exactly where I was the night *Coronation Street*'s Renee Roberts was killed in a car accident. Television also, as my second anecdote suggests, structures the ways in which others perceive us. Which is more odd – the fact that an august Romantic scholar in the United States would assume that, as a Brit, I would automatically recognise a catch-phrase from a 1970s British sitcom, or the fact that I did?

In writing this book I made a number of decisions that are worth mentioning here. I have not considered every sitcom episode co-written by Perry and Croft. This was, in part, a result of availability: some of their series are more readily available on VHS, DVD, or UK Gold than others – *You Rang, M'Lord?*, in fact, has not been released for public viewing. But since this book was never to be an exhaustive 'episode guide', I chose to limit myself to close analysis of a few key episodes, particularly those early in each series when Perry and Croft's concept was at its freshest. I hope, then, to have achieved an appropriate balance between a consideration of a sufficient range of each of the sitcoms and a closer analysis of individual episodes and scenes. I have tried to restrict my close analysis to episodes that are readily available, though readers may have difficulty tracking down copies of *You Rang, M'Lord?* Although scripts have been published for *Dad's Army*, I have chosen to transcribe lines from the episodes; this was done partly to remain consistent throughout all four series, but also to represent the sitcoms as they were originally received. In the case of *Dad's Army*, for example, Arthur Lowe's rendition of Captain Mainwaring's lines often deviated from the script. Readers will also find that I have focused on a fairly narrow range of secondary material, which includes theoretical work as well as what we might call 'fan-criticism'. The latter is not necessarily to be derided, since it often provides accurate information unavailable elsewhere; some examples, like Graham McCann's *Dad's Army: The Story of a Classic Television Show*, show good scholarship even if they take a largely uncritical position in response to the series themselves. There is certainly not a large volume of critical analysis of Perry and Croft's work to begin with, though there is a considerable body of scholarship on television studies. By focusing on key articles, and by demonstrating how they operate in context, I hope to have kept the emphasis in this book on Perry and Croft's work.

Finally, I feel compelled to point out that while *Jimmy Perry and David Croft* might be of interest to fans of Perry and Croft's sitcoms, it is principally a work of critical scholarship. Readers will not find here, as I mentioned above, an exhaustive guide to episodes, or a text dependent on insider anecdotes and unqualified celebration. Later in this book I discuss the inability of authors to retain control of a text's meaning once it enters the public domain, and so I should, perhaps, be a little less concerned about my own book's reception. But the opinions of two particular readers are a source of some anxiety to me: those of Jimmy Perry and David Croft themselves. I hope that they feel I have not misrepresented their work too much, that they understand I have undertaken this project from a position of respect for their significant contributions to British television, and that they don't roll their eyes too often if they read it.

All writers owe great debts to those friends and colleagues who have supported them during their writing process. I would like to acknowledge here some individuals important to the writing of *Jimmy Perry and David*

Croft. This book could never have been written without a sabbatical, and I would like to thank the former Chair of the English Department at Bowling Green State University, Thomas L. Wymer, for supporting my proposal, and Donald G. Nieman, Dean of the College of Arts and Sciences, for granting my Faculty Improvement Leave (the state of Ohio's term for a sabbatical). I would like to thank my colleagues in Literature for trusting me enough to offer courses in British television, and the students in those courses for helping me think through ideas and problems. One colleague particularly deserves special mention: Ellen E. Berry and I met weekly during our sabbaticals to discuss each others' work, to provide mutual encouragement and to gossip in cafes – without Ellen's sustaining friendship over the last decade, I would never have made it this far.

I am grateful to the many sources of professional help that enabled this book to be written. Bowling Green State University's Center for Teaching, Learning and Technology was very helpful to me as I negotiated minidisk recorders for interviews and as I prepared illustrations. Linda Meek, in the Department of Romance Languages, very generously allowed me access to a PAL VCR. I would also like to recognise the cheerful and accommodating staff at the British Film Institute, where I spent many, many hours poring over episodes of *You Rang, M'Lord?* Sarah Cardwell has taken a lot of time out of her own work to give me feedback at various points in my project, and the staff at Manchester University Press have been exemplary in their responses to my questions. Other individuals provided help or information: Rob Cope, Su Pollard's PA, very generously provided me with interviews and tapes, and Dave Homewood of the *Dad's Army* Appreciation Society – New Zealand took time to give interesting insights into *It Ain't Half Hot, Mum*. My greatest debt here is to David Croft, who allowed himself to be interviewed – once again – and who very generously sent me a copy of his unpublished autobiography, 'You Have Been Watching', which was invaluable in the preparation of my own book. Thanks again, Mr Croft.

I have benefited immeasurably from the support of friends and family, all of whom deserve a mention: Jerry C. Jaffe Jr (for our many conversations about comedy), David Wall (for his wit and repartee), Mark Nelson (for his loyal friendship), Frederick Zackel (for drawing my attention to Manchester University Press's Television Series in the first place), John Cheall (who I suspect *is* John Shuttleworth), and Jonathan Pollard (for granting me a piece of floor during my research visit to London). My parents, Bob and Margaret Russell, have always supported me during my various unlikely projects. Finally, my wife Kim Greenfield deserves the greatest share of thanks. She *claims* to have a sense of humour, of course, and she did come up with a very funny sketch involving a trampoline, but she doesn't find Perry and Croft's sitcoms at all amusing. I love her in spite of this obvious character flaw, and thank her for putting up with me.

All that remains here is to dedicate this book, with love, to memory of my grandparents: Alderman John Morgan BEM, who taught me the lifelong pleasure that can be taken in language, and Rhoda B. Morgan, with whom I shared countless, golden hours of television viewing.

Introducing the situation comedies of Jimmy Perry and David Croft

A short history of situation comedy

In order properly to situate Jimmy Perry and David Croft's contribution to the genre of situation comedy, it is necessary to trace a brief history of broadcast comedy in Britain from the early days of radio and television through the late 1960s when *Dad's Army* was first transmitted. It is important to recognise, I think, that Perry and Croft's work did not simply emerge in a vacuum, but derived from a sequence of comic traditions, and from the particular circumstances of broadcast media's development. What follows, then, is only a partial history of British broadcast comedy, drawn from a variety of sources that each give more detailed accounts of radio and television history.

In November 1922, the British Broadcasting Company (which became the British Broadcasting Corporation on 1 January 1927) began transmission under the leadership of the BBC's first General Manager, and later Director General, John Reith. Reith's Calvinist morality is frequently cited as a structuring influence on the BBC's ideology (a legacy some might claim still persists), but particularly significant to the BBC's initial broadcast output was his commitment to resist an 'American', commercial model of radio entertainment in favour of an explicitly didactic agenda. Early radio broadcasts were dominated by classical and orchestral musical performance, and the smaller output of spoken word broadcasts was dominated by serious or informative programming. Light entertainment in the 1920s and early 1930s consisted largely of broadcasts of music hall or theatre acts, a mixture of music and comedy that persisted as the standard of the 'variety show'. As Andrew Crisell points out in *An Introductory History of British Broadcasting*, the radio broadcast of music hall acts had significant ramifications for writing and performance. 'Radio simply devoured their material', he remarks, '[t]he two or three routines which in the halls could last them a lifetime now vanished into the ether and could never be used again'.[1] This consumption of available material had several long-term effects, not least the necessary reconceptualisation of comedy writing; in the most immediate sense, however, it resulted in the foundation in 1930 of a variety department within the BBC, and in the production of 'in-house' series such as *Songs from the Shows* (1931) and *Music Hall* (1932). Perhaps the first watershed in comedy broadcasting, though, was *Band Waggon* (1938), cited by many commentators as both an original comic contribution and a significant influence on future writing.[2] The hour-long show was dominated by musical and other variety performances: as Barry Took points out, the comedy sketches featuring Arthur Askey and Richard Murdoch occupied only ten minutes of the show's sixty. These sketches, however, approached the format of situation comedy (Steve Neale and Frank Krutnik suggest that *Band Waggon* 'represented a move towards a comedy of character and situation'), with Askey and Murdoch, putative custodians of the Greenwich Time Signal's 'pips', sharing a flat at the top of the BBC's Broadcasting House.[3] Another development attributed by Neale and Krutnik to *Band Waggon*'s regular broadcast schedule, and to its status as the 'first BBC variety show to use a regular writing team', is the evolution of the running gag and the catchphrase, both important staples in most situation comedies, including those of Perry and Croft.[4]

Most historians of radio cite *ITMA* – the acronym of *It's That Man Again*, which was a reference in common parlance to Adolf Hitler – as the heir to *Band Waggon*, both in its mining of what Crisell dubs a 'radiogenic seam', and in its landmark innovation. The significance of the series, which ran between 1939 and 1948, certainly can't be called into question: Crisell states that '*ITMA* was one of the most popular comedy shows in radio history', even if its 'jokes may now be so dated as to be scarcely comprehensible'.[5] Ultimately, though, *ITMA* contributed less to the development of situation comedy than many of its contemporaries and successors: the show consisted of thirty minutes of fast-paced and often surreal comedy, what scriptwriter Ted Kavanagh referred to as an 'illusion of rather crazy or inverted reality'.[6] In this regard the show was more influential on a tradition of comedy carried through, for example, radio's *Goon Show* (1952–59) and television's *Monty Python's Flying Circus* (1969–74). And despite *ITMA*'s popularity, Paul Alan Taylor suggests that during the war years, broadcast comedy moved away from 'variety' comedy towards models of situation comedy, such as *Ray's a Laugh* (1949–61), *Life with the Lyons* (1950–61), or *The Clitheroe Kid*.[7] Although not a situation comedy, Frank Muir and Dennis Norden's *Take it from Here* is often cited as a source in the development of the genre; the thirty-minute show combined sketches, quick verbal gags and sustained parodies with what Philip French calls 'a marvellously (for its time) insouciant, unsentimental, non-patronising attitude towards its material and its listener'.[8] French goes on to characterise the show as 'calculated heartlessness', escaping the nostalgic inflection of other post-war shows: '*TIFH* was the *New Yorker* to the *Saturday Evening Post* of the warm-hearted family series like *Life with the Lyons*'.[9] Though initially not particularly well received, the show gathered strength, reaching its peak in 1953 with the replacement of the parodies of literary and high cultural topics with a glimpse into the life of a working-class family, 'The Glums': Pa Glum (Jimmy Edwards), his son Ron (Dick Bentley), and Ron's eternal fiancée, Eth (Joy Nichols, June Whitfield). According to French, 'The Glums' began as a parody of radio's familiar 'didactic, instructional playlets', in which '[t]hey were presented as "our ordinary family coping intelligently with life's problems"'.[10] Gradually, however, the role of 'The Glums' in *TIFH* expanded to occupy half of the show, effectively evolving into a self-contained situation comedy within *TIFH*. Although French's adulation of Muir and Norden's show is clear in this essay, he is less convinced of the brilliance of 'The Glums', which, contrary to his assessment of *TIFH*'s original format, he feels relied on 'rib-nudging malapropisms', and which could be 'socially patronising'. He does, however, identify a feature of this situation comedy that connects it both with future expressions of the genre and with some of the critical suggestions covered later in this chapter. For French, '[The Glums] became a sadly touching ménage, trapped by the limitations of their lives and aspirations. Like the figures of Keats's Grecian Urn, for ever would Eth love and Ron not stir'.[11] Both practitioners and critics have commented on the necessary of such limitation in situation comedy: Barry Took, for example, proposes that all successful comedies must have a 'trap' in which the characters exist, 'a little enclosed world where you have to live by the rules', and Mick Eaton, whose essay we will consider in more detail later in this chapter, suggests that the situation comedy's 'formal necessities ... provide the existential circle from which the characters cannot escape'.[12]

Perhaps the most significant contribution made by radio to the development of television situation comedy, however, was *Hancock's Half-Hour* (1954–59), not least because it transferred successfully from the radio to television. The series was innovatory in several ways, and positioned itself against the various types of radio comedy described above: each episode saw a full-length narrative in a distinct situation comedy format rather than the surreal fantasies of *The Goon Show*, and the series' writers, Ray Galton and Alan Simpson, insisted on a level of

'realism' or 'naturalism' that distinguished their writing from that of other radio sitcoms – a distinct contrast with what Peter Goddard has called the 'cosiness' of series like *Life with the Lyons*.[13] It took a little while for this comic philosophy to settle in; Barry Took's *Laughter in the Air* cites Galton and Simpson's desire for a vehicle that was 'non-domestic with no jokes and no funny voices, just relying on caricature and situation humour', but Kenneth Williams – the acknowledged master of the 'funny voice' – was a regular performer in the radio series, and Hancock's installation at the infamous 23 Railway Cuttings, East Cheam only gradually took place.[14] Nevertheless, the comedy of *Hancock's Half-Hour* depended on naturalistic character development. Peter Goddard maintains that Tony Hancock and other regular performers 'were funny because they behaved in familiar ways in situations with which their audience could identify', an assessment borne out by producer Dennis Main Wilson's remark to the BBC's Assistant Head of Variety Productions that this 'purely situational' comedy would 'try to build Tony as a real character in real life surroundings. There will be no "goon" or contrived comedy approaches.'[15] The key component of the comedy, of course, was the development of Tony Hancock's character, the infamous 'Anthony Aloysius St John Hancock II', a tragicomic, Everyman figure, whose legacy persists in British comedy. Eloquently described by a number of critics, Hancock's character is 'lower middle-class … idle, pompous, and tetchy … constantly thwarted by the earthiness of his companions' according to Andrew Crisell, and Peter Black writes that he is possessed of 'seedy grandiloquence and unavailing pretensions' and 'visions of nobler things' destined to be kiboshed by his 'natural bad taste and indolence.'[16] He is a British comic archetype easily traceable through *Steptoe and Son*'s Harold Steptoe and *Fawlty Towers*'s Basil Fawlty to Steve Coogan's Alan Partridge in the present day.

Hancock's Half-Hour is also a milestone in the history of situation comedy because it made a successful transition between radio and television – in fact, the two media overlapped, with television broadcasts beginning in 1956 and the radio series not ending until 1959. A detailed discussion of the rise of television is not appropriate to this book, and has been undertaken by the media historians cited earlier in this chapter, but it is worth quoting, I think, a statistic cited by Andrew Crisell which reveals the shift in popularity from radio to television: '[t]he BBC's average evening [radio] audience in 1949 was almost 9 million: by 1958 it had shrunk to less than 3.5 million, three-quarters of whom had no access to a television set'.[17] The moment in British cultural history that has assumed a legendary, pivotal status in this process is the coronation of Elizabeth II in 1953, the event that prompted many British families (including my own) to acquire their first television sets. *Hancock's Half-Hour* was not the first British situation comedy to appear on television, nor was it the only series to make the transition between radio and television – *Life with the Lyons*, for example, was broadcast as a television situation comedy in 1955. But several historians and critics have identified it both as the 'breakthrough' moment in sitcom's transfer to television, and as the precursor to subsequent examples of the genre.

Peter Goddard maintains that Galton and Simpson's emphasis on 'reality' in the writing for *Hancock's Half-Hour* assured its success as television comedy; unlike the strand of radio comedy dubbed by Crisell as 'radiogenic', which resists easy visual representation, the distinctive naturalism of the characterisation and physical location of *Hancock* seem suited to a visual medium, although Galton and Simpson famously claim that they made very few concessions to writing for television as a medium rather than radio. Goddard's notion of 'realism' needs to be contextualised, however, in relation to what he calls 'sitcom naturalism'.[18] *Life with the Lyons* manifested what might seem like an absurd level of preoccupation with realism: Ben Lyons and his wife Bebe Daniels, American expats living in London, played themselves, as did their children, and the series dramatised real-life events (subject, of course, to some comic exaggeration) – to the extent that when the 'actual' Lyons moved house from Marble Arch to Holland Park, the studio sets matched 'reality as closely as possible, right down to the colour schemes, decorations and furniture'.[19] The important distinction to make between *Hancock* and *Life with the Lyons* is one of audience identification: as Americans living an affluent lifestyle, the Lyons and their meticulously constructed 'reality' were necessarily removed from the social reality of most of their audience; but Hancock, the 'dyspeptic, status-anxious, petit-bourgeois suburbanite', in many ways an outsider looking in on what (he assumed) he was missing, was more immediately recognisable. As Goddard expresses it: '*Hancock's Half-Hour* had become ... a comedy of observation with which viewers were invited to identify and to find believable', or, as Galton and Simpson themselves remark, the series succeeded because they were able to put 'Hancock in the sort of situation where we all feel ineffectual'.[20] An alternative position is argued by Stephen Wagg, who claims that *Hancock*, in fact, lacks a sense of social realism, and that the key to the series' success (and that of 'most other successful sitcoms on British television') is the 'interplay between realistic and romantic notions of the relationships between the social classes'.[21] Both of these readings of the success of *Hancock's Half-Hour* seem entirely feasible; perhaps the most important point made here is that the series introduces issues of class and class conflict that continue to play a significant role in British situation comedy even today.

Hancock's Half-Hour contributed to the evolution of situation comedy in other significant ways that deserve mention, particularly through innovations in production techniques. The first of these is the use of the close-up, a technique that, from today's perspective, seems so intrinsic to television as to lack a specific point of origin. *Hancock* was certainly not the first comedy broadcast on British television to use the close-up: American situation comedies in the 1950s, such as *The Burns and Allen Show* and *I Love Lucy*, used two or three cameras to capture the joke told or enacted but also to capture other characters' facial reactions to the joke. Terry-Thomas, in the BBC's own *How Do You View* (1949–53), used close-up extensively to orchestrate the 'fine-grain comedy that can be touched off by a flicker of an eyebrow, the roll of the eyes, a twitch of the mouth', the sort of technique that any observer of stand-up comedians like Tommy Cooper or Frankie Howerd knows very well.[22] Tony Hancock's undisputed talent was for facial comedy, and Galton and Simpson came to write their scripts for the show in ways that allowed him to showcase this ability. Moreover, as Goddard reports, Hancock's facial comedy prompted innovations in television production. The series' producer, Duncan Wood, 'developed more precise plotting, cutting and camera techniques than had hitherto been necessary in British television comedy'.[23] Lines were broken in half to allow cutting between close-ups of Sid James and Hancock, so that, in Wood's own words: 'Whereas you used to shoot situation comedy on 150 shots in half-an-hour, you were now taking 250 to do the same amount of dialogue ... It was one of the greatest revolutions, I think, reaction as against action'.[24] If this 'revolution' is apparent in situation comedy after *Hancock*, it is put to particularly good use in Perry and Croft's collaborations – in *Dad's Army*, for example, close-ups are used to capture the facial expression of Captain Mainwaring after one of Corporal Jones's improbable suggestions, or Sergeant Wilson's bemused eye-rolling at Mainwaring's pompous pronouncements.

The other breakthrough in production brought about by *Hancock's Half-Hour* was the use of Ampex telerecording for situation comedy. Although the BBC had invested in an Ampex machine in 1958, Asa Briggs reports a reluctance to use it extensively because of the prohibitive cost of videotapes – £100 – which could not be reused once cut. However, at the insistence of Wood and Hancock (who refused to sign his contract), the use of Ampex was authorised in 1959 as an experiment, allowing each episode to be recorded in six takes and enabling changes of scene and costume. The experiment was clearly successful, and 'the new technique proved immediately effective on the screen, and was subsequently used by many other producers, particularly producers of sitcom'.[25]

I have spent some time discussing *Hancock's Half-Hour*, in both its radio and television forms, because of its significance in the development of sitcom. I don't think that Peter Goddard is over-stating the case when he says that the series was responsible for 'popularising and "fixing" situation comedy' as the dominant expression of television comedy.[26] Interviewed by the *Radio Times* in 1958, Frankie Howerd famously announced: 'I now prefer being funny in a situation, rather than just telling jokes. That, after all, isn't fashionable any longer'.[27] Goddard also maintains that 'the indirect influence of *Hancock's Half-Hour* can be traced in almost every subsequent television comedy series', which, while being rather a broad claim, is perhaps true of the next generation of sitcoms in the 1960s, the immediate context for the first of Perry and Croft's situation comedies. Discussions of sitcom in the 1960s inevitably revolve around the comparatively few perceived 'classics' of the genre, but Stephen Wagg's 'Social Class and the Situation Comedy in British Television' reminds us that the 1960s saw around one hundred situation comedies made for British television, expressing what Wagg sees as a significant diversity of interests and settings.[28] Wagg claims that only about half of 1960s sitcoms have a domestic situation, that '[s]traightforward married couples with or without children are on the whole rare and account for only around a dozen sitcoms', and that representation of the 'suburban lower-middle classes' is both scarce and unfavourable.[29] Despite this diversity, however, Wagg is able to identify three dominant themes in British sitcoms of the 1960s: a 'concern, variously expressed, to represent working class life'; 'a marked determination ... to explore the interior life of the different social classes'; and a 'sharper treatment' of the 'issue of social mobility'.[30] All of these themes, arguably, are traceable to *Hancock's Half-Hour*. *Steptoe and Son* (1962–74) is usually identified as *Hancock*'s heir, not least because Galton and Simpson wrote, and Duncan Wood produced, the series. There are obvious thematic connections with *Hancock*, too. Harold Steptoe has aspirations to a 'better', more culturally refined life, as does Hancock; and he explores the possibility of social mobility through a number of doomed 'middle-class' scenarios: amateur dramatics, a badminton club, interior decorating. However, just as Hancock's flights of fancy were inevitably grounded by Sid's earthiness, Harold's aspirations are ultimately undone by his father, Albert. In 'A Star is Born', for example, Harold seeks to escape from his surroundings by taking a part in a local amateur theatre production, invoking

Sean Connery's rise to success and stardom from humble beginnings. By cruel circumstance, Albert also gets a part, and, despite Harold's insistence that his father will ruin the production, becomes the star of the show. The episode concludes with a disillusioned Harold leaving the theatre alone by the stage door and acknowledging his failure: 'I'm just a rag and bone man, and that's all I'll ever be'.

Another sitcom that explored the social mobility of the working classes was Dick Clement and Ian le Frenais's *The Likely Lads* (1964–66), which represented the lives of two factory workers in Newcastle, Bob Ferris and Terry Collier. The dynamic between Bob and Terry is not quite the same as that between Harold and Albert, or Hancock and Sid. Bob aspires to the perceived qualities of middle-class life, and Terry's relentless pragmatism serves as a grounding influence, but, unlike *Steptoe and Son*, *The Likely Lads* and its sequel, *Whatever Happened to The Likely Lads* (1973–74), depict successful social mobility, since Bob manages to escape to the white-collar world, becoming engaged (and subsequently married) to his boss's daughter, Thelma.

Working-class life is perhaps most famously represented, though, in the other touchstone of 1960s British sitcom, Johnny Speight's *Till Death Us Do Part* (1965–75). Asa Briggs suggests that although '[m]ost of the episodes had a nightmarish quality', they nevertheless 'reflected a 1960s society ... which, for all the talk of ideas, was still propped up by prejudices'.[31] Speight's central character was Alf Garnett, a middle-aged East End docker, a working-class Tory, a strong supporter of British royalty, and perhaps the most bigoted character British television has seen. Speight puts Alf in dialogue with his resident daughter and son-in-law, Rita and Mike, the latter of whom is unemployed and – to Alf's disgust – a socialist. *Till Death Us Do Part* articulated what Stephen Wagg has called 'a complex and contradictory politics', one which was often difficult for the audience to read: attacked by both the Left and the Right, the screening of the first episode, 'Pride and Prejudice' attracted 130 letters of complaint.[32] I will return to the controversial politics of *Till Death Us Do Part* in more detail during my discussion of *It Ain't Half Hot, Mum* in Chapter 3.

All of the above-mentioned series were products of the BBC, and Wagg finds little politically radical potential in ITV's situation comedies from the 1960s, which, in his view depended on a caricatured representation of the working classes. *On the Buses* (1969–73), for example, offered escapism and 'low farce' and 'made no pretence to social or political realism'.[33] For quite different reasons, however, he also singles out the work of Perry and Croft as lacking any sense of radical cultural critique: in *Dad's Army* (1968–77), for example, there is no (lasting) subversion of Captain Mainwaring's authority, which 'harks back to a world in which social positions were more rigid and relationships more straightforwardly authoritarian'.[34] Wagg suggests that, by contrast with the more controversial representation of 'real' issues that we see in most of the other sitcoms surveyed above, *Dad's Army* offered its audience a 'reassurance' derived its historical situation in a social system 'in which people do not look beyond their social positions and hierarchy is undermined, not by deliberate subversion but by mounting, unintended chaos'. This claim will be evaluated in later chapters, but it is important to note here that *Dad's Army* is generally perceived as a 'gentler' situation comedy (Crisell, for example, refers to its 'delightful gallery of characters') than many of its more radical contemporaries, and one which did not demonstrate the 'bad taste' of the more raucous members of its generation.[35]

Perry and Croft, then, inherited a televisual genre that had, even by the late 1960s, acquired recognisable characteristics – a lexicon of character-types, of situations, and of styles that had evolved since the beginnings of British broadcast comedy. Both Croft and Perry bring other comic traditions to their work, however, as the following short biographies will reveal.

David Croft

David Croft was born on 7 September 1922, to Anne Croft and Reginald Sharland, near Poole in Dorset. Croft's father was billed as a 'Theatrical Actor' on Croft's birth certificate, and both of his parents, in fact, were 'theatrical', playing in a revue called 'The Peep Show' at the London Hippodrome just before Croft's birth. Sharland left the family early in Croft's life to attempt a Hollywood career, and after a few small parts in RKO productions, he became the star of a popular radio show, playing the role of 'The Honourable Archibald Chislebury', whom Croft describes as a 'Wooster-like' figure living in California with a 'Japanese Jeeves'.[36] Croft's mother was a popular theatrical star of the 1920s and 1930s, and, as a result, Croft was introduced to the world of the theatre at a very early age, initially as the object of unwanted attention from chorus girls, but later as a performer himself. Croft was educated at Arnold House (a day school in St John's Wood), Durlston Court in Dorset, and finally at Rugby, which he was ultimately compelled to leave because of a short-fall in the family's finances resulting from his mother's theatrical venture, *Primrose Time*. With money sent by his father, Croft was treated to a series of very practical courses of education: typing, shorthand and book-keeping; horse-riding; singing and dancing. Around this time he helped in his mother's production company, and took a number of small roles in radio and film – notably as a butcher's boy in *Goodbye Mr Chips* (in which his elder brother, Peter, played the part of John Mills's batman). Croft was on the verge of joining his father in Hollywood when the Second World War broke out, and his family moved to Bournemouth. Croft served as Air Raid Warden; he maintains that while this period gave him ample experience for his later work on *Dad's Army*, he was not at all like Air Raid Warden Hodges.

In 1942, Croft joined the RAF, undertaking Royal Artillery basic training in Blandford, and acquiring the rank of Bombardier. His experiences in the armed forces were quite varied, and so difficult to summarise briefly. During a posting to Bone, North Africa, he contracted impetigo as a result of vitamin deficiency, was hospitalised with rheumatic fever, and was sent home to England to convalesce. Croft hoped that he might be invalided out of the armed forces, but when this failed to happen he succeeded in obtaining a commission and entered officer training at Sandhurst. He was posted to India, arriving in Bombay just as victory in Europe was declared. Croft was assigned to the Essex Regiment, and undertook jungle training, landing finally in the Urulli camp outside Poona. While there he was made Brigade Entertainments Officer (among other things), and he was promoted to Captain. During this time he worked briefly with ENSA and the Combined Services Entertainment (CSE). Ultimately promoted to the rank of Major, Croft completed his time in the Far East in Singapore, overseeing the evacuation of Japanese prisoners of war, before returning to work in London's War Office. Croft details his military career extensively in *You Have Been Watching*, and it's clear that his experiences had a direct bearing on his writing for *Dad's Army* and *It Ain't Half Hot, Mum* – particular episodes, locations and characters stand out clearly in his autobiography as models for their counterparts in his sitcoms, demonstrating again his claims to authenticity of representation. Croft notes particularly the train departure in *It Ain't Half Hot, Mum*'s 'The Road to Bannu' as an example of a scene inspired directly by personal experience.

On his return to England, Croft tried his hand at a number of theatrical ventures, starring in a diverse range of productions in repertory – during which he encountered several notable individuals, including Arthur Lowe, Ian Carmichael, and his wife-to-be. He also became involved in producing summer shows in Butlin's holiday camps. Although Croft remarks that 'I don't think I ever put a show into any of the camps of which I was not deeply ashamed', the experience clearly generated valuable material for what would become *Hi-de-Hi!*[37] He took several small roles in BBC television as a consequence of his acquaintance with Michael Mills, and was a member of the BBC Show Band Singers, writing songs, and, eventually, pantomimes – as vehicles for famous figures such as Tommy Steele, Norman Wisdom, Harry Secombe, Bruce Forsythe, Charlie Drake, Roy Castle and Cliff Richard. Croft's work as an actor for the BBC in the early 1950s caused him frustration with the technical difficulties that dogged television production at that time; as a result, his wife suggested that he might consider becoming a producer and director himself. Encouraged by Michael Mills, Croft was offered a job as a trainee television producer with the BBC, but the salary was so meagre (a six month provisional contract for £300) that he took a position as a Light Entertainment script editor with Associated Rediffusion at the more substantial yearly salary of £1,500.

Croft's time with Rediffusion was relatively short-lived (though while he was there he produced Spike Milligan's *Idiot Weekly, Priced 2d.*), and he joined Tyne Tees Television as a producer at the suggestion of Bill Lyon Shaw, a friend who was Controller of Programmes. Although Croft and his family didn't much enjoy their time in the North, it was profitable in career terms: he reports that by the time he left Tyne Tees he had produced around 250 shows for commercial television. Croft's first assignment at Tyne Tees was to direct an advertising magazine, or 'admag', called *Ned's Shed*, a fifteen-minute magazine programme about do-it-yourself products, but he went on to produce another admag (*Mary Goes to Market*), and *The One O'Clock Show*, a 45–minute live variety programme of sketches, band numbers and interviews. At one point, Croft relates, he was producing two admags and three editions of *The One O'Clock Show* each week. Importantly for this book, Croft also did his first work on situation comedy at Tyne Tees, producing *Under New Management*, which was set in a derelict pub in the North of England, and writing a 'situation comedy with music' called *Sunshine Street*.[38] Croft continued to work in Light Entertainment on joining the BBC, inheriting a project about university life from Dennis Norden and Frank Muir, the 'Comedy Advisers' of the Light Entertainment department.[39] Although the sitcom, which Croft called *The Eggheads*, gradually improved its 'appreciation index' from a 'record low' of 45 to a somewhat more acceptable 65, the series did not prove popular with critics and managed only eleven episodes.[40]

Despite this awkward start, Croft went on to produce *The Benny Hill Show*, before Benny Hill left for ITV, and *This is Your Life*. Having doubts about his career as a producer with the BBC, Croft began to observe the work of Duncan Wood, who had produced *Hancock's Half-Hour* and was at that time working again with Ray Galton and Alan Simpson on *Steptoe and Son*. In Croft's words, 'Duncan was the first to realise that television comedy lies more in the reaction of the characters to a line than in the line itself', and he also suggests that '[t]elevision comedy owes more to [Galton and Simpson] than to any other writers'.[41] Croft claims that he never missed either a rehearsal or a transmission of *Steptoe and Son*, and the education that this experience gave him is clearly evident in his own later work. In 1962, he began to produce the long-running sitcom starring Terry Scott and Hugh Lloyd called *Hugh and I* (1962–68), and he worked with a variety of comedians, including Roy Kinnear and Dick Emery, in sitcoms and sketch comedy shows. It was during *Beggar My Neighbour* (1966–68) that Croft met Jimmy Perry, casting him in one episode as the loud-mouthed brother of Harry Butt (Reg Varney).

Perry and Croft's professional partnership is, of course, more extensively discussed in the remainder of this book, but I think that its worth mentioning here the particularly unusual way in which they wrote their sitcoms. Meeting for two or three days together, they discussed the plots of two episodes and made notes about potential scenes to be included in them. Then each would write an episode independently of the other – 'in this way', Croft explains, 'we would each feel personally responsible for the episode we had written'.[42] In my interview with David Croft, he confessed to me that he was unable to remember which episodes were his and which were Perry's; and I was unable, despite extensive viewing of their work in a relatively short space of time, to discern two clearly separate authorial voices in their sitcoms – a testament, I think, to the peculiar symbiosis of their collaboration.

In addition to the four long-running sitcoms that Croft co-wrote with Perry (and that, in part at least, he produced and directed), he also worked extensively with Jeremy Lloyd to generate the other famous 'ensemble' British situation comedies: *Are You Being Served?* (1972–85), *Come Back Mrs Noah* (1977–78), *Oh Happy Band!* (1980), *'Allo, 'Allo!* (1982–92), *Grace and Favour* (1992–93) and *Which Way to the War?* (ITV, 1 episode, 1994). He worked, in most cases, as co-writer, producer and director. He also worked as a producer on *Up Pompeii!* (1970) (and on *Further Up Pompeii!* five years later), accommodating the unusual working habits and performance style of Frankie Howerd, and he collaborated with other writers – *Oh, Doctor Beeching!* (1995–97) was written with Richard Spendlove.[43] David Croft was given the Writers' Guild of Great Britain Award for Best Comedy Script with Jimmy Perry in 1969, 1970 and 1971 for *Dad's Army*; the SFTA Award for Best Light Entertainment Production and Direction in 1971 for *Dad's Army*; and the prestigious Desmond Davis Award at BAFTA in 1982. He was awarded the OBE in 1978 for services to television.

Jimmy Perry

Unlike David Croft, Jimmy Perry was raised in what he describes as a 'middle-class London suburban family'.[44] He was born in Barnes on 20 September 1923, the son of an antiques dealer, Arthur Perry. Perry describes an early life of middle-class security; his parents employed a housemaid and a 'daily woman' called Mabel – the model for *You Rang, M'Lord?*'s scullery maid of the same name. Perry's paternal grandfather had been a butler in Belgrave Square, and many of the stories his father had passed on served as the foundation for Perry and Croft's final series. Perry's early education was fairly prestigious; as a five-year-old he attended a 'small private kindergarten for posh middle-class kids', before starting at St Paul's Preparatory School, Colet Court, at the age of eight.[45] Perry did not enjoy his time at the school, and he was not academically inclined, so when he was fourteen his parents removed him from school and enrolled him at Clark's College, where he was taught shorthand, typing and bookkeeping. This did not prove to be a success either and, after a period of truancy was discovered, Perry left school and became an apprentice at Messrs Waring and Gillow, a furniture store where he was 'to do a year in the carpet department, another year in soft furnishing and my final year in furniture'.[46] Throughout the early years of his life, Perry was a keen follower of popular entertainment. He was fascinated with the 'silver screen', emulating the accents and movements of the movie stars he had seen in the Ranelagh Cinema in Barnes, and he was sometimes taken by his father to variety theatre, where he saw legendary figures such as Max Miller and Tommy Trinder. He also harboured an early ambition to become a comedian, and his autobiography returns repeatedly to what he feels is a strong, clear distinction between the amateur comedian and the professional.

Perry's career as a furniture salesman was suspended by the outbreak of the Second World War. His family moved to Watford to live in the premises of his uncle's shop, and this move was to play a significant part in Perry's life: 'it was there I did my service in the Home Guard and made my first appearance on any stage'.[47] He joined the Watford Company of the Home Guard of the Bedfordshire and Hertfordshire Regiment, and maintains that their exploits and those of *Dad's Army*'s Home Guard were largely identical. Perry, in fact, was the model for Private Pike, and his mother, who was opposed to his joining the Home Guard, fussed over him much like Pike's mother. Perry also mentions the original Lance Corporal Jones, an elderly French-polisher who had served in the Battle of Omdurman in 1898. Perry's first stage appearance came in 1941, at a 'smoking concert' announced after a Home

Guard parade, and he also did a 'turn' before 2,000 people at the Gaumont Cinema, Watford – a series of gags, some impressions (including his much-loved Charles Laughton in the role of Captain Bligh) and a song. He experienced his 'first really big laugh' but felt, ultimately, that he had lost his audience in the middle of his performance. Nevertheless, Billy Cook, a professional comedian running a local amateur concert party, 'Hello, Watford, Hello', saw the show and asked Perry to join his company, performing two or three shows a month.

At his mother's insistence, Perry worked at an ammunitions factory as a means of delaying his conscription. At the end of 1943, however, he was called up, reporting first to a training camp in Colchester, and ending up at Oswestry in the First Mixed Heavy Anti-Aircraft Regiment of the Royal Artillery. He joined the camp's concert party, with what he refers to as 'quite a polished act', and his comic talent saved him from being posted to D-Day; the regiment's colonel (the inspiration for Colonel Reynolds in *It Ain't Half Hot, Mum*) kept him back to keep up morale with his performances.[48] After a brief encounter with officer training, which he chose not to pursue, Perry was posted to the Far East in 1944, after a professional altercation with a Captain at Oswestry who 'fancied himself as a comedian'.[49] Teamed with a fellow performer, Harry Waller, Perry performed in the transport's concert party, before arriving in Bombay. From there he was posted to Burma, having been promoted from Gunner to Bombardier along the way. After a burst appendix, he was posted to Deolali, a large Royal Artillery base and former mental hospital. There he was reunited with Harry Waller, with whom he joined the Royal Artillery concert party. Perry's time in Deolali obviously inspired *It Ain't Half Hot, Mum*, which, like *Dad's Army*, he insists was drawn largely from life experience. In fact, his accounts of this period of his life, along with those of his later stint in the Combined Services Entertainment, are replete with characters, episodes and lines that were to crop up in his second collaborative sitcom with Croft.

On his return to England, Perry set out to find a career in show business. After a failed attempt to get into the Windmill Theatre – a venue famous for its comics – he was persuaded by an old Royal Artillery acquaintance to try out for RADA. His fellow students there included Joan Collins, Lionel Jeffries, Robert Shaw, and – especially noteworthy in a book about situation comedy – Warren Mitchell. In the summers between RADA terms, Perry took a job as a Redcoat at Butlin's in Pwllheli, North Wales, where he graduated rapidly from sports organiser to competition compère and, ultimately, to camp producer. Once more, Perry's experiences inspired his work as a comedy writer, and his autobiography cites several anecdotes that were to turn up later in *Hi-de-*

Hi! After RADA Perry served a long apprenticeship in the theatrical profession, performing in a variety of West End musicals, weekly rep and situation comedies before ending up in Joan Littlewood's Theatre Workshop. It was as this time he developed the idea for a television situation comedy based on the Home Guard that would eventually become *Dad's Army*.

Perry is the first to admit that not all his ventures into comedy writing for television have been successful. His first solo project – and the 'first ever sitcom made in colour' – *The Gnomes of Dulwich* (BBC2, 1969) got good reviews, but his next attempt, a domestic comedy called *Lollipop Loves Mr Mole* (ATV, 1969), was, in Perry's own words, 'rub-bish'.[50] A much later sitcom about hotel service – *Room Service* (ITV, 1979) – was a '[d]isaster', and Perry doesn't even mention *High Street Blues* (LWT, 1989), co-written with Robin Carr, which Mark Lewisohn pronounces 'pitiful'.[51] There are two conclusions that we might draw from this: that Perry worked best in his relationship with Croft, or that he was more comfortable writing in the 'middle-class, rather snobbish environment of the BBC'.[52] But, as Perry's otherwise successful career makes clear, he is a more effective writer when, to use a cliche, he writes about what he knows. As he says of *Room Service*, 'What did I know about hotels? I'd no interest in the subject whatsoever, so I deserved everything I got'.[53] Indeed, where Jimmy Perry's own life experiences coincide, almost uncannily, with those of David Croft, the result has been a tradition of emblematic British comedy that spans twenty-five years. Along with Croft, Perry was given the Writers' Guild of Great Britain Award for Best Comedy Script 1969, 1970 and 1971, but he was also given the BAFTA Award for Best Television Episode in 1971 (*Dad's Army*) and the Ivor Novello Award for Best Television Signature Tune in 1971 (again for *Dad's Army*). He was awarded the OBE in 1978.

A brief survey of situation comedy criticism

Given the considerable scope of film and television criticism, and given situation comedy's significant presence in contemporary television broadcasts, the comparative dearth of critical analysis of sitcom is sur-prising. Essays devoted to British situation comedy, of course, form only a part of the broader critical discourse about the genre, and, of this limited number, the essays that consider the work of Jimmy Perry and David Croft in anything other than a cursory way comprise a small fraction indeed. Since so little critical work addresses their output directly, it would be inappropriate to devote a great deal of space in this book to a survey of sitcom criticism at large. But I think that it is worth tracing the general trends in the criticism of situation comedy, and some of the most immediately relevant ideas in television studies, as a means of establishing a critical foundation for my discussions of Perry and Croft's collaborations. This survey will be necessarily selective, representing the ideas that I think have contributed most significantly to the investigation of situation comedy generally, and that will be most useful to an evaluation of Perry and Croft's specific contributions to the genre.

Despite their comparatively small number, critical investigations of situation comedies range in subject from *I Love Lucy* to *Roseanne*, from *The Flintstones* to *The Simpsons*, from *Ellen* to *Home Improvement*. The tradition of US sitcom is certainly well-represented in criticism, especially – and unsurprisingly – within the discipline of Popular Culture in the United States, but individual British situation comedies have also generated critical responses. 'Classics' such as *Hancock's Half-Hour*, *Steptoe and Son* and *Fawlty Towers* seem to be perennial favourites, but other series such as *Absolutely Fabulous*, *Yes Minister*, *The Young Ones* and *On the Buses* have also been subject to investigation. Comparatively few of these critical approaches come to grips with the nature of situation comedy itself: Michael J. Apter's '*Fawlty Towers*: A Reversal Theory Analysis of a Popular Television Comedy Series', for example, ultimately has less to say about sitcom as a televisual genre or a cultural phenomenon than about the particular psychoanalytic theory that forms the essay's framework.[54] Situation comedies have been interpreted using most of the discourses of contemporary critical theory, from Kirkham and Skaggs's feminist analysis of *Absolutely Fabulous* and Steve Neale and Frank Krutnik's ideological account of *Steptoe and Son*, to Leon Hunt's Bakhtin-inflected cultural criticism of *On the Buses*, *Man About the House* and *Love Thy Neighbour*.[55]

Mick Eaton's 'Television Situation Comedy' is a good place to begin, because it articulates some of the key questions about sitcom criticism and, as perhaps the most frequently cited early essay on sitcom, it has established some of the standards for debate.[56] From Eaton's perspective, writing in the late 1970s, there had been 'nothing written about the television situation comedy as a specifically televisual form', so that discussion 'from within the television industry' circulated around questions of realism or naturalism (such as we encountered in Galton and Simpson's concerns with 'realism' in *Hancock's Half-Hour*), while academic work from without seemed poised on the brink of a 'collapse back into a culturalist and sociologistic reading of individual television programmes in which "criticism" becomes just another "point of view" from a position along an ideological spectrum'.[57] Eaton's purpose, however, is to develop a typology of situation comedy by concentrating on 'production' rather than 'communication'; by emphasising television's role as a 'signifying practice', he intends to consider the sitcom in its 'formal effectivity, not as aesthetic device or evidence of televisuality'.[58] Firstly, he establishes the parameters of the situation comedy, as they are defined by the thirty-minute time-slot that sitcoms occupy in the broadcast schedule. Most sitcoms are *series* rather than *serials*, which is to say that they are structured by a concept that can be reproduced across a number of programmes in an episodic or strictly self-contained fashion; a *serial*, by contrast, has an ongoing narrative, spilling over from one episode to the next. One exception he cites to this general statement is *The Fall and Rise of Reginald Perrin*, but a more recent example might be *The League of Gentlemen*, which explores a developing narrative throughout each of its series that results ultimately in a degree of narrative closure (such as the building of the 'New Road', or Royston Vasey's mysterious epidemic). The *series* must effectively 'forget' the events of previous episodes, returning to the sitcom's original, endlessly 'reproducible' concept:

> The 'situation', to fill the demands of the time-slot, the demands of constant repetition of/in the series, needs to be one whose parameters are easily recognizable and which are returned to week after week. Nothing that has happened in the narrative of the previous week must destroy or even complicate the way the situation is grounded.[59]

One significant implication of the stability of the series' situation is the necessity for a clearly demarcated dichotomy of 'inside' and 'outside', which precludes every aspect of the sitcom's production, even, Eaton emphasises, 'its finest budgetary details'.[60] The 'inside' is constituted by stock sets, consistent exterior location shots, and regular characters and their relationships to each other, and the 'outside' by events or characters that temporarily interrupt the stability of the established situation. By the episode's end, the outside influence must be expunged, leaving the inside unaffected in any permanent way and 'reset' for the next episode. Eaton makes clear that his usage of 'inside' and 'outside' has no political or ideological implications, because the 'ideology resides institutionally in the structure', so that the series' insistence upon stability is not a product of any conservatism in content, but rather of the material demands made by the time-slot.[61] Eaton finds that there are two recurring 'situations' used in sitcom – the 'home' (or 'family'), and 'work'. This, again, he attributes less to ideological reasons than to the situations' simple provision of repeatable, familiar ideas, and their easy accommodation within the 'economic demands of the company's budget'.[62]

John Ellis, and the co-authors Steve Neale and Frank Krutnik, address this inside/outside dichotomy in terms that venture beyond Eaton's production-based approach, however. In *Visible Fictions*, Ellis makes a distinction between the cinema viewer and the viewer of broadcast television, for whom 'the regime of viewing is rather one of complicity with TV's own look at the passing pageant of life'.[63] Television underscores the viewer's separation from the events represented, or, as Ellis puts it, 'confirms the domestic isolation of the viewer' which inscribes him or her in the dichotomy of the inside/outside: the 'inside' is the world of the private life, the home, family, security, 'confirmation of identity' and the 'outside' is that of the public life, work, potential danger, 'challenge to identity'.[64] The inscription of the viewer within this dichotomised model of inside vs. outside (or 'self' vs. 'other') seems to me necessarily ideological – as culturally significant, in fact, as the distinction between the 'inside' and the 'outside' itself. As Ellis states, the effect of this dichotomy on the television viewer is 'to confirm the normality of the domestic and the abnormality of the world upon which TV's look is turned'.[65] Ellis is referring to broadcast television generally, of course, and he places the world of 'work' on the opposite side of the dichotomous division from 'home' and 'family'. In *Popular Film and Television Comedy*, however, Neale and Krutnik take up a discussion of the inside/outside dichotomy, in terms similar to Ellis's, specifically in relation to the domestic situation comedy. Quoting from Eaton, they identify the 'inside' of the domestic sitcom as the 'highly recognizable conception of the middle-class nuclear-family unit', and by considering several examples of this situation, they show that the return to stability through the expulsion of disruptive 'outside' influences is as much a consolidation of the values associated with the bourgeois family unit as a demand of the medium.[66] Thus, for Neale and Krutnik, domestic situation comedy reveals its 'investment ... in the bourgeois family as a model of stability, of "normality"'.[67] The consolidation of the relationships within the family that occurs as a result of the expulsion of 'outside' forces is described by Neale and Krutnik as an act of 'communalization', an act that they see as representative of broadcast television in general, which itself 'attempts to inscribe the viewer as part of its own "family"'.[68] This echoes Ellis's statement about television's 'complicity of viewing'; as Neale and Krutnik write, '[b]oth the sitcom and television in general are concerned with reaffirming cultural identity, with demarcating an "inside", a community of interests and values, and localizing contrary or oppositional values as an "outside"'.[69] Even in the case of *Steptoe and Son*, which inverts the 'normality' of an inside/outside dichotomy, they argue, this ideological imperative is maintained, because, of course, 'one has to know the 'rules' [of bourgeois decorum] in order to recognize and to find funny the ways in which they are broken'.[70]

If Ellis places Eaton's other basic sitcom situation – work – in an oppositional relationship to the family, Neale and Krutnik rehabilitate it as a 'surrogate family', with its unity and the stability of its relationships firmly established as the 'inside'. It is certainly as easy to appreciate the cultural centrality of the stable bourgeois work ethic as that of the bourgeois family unit. These ideas are particularly important to our understanding of Perry and Croft's situation comedies, all of which are apparently structured around the situation of 'work' – the Local Defence Volunteers, a Royal Artillery concert party, a holiday camp, the 'below stairs' environment of an aristocratic household. With the exception of *Dad's Army*, however, the other sitcoms also accommodate the domestic in several unusual ways: in *It Ain't Half Hot, Mum*, *Hi-De-Hi!* and *You Rang, M'Lord?*, the characters who *work* together also *live* together and comprise a distinctly non-normative family unit. The concept of the inside/outside dichotomy, in its purely materialist and in its ideological formulations, then, will necessarily become an important part of our subsequent investigations of Perry and Croft's sitcoms, and I shall return to these formulations of the model frequently.

Another text that is important to recognise in this critical survey is the BFI dossier *Television Sitcom*, a collection of essays written by participants in a BFI summer workshop, which offers a range of politically engaged analyses of British situation comedies, including those of Perry and Croft.[71] Perhaps because of the common, collective origin of the dossier, the essays are closely linked, referencing each other and returning to the same recurring issues and ideas. I will refer more directly to some of the essays in later chapters in the context of specific Perry and Croft sitcoms: Andy Medhurst and Lucy Tuck's 'The Gender Game' discusses Gloria in *It Ain't Half Hot, Mum*, and Susan Boyd-Bowman's 'Back to Camp' is an extended discussion and analysis of an episode of *Hi-De-Hi!* But I think it is most useful here to consider some of the ideas articulated across several of the essays rather than to offer a summary of individual pieces.

A number of the concepts, such as the relationship of sitcom to 'reality' or the question of the conservative or progressive nature of the genre, have, of course, already seen discussion above. Several of the dossier's essays discuss the function of 'reality' in situation comedy including Barry Curtis's in 'Aspects of Sitcom'. Starting, like a number of others from *Hancock*, Curtis perceives that sitcom reality is ultimately that of the realist dramatic convention, what he calls 'plausibilities of setting and character', used as a foundation for comic interruption; he also suggests that the realism of props or setting provides implicit social commentary, such as an articulation of class anxiety or social preten-sion.[72] He proposes that this realism allows the assertion of 'common-sense' or 'reasonableness', so that there is a 'sense in which the simple assertive truths of comedy are accorded a special social status'.[73] Curtis' discussion of realism here is curiously detached from any consideration of ideology – one might ask 'Sense common to whom?' or 'Reasonable by whose standards?' – even though he does acknowledge one model of sitcom as 'an ideological apparatus for asserting dominant values' later in the essay.[74] Ultimately the familiarity embodied for the viewer by the sitcom's realism seems to serve for Curtis as a 'ludic space', the televisual equivalent of Shakespeare's famous 'Green World' where the 'temporary challenge to hierarchies of value and ordered social relation-ships effects a temporary relief from the constraints of social domin-ance and subordination, a space for a sense of liberated community'.[75]

The relationship of realism to comedy is taken up by both Jim Cook and Terry Lovell in their contributions to the dossier, through their discussions of comedy, narrative and social transgression.[76] Jim Cook begins by establishing that the temporal sequence of cause and effect in the dramatic narrative can be read in two ways – in terms of its content (i.e. *what* the narrative is 'about'), and of its structure (i.e. *how* this sequence of cause and effect is assembled). The former understanding of narrative, however, has predominated and become naturalised – an 'expressive realist [way of reading] … characterised by a privileging for consideration of the "told" at the expense of the "telling"' – although, Cook claims, the operation of some situation comedies (including *Hi-De-Hi!*) subverts this otherwise dominant understanding of narrative.[77] (Re)evaluating Gerald Mast's list of eight basic structures for film come-dies, Cook concludes that the narratives Mast identifies are not in them-selves comic, but rather that their comedy arises from the intention to indicate comedy through an incongruous or unexpected interruption – in other words, that comedy is not implicit in the cause and effect of the 'told', but rather in the 'telling'. This conclusion might seem like a generally held truism ('It's the way I tell 'em', insists Frank Carson), but it does have a bearing on the relationship of 'realism' to comedy: the intention to produce comedy is not itself 'naturalistic', and so finds itself at odds with the 'realism' of the narrative.

Terry Lovell's essay, 'A Genre of Social Disruption', acknowledges Cook's argument, but continues to think about realism's relationship to comedy, suggesting that 'comedy and realism are not in fact inimical'.[78] She proposes the existence of 'social realist comedies' as the genre into which most television situation comedies fall, and adds '[r]ather than defining comedy against realism ... it may be seen as a mode which creates different problems for different genres'. Lovell's treatment of 'reality' (or, more precisely, 'social reality') as the foundation of the sitcom is a little more developed than Curtis': '[t]he social order which sitcom references comprises two levels: the normative order, (roughly what people think ought to be the case) and the typical social order (what they think is usually the case)'. Thus, rather than representing a stable, fixed point of reference for comic intervention, 'reality' is a construct predisposed towards ideological conflict, and comedy is produced at those moments when the 'two levels' of social reality do not precisely align. Furthermore, claims Lovell, social realist comedy seeks to obscure the narrative's 'how' (or the characteristic of 'telling' identified by Cook as essential to comic intention) by naturalising the comic as 'found' – in other words 'by constructing narratives which "bring out" comedy as seen as inherent in the "human condition"' of plausible, 'realistic' characters.[79]

Lovell's essay problematises any easy relationship between comedy and reality, but its principal purpose is to investigate the ideological underpinnings of comedy – is it implicitly conservative, or progressive? David Grote, for example, proposes that the sitcom is the 'end of comedy' because of its non-progressive 'conservatism': having established a comedic tradition from the Menandrian origins of New Comedy up to the twentieth century which is identified by its 'dedication to change and progress, in people, in society, and in the species', he discovers that US television 'has suddenly and completely rejected it' because '[t]he principal fundamental situation of the situation comedy is that things do not change'.[80] What Grote sees as the sitcom's rejection of progressiveness, however, is itself grounded in a conservative, liberal humanist agenda, and other critics, such as David Marc and Jane Feuer, see the genre as potentially progressive; Barry Curtis proposes sitcom as a temporary subversive space for a 'liberated community'.[81] Does the sitcom have subversive potential? For Lovell, 'the fact that we cannot produce an example of a "subversive" sitcom' is irrelevant, and not surprising given that they are characteristically broadcast at peak viewing times.[82] Andy Medhurst and Lucy Tuck concur: '[s]itcom must not be approached in the spirit of searching for the great lost progressive text. We must sift through texts to see if any use can be made of them.'[83] If we recognise that situation comedies are subject to the same contradictions that are inherent in the ideology that produces them, or – as Lovell writes – that they 'are not, or not always, completely hegemonised by bourgeois ideology', then the possibility for subversion exists. If we return to the 'inside/outside' model of situation comedy discussed earlier, we can see how some of these possibilities work. Although the stable, normative 'inside' of the sitcom's situation is restored at each episode's end, thus expelling or containing the potentially subversive intrusion of the non-normative 'outside', is it the case that this always results in immutability or a restatement of hegemony? Is it possible that the mere act of representing the non-normative is progressive or ideologically subversive – a Pandora's Box of possibility? Or is the dominant ideology's strategy in permitting representation of the subversive only a means of recuperation, or disempowerment of the non-normative? These questions, of course, are unanswerable in an abstract sense, and are certainly larger concerns than this book can attempt to resolve. Lovell's conclusion is that those sitcoms that reference social reality most strongly tend to be less subversive, 'not because this form of comedy is immune to subversion, but because the conventions of realism invite the audience to take its action and characters as typical'; this is a statement to which we will return in our investigation of Perry and Croft's comedies. Commentators routinely categorise their sitcoms as anything but progressive or subversive, and while I do not intend to make grand claims to contrary, I think that their work needs closer examination in this respect.

This survey has necessarily been selective, and I will certainly have occasion to cite other critical work throughout the rest of this book. But the principal issues outlined above – the delineation of the sitcom's 'formal structures', the role of the television audience, the function of 'reality', the 'inside/outside' dichotomy in its various political guises, the inherent conservatism (or, alternatively, subversive potential) of the sitcom – will all figure prominently in my later discussions of Perry and Croft's work.

A cultural studies approach to Perry and Croft

This study of Perry and Croft's situation comedies operates within what might be called a 'cultural studies' paradigm. There is no place for a detailed defence of cultural studies as a critical practice in this book, and I have not worked within any particular school or single tradition, but I think that it is worth enumerating some of the assumptions and ideas that underlie my approach to the sitcoms that follow. My explorations of *Dad's Army*, *It Ain't Half Hot, Mum*, *Hi-de-Hi!* and *You Rang, M'Lord?* are of the kind that Mick Eaton described as 'culturalist and sociologistic reading', a type of critical practice that 'becomes just another "point of view" from a position along an ideological spectrum'.[84] Despite Eaton's pejorative characterisation of this type of criticism, it has now been a prominent mode of scholarship for about twenty years, with its roots in earlier scholarly traditions.

One source of cultural criticism worth tracing is the grand tradition of historical criticism, which sought to explain a text through consideration of its historical background, often in tandem with biographical criticism. In many ways this type of critical investigation seems eminently suitable to a study of Perry and Croft's sitcoms; all of their collaborative efforts are set in the past (unusually for situation comedy) and make some claims for historical authenticity. One response might be, then, to render these sitcoms comprehensible to audiences in the new millennium through an explication of the history that informs them – of the aristocratic households of the 1920s, for example, or of the Royal Artillery concert party's activities during the Second World War. This approach also seems appealing because of the uncannily similar life experiences of the two authors informing the four series: each sitcom reflects aspects of both Perry's and Croft's personal histories, as my earlier biographical sketches clearly demonstrate. As with any critical approach, this type of work has its limitations. It often supposes, for example, that history is transparently accessible, or that it speaks with a single voice, and that the author represents this historical certainty without any mediation through his or her own consciousness. Indeed, Perry and Croft's autobiographies frequently justify criticisms of the themes that occur in their sitcoms (such as the accusations of homophobia or racism in It Ain't Half Hot, Mum) by insisting 'that's the way things were'; while Perry and Croft, as individuals, found these attitudes unpalatable or unreasonable, they claim to have offered them only as accurate representations of historical fact.

Cultural criticism might be able to address these particular shortcomings. It does not, certainly, seek to ignore a text's historical context, since, as a critical practice, it is often marshalled against formalist approaches which reads texts as universal or transcendent of history. But cultural criticism recognises that history itself is a complex structure of discourses competing for predominance, and that products of any historical moment – whether texts or authors – are themselves necessarily caught up in the struggle for meaning. Some of the more recognisable manifestations of cultural criticism, such as the American 'new historicism' or British 'cultural materialism', attempt to recover some of the marginal voices that occur in texts, voices which are a component of any culture divided by dominant and subordinate subcultures, across class, for example, or gender. Some critics would even argue that these marginal voices are included in texts in order to bolster the expression of dominant culture, which is strengthened by their dismissal, exclusion or – in the case of comedy – ridicule. But beyond this, cultural criticism recognises the implication of the text's reader (or, in the case of television, the medium's viewer) in the interpretive process, which makes the claim of the critic to a purely objective response difficult to maintain. This emphasis on the importance of the subjective response is, in part, an acknowledgment of the polysemic nature of cultural productions – that is, the fact that culture, like language, has 'many meanings' or rather, means different things to different individuals depending on their ideological biases or social and political formations. Opponents of cultural studies often cite this characteristic as a limitation of the critical method – that it is 'too subjective' or 'too partial' in its investigation, driven by personal politics or 'faddish trends' imposed upon the texts under investigation. But cultural critics would defend themselves against this criticism by arguing that they are merely acknowledging that all critics themselves are products of culture, and thus cannot step outside their own subjective positions: the critic is necessarily implicated in the text he or she investigates, because they are both implicated in the cultures that produced them.

Clearly, this is only a brief sketch of a complex and varied critical field. A good introduction to the theoretical assumptions underlying cultural studies can be found in Graeme Turner's *British Cultural Studies: An Introduction*, which outlines the dominant ideas in the discipline, from the formative work of Raymond Williams, Stuart Hall and the Birmingham Centre for Contemporary Cultural Studies, through more recent manifestations, including work on television by individuals like John Fiske, John Hartley and David Morley. My summary, however, should be adequate to demonstrate why I consider it to be a suitable critical methodology with which to approach Perry and Croft's sitcoms. Although their collaborative sitcoms are based on their own life experience, and as such are 'about' the Home Guard or the Royal Artillery concert party, they are also written to appeal to an audience watching several decades after the events took place. A useful point of comparison would be Shakespeare's history plays: although depicting the lives of fifteenth-century Plantagenet kings, the plays are understood by modern critics to represent the attitudes of Shakespeare's own, late sixteenth-century culture – they are thus as much (if not more) 'about' Shakespeare's culture as they are about what they purport to portray. *It Ain't Half Hot, Mum* likewise functions as a representation of life in the Royal Artillery concert party in India at the end of the Second World War, authenticated by the real life experiences of its authors. It is, therefore, meaningful in this context. But the sitcom is also a product of the early 1970s and is necessarily implicated in the discourses of the culture in which it was produced. *It Ain't Half Hot, Mum* is a particularly good example for my purposes here, since there are obvious 'slippages' between the two contexts: accused subsequently of racist and homophobic representation, Perry and Croft both defended the series by invoking its historical context ('that's the way things were'). But within the context of debates about immigration and sexuality in the early 1970s, *It Ain't Half Hot, Mum* also becomes meaningful in other ways, not all of them intended by the series' authors. As the subject of criticism, then, *It Ain't Half Hot, Mum* constitutes a polysemic text poised for the type of critical investigation afforded by cultural studies.

In the four chapters that follow I consider each of Perry and Croft's sitcoms, working from the themes and ideas I see represented in each series. I have acknowledged in each case the historical background of the setting and Perry and Croft's own biographical implication; this is important, I think, to an understanding of the authors' intentions for each series, and to establish a context for what they see as their principal goals and ideas. But this historical contextualisation also serves to establish a background against which to explore the slippage between, for example, the attitudes towards class, gender roles and sexuality in the 1920s and those represented in *You Rang, M'Lord?*, a sitcom written and received in the 1990s – that is, between the historically positioned concept and the reality of its contemporary representation. While the ideas I address in this book might seem all too familiar as the concerns of cultural studies – a preoccupation with the ideologies of class, gender and sexuality – I would argue that these discourses are inherent to the operation of Perry and Croft's sitcoms, to British sitcoms generally, and perhaps even to comedy itself. As Andy Medhurst neatly observes, 'Comedy is, to put it mildly, political. If you want to understand the preconceptions and power structures of a society or a social group, there are few better ways than by studying what it laughs at'.[85]

Notes

1 Crisell, *An Introductory History*, p. 34.
2 Roger Wilmut writes of *Band Waggon* that '[f]or the first time, a Variety program-me was placed on a regular day, at a more-or-less regular time, and with a regular comedian' (Wilmut, *Kindly Leave the Stage*, p. 130); Andrew Crisell suggests that series provoked '[t]he first realization that radio might be able to create its own distinctive kind of comedy' (Crisell, *An Introductory History*, p. 57).
3 Neale and Krutnik, *Popular Film and Television Comedy*, p. 221.

4 *Ibid.*

5 Crisell, *Understanding Radio*, p. 168; Crisell, *An Introductory History*, p. 58.

6 Quoted in Took, *Laughter in the Air*, p. 30.

7 Taylor, 'Theories of Laughter', p. 266. Cited in Neale and Krutnik, *Popular Film and Television Comedy*, p. 233.

8 French, 'The Golden Shows of Radio Comedy', p. 781.

9 *Ibid.*, p. 782.

10 *Ibid.*

11 *Ibid.*

12 Took, cited in Wheen, *Television*, p. 205; Eaton, 'Television Situation Comedy', p. 74.

13 Goddard, '"Hancock's Half-Hour"', p. 78.

14 Took, *Laughter in the Air*, p. 128.

15 Goddard, '"Hancock's Half-Hour"', p. 78; Dennis Main Wilson's memorandum is cited in Briggs, *History of Broadcasting*, p. 210.

16 Crisell, *An Introductory History*, p. 70; Black, *Biggest Aspidistra in the World*, pp. 191, 193.

17 Crisell, *An Introductory History*, p. 76.

18 Goddard, '"Hancock's Half-Hour"', p. 79.

19 Lewisohn, *Radio Times Guide to TV Comedy*, p. 400. I am reminded of Alan Partridge's insistence in *Knowing Me, Knowing Yule* that the television studio is a very expensive 'actual mock-up' of his Norwich home.

20 Wagg, 'Social Class and Situation Comedy', p. 7; Goddard, '"Hancock's Half-Hour"', p. 79; Galton and Simpson, *The Times*, 2 March 1959, quoted in Goddard, '"Hancock's Half-Hour"', p. 82.

21 Wagg, 'Social Class and Situation Comedy', p. 8.

22 Terry-Thomas, *Radio Times*, 14 September 1951, p. 47, cited in Goddard, '"Hancock's Half-Hour"', p. 81. Goddard suggests that even though Terry-Thomas used the 'very close close-up' in the early 1950s, *How Do You View* was 'not the breakthrough which television comedy needed', and so the close-up reaction shot remained 'not fully understood, even five years later, by many performers'.

23 Goddard, '"Hancock's Half-Hour"', p. 82.

24 Quoted in Wilmut, *Tony Hancock – Artiste*, p. 100.

25 Briggs, *History of Broadcasting*, vol. 5, p. 213.

26 Goddard, '"Hancock's Half-Hour"', p. 86.

27 *Radio Times*, 28 March 1958, quoted in Goddard, '"Hancock's Half-Hour"', p. 87.

28 Wagg, 'Social Class and Situation Comedy', p. 8.

29 Ibid., pp. 8–9.

30 Ibid., pp. 9, 11.

31 Briggs, *History of Broadcasting*, vol. 5, p. 528.

32 Wagg, 'Social Class and Situation Comedy', p. 10; Briggs, *History of Broadcasting*, vol. 5, p. 529.

33 Wagg, 'Social Class and Situation Comedy', p. 10. He goes on to characterise the sitcom as one populated with 'bus drivers, apopleptic at the sight of girls in mini-skirts, lugubrious inspectors, and looming wives'. Hunt, *British Low Culture*, offers an analysis of *On the Buses* in his chapter 'From Carnival to Crumpet'.

34 Wagg, 'Social Class and Situation Comedy', p. 14.

35 Crisell, *An Introductory History*, p. 121; Crowther and Pinfold, *Bring Me Laughter*, p. 112.

36 Croft, 'You Have Been Watching', p. 30.

37 *Ibid.*, p. 112.

38 *Ibid.*, p. 138.

39 *Ibid.*, p. 142.

40 Lewisohn counts only 7 episodes for *The Eggheads* (Lewisohn, *Radio Times Guide to TV Comedy*, p. 217).

41 Croft, 'You Have Been Watching', p. 146.

42 *Ibid.*, p. 158.

43 Croft reports that he tried, unsuccessfully, to interest Jimmy Perry in *Oh, Doctor Beeching!*, but 'Jimmy was not interested in a series about Railways and in fact didn't like trains' (*ibid.*, p. 212). He also mentions another sitcom devised with Jeremy Lloyd that exists only as a script for a pilot episode: *Here Comes the Queen*, a vehicle for Molly Sugden and John Inman, as a sister and brother who own a 'wool shop in the North' but who turn out to be the only heirs to an obscure foreign throne.

44 Perry, *A Stupid Boy*, p. 10.

45 *Ibid.*, p. 39.

46 *Ibid.*, p. 80.

47 *Ibid.*, p. 89.

48 *Ibid.*, p. 138.

49 *Ibid.*, p. 149.

50 *Ibid.*, pp. 274, 275.

51 *Ibid.*, p. 276; Lewisohn, *Radio Times Guide to TV Comedy*, p. 317.

52 Perry, *A Stupid Boy*, p. 12.

53 *Ibid.*, p. 275.

54 Apter, '*Fawlty Towers*: A Reversal Theory Analysis', pp. 128–138.

55 Kirkham and Skaggs, '*Absolutely Fabulous*: Absolutely Feminist?'; Neale and Krutnik, *Popular Film and Television Comedy*, chapter 9, 'Broadcast Comedy and Sitcom'; Hunt, *British Low Culture*, chapter 3, 'From Carnival to Crumpet'. For a range of critical approaches to televisual media generally, see Allen (ed.), *Channels of Discourse*.

56 Eaton, 'Television Situation Comedy', pp. 61–89.

57 *Ibid.*, pp. 61, 62.

58 *Ibid.*, p. 68.

59 *Ibid.*, p. 69.

60 *Ibid.*, p. 70.

61 *Ibid.*, p. 70.

62 *Ibid.*

63 Ellis, *Visible Fictions*, p. 160.

64 *Ibid.*, p. 166.

65 *Ibid.*, pp. 166–167.

66 Neale and Krutnik, *Popular Film and Television Comedy*, p. 237.

67 *Ibid.*, p. 239.

68 *Ibid.*, pp. 240, 241.

69 *Ibid.*, p. 242.

70 *Ibid.*, p. 251.

71 Cook (ed.), *BFI Dossier No. 17: Television Sitcom*.

72 Curtis, 'Aspects of Sitcom', pp. 7, 8.

73 *Ibid.*, p. 7.

74 *Ibid.*, p. 11.

75 *Ibid.*, p. 11.

76 Cook, 'Narrative, Comedy, Character and Performance', and Lovell, 'A Genre of Social Disruption?'

77 Cook, 'Narrative, Comedy, Character and Performance', p. 13.

78 Lovell, 'A Genre of Social Disruption?', p. 22.

79 *Ibid.*, p. 23.

80 Grote, *The End of Comedy*, pp. 55, 56, 105.

81 Marc, *Demographic Vistas*; Feuer, 'Genre Study and Television', pp. 113–133; Curtis, 'Aspects of Sitcom', p. 11.
82 Lovell, 'A Genre of Social Disruption?', p. 27.
83 Medhurst and Tuck, 'The Gender Game'. I will return to this essay in Chapter 3.
84 Eaton, 'Television Situation Comedy', pp. 61, 62.
85 Medhurst, 'Introduction', p. 1.

1 *Dad's Army*, 'The Test' (1970): platoon on parade

2 *Dad's Army*, 'The Man and the Hour' (1968): the ordinary man

3 *Dad's Army*, 'Big Guns' (1969): playing in the sandpit

4 *Dad's Army*, 'The Deadly Attachment' (1973): 'Don't tell him, Pike!'

5 *Dad's Army*, 'The Test' (1970): gentlemen and players

6 *It Ain't Half Hot, Mum*, 'Forbidden Fruits' (1975): Atlas as Marlene Dietrich

7 *It Ain't Half Hot, Mum*, 'Meet the Gang' (1974): Gloria's reaction

8 *It Ain't Half Hot, Mum*, 'Whispering Grass': the hypermasculine body

9 *It Ain't Half Hot, Mum*, 'Whispering Grass': the object of desire

10 *It Ain't Half Hot, Mum*, 'My Lovely Boy' (1974): 'Rule Britannia!'

11 *Hi-de-Hi!*, 'Hey Diddle Diddle' (1980): open and closed bodies

12 *Hi-de-Hi!*, 'Peggy's Big Chance' (1981): Barry and Yvonne's gender reversal

13 *Hi-de-Hi!*, 'Peggy's Big Chance' (1981): 'I'll get there somehow … you'll see'

14 *Hi-de-Hi!*, 'On with the Motley' (1981): famous people on the karsy

15 *Hi-de-Hi!*, 'Peggy's Big Chance' (1981): 'Step, heel, slide, slide, slide, recover, trip, in'

16 *You Rang, M'Lord?*, 'Royal Flush'
(1990): the family above stairs

17 *You Rang, M'Lord?*, 'Royal Flush'
(1990): the family below stairs

18 *You Rang, M'Lord?*, 'Royal Flush'
(1990): Cissy and Poppy

19 *You Rang, M'Lord?*, 'Royal Flush'
(1990): 'Do girls usually kiss each other
on the lips these days?'

Dad's Army

2

Whatever else may be said about the situation comedies of Jimmy Perry and David Croft, the recognition that *Dad's Army* had 'classic comedy' status even during its original broadcasts seems well established. In various histories of British comedy, the series almost always receives positive mention alongside *Hancock's Half-Hour*, *Steptoe and Son*, and *Till Death Us Do Part* as one of the milestones of British sitcom, overshadowing its contemporaries as well as the later collaborative work of Perry and Croft. It has attracted a formidable international fan-base and a variety of attendant discourses of appreciation, in the form of published scripts, DVD and VHS releases, celebratory books, cast autobiographies, appreciation societies and internet resources. In keeping with the critical response to situation comedy generally, however, *Dad's Army* has attracted very little serious critical discussion; more often than not it is characterised as gentle, delightful, whimsical, or 'middle-of-the-road' when compared with other 'classic comedy' products of the 1960s.[1]

The show first aired on BBC1 in July 1968 and continued, with a two-year hiatus between series eight and nine, until November 1977. Mark Lewisohn counts 83 episodes (77 × 30 mins; 1 × 60 mins; 1 × 40 mins; 1 × 35 mins; and 3 × short Christmas specials), of which the first 13 (the first two series and the first short special) were black and white.[2] This places it in the 'top fifteen' long-running sitcoms according to Lewisohn, far exceeding Perry and Croft's other collaborations: *It Ain't Half Hot, Mum* (56), *Hi-de-Hi!* (58), and *You Rang, M'Lord?* (26).[3] Although they are strictly beyond the purview of this book, it is worth pointing out that like many successful sitcoms *Dad's Army* generated a feature film (directed by Norman Cohen, 1971), and also a musical stage-play (1975), guest appearances by cast members on *The Morecambe and Wise Show* and *Blue Peter*, and a BBC Radio 4 adaptation of the television scripts that ran for 67 thirty-minute episodes between January 1974 and

September 1976. A BBC Radio 2 peace time sequel, *It Sticks Out a Mile* (a reference to the town pier), made a brief appearance in November and December 1983. The enduring nature of the series, and the proliferation of adaptations and spin-offs, testify to its popularity; as Lewisohn sums up: 'In Britain, few series have garnered such deeply entrenched and deserved love and affection'.[4] In the chapter that follows, I will first establish a historical context for *Dad's Army*, before moving on to a formal analysis of the series using some of the models of sitcom criticism I outlined in the last chapter. I shall focus specifically on how *Dad's Army* negotiates the particularities of realism, how the various configurations of the dichotomy of 'inside/outside' function in relation to the dynamics of the work-based sitcom, and how Perry and Croft represent the internal relationships of within and between classes.

Dad's Army follows the activities of the Local Defence Volunteers (or LDV) of Walmington-on-Sea, a fictitious south-coast town, during the Second World War. The LDV, which became known as the 'Home Guard' shortly after its inception, was formed by Home Secretary Anthony Eden in 1940 as a final line of defence against German invasion. Drawn from individuals too elderly or too young for the army, physically unfit, or in 'reserved' occupations, units of Home Guard were often a diverse group of volunteers – if generally senior, which gave rise to the colloquial moniker 'Dad's Army'. As I mentioned in the last chapter, Jimmy Perry himself was a member of his local Home Guard.

The cast of characters consists of the platoon's commanding officer, Captain Mainwaring (Arthur Lowe), a pompous bank manager in civilian life; Sergeant Wilson (John Le Mesurier), his languid chief clerk; the over-enthusiastic Lance Corporal Jones (Clive Dunn); and a motley collection of Privates – Pike (Ian Lavender), a 'mother's boy'; Godfrey (Arnold Ridley), a gentle and infirm old soul; Frazer (John Laurie), a doom-laden Scot; and Walker (James Beck), an archetypal 'spiv' (figure 1). This central core of characters (often fondly remembered as 'The Magnificent Seven') was joined by other adversaries and allies: Pike's doting mother and Sergeant Wilson's paramour, Mrs Pike (Janet Davies); a nasal, ineffectual Vicar (Frank Williams) and his belligerent Verger (Edward Sinclair); and – Mainwaring's chief oppositional influence – Air Raid Warden Hodges (Bill Pertwee). In addition to having stock studio-sets (the church-hall, Mainwaring's bank and requisitioned church hall offices, and the parade ground), the series saw quite a bit of exterior location filming in the Stamford Practical Training Area, owned by the Ministry of Defence, near Thetford in Norfolk.

While the principal source of *Dad's Army* was obviously Jimmy Perry's own experience in Watford's Home Guard, the particular moment of inspiration that Perry cites occurred only in 1967, during a walk through St James's Park. Hearing the changing of the guard, Perry remembered his own experiences during the war: 'The red tunics of the soldiers made a brave sight – what a difference from the drab khaki battle dress of the war years, when the Home Guard had a spell of duty at the Palace'.[5] Subsequently Perry imagined that the Home Guard would provide a perfect situation for a television sitcom. The other formative influence that he cites was *Oh! Mr Porter*, a Will Hay comedy from 1937, which Perry saw on television by chance as his initial concept for *Dad's Army* began to develop. The dynamic that Perry took from this film was the tripartite relationship between main characters: 'a pompous man, a boy, and an old man'.[6] Tempting as it is to identify these character types as Mainwaring, Pike and Jones, the scope of the relationships in *Dad's Army* clearly extends and complicates this structure.[6] Perry presented an initial script called *The Fighting Tigers* to David Croft, with whom he had some professional acquaintance, and together they produced an additional script and presented both to Michael Mills, the BBC's Head of Light Entertainment. Mills approved the project, but suggested the series' change of title to *Dad's Army*.

Perry and Croft's first collaboration was certainly not the first military situation comedy broadcast on British television – although, as many commentators point out, *Dad's Army* is not strictly about the armed forces. The late 1950s and early 1960s saw several imports with a military setting. *The Phil Silvers Show*, better known as *Bilko*, was broadcast by the BBC between 1957 and 1960, and was set in Fort Baxter, Kansas, though the series' military situation often seems incidental to the plots designed to showcase Sergeant Bilko's wily, double-dealing activities. Another popular US sitcom, which made only a brief appearance on the BBC in 1963, was *McHale's Navy*. Set on a ship in the South Pacific during the Second World War, the sitcom had an eponymous character (Ernest Borgnine) cast very much in Bilko's mould; the series' plots revolved largely around McHale's schemes to shirk his responsibilities. In these shows the oppositional or 'outside' influence was provided by Bilko's and McHale's commanding officers – Colonel 'Melonhead' Hall and Captain Binghamton respectively – and not by the historically 'real' enemy: the Japanese in the case of the latter. As with *Bilko*, the military setting seems incidental to *McHale's Navy*; although the show's later episodes were relocated to Italy, there was, according to Bruce Crowther and Mike Pinfold, 'no appreciable increase in the reality content'.[7] The other significant US sitcom with a military setting from this period was *Hogan's Heroes*, which ran on ITV between 1967 and 1971. Set in a German prisoner-of-war camp, Stalag 13, during the Second World

War, the series depicted the activities of a group of Allied prisoners; contrary to the grim conditions in POW camps, life in Stalag 13 is presented as tremendous fun – so much so that the prisoners don't have any desire to leave. The camp's commanding officer is a ridiculous German stereotype: Colonel Klink (Werner Klemperer) is bald and monocled like Eric Von Stroheim, speaks with an absurd accent, and is portrayed as cowardly and inept beside the (predictably) wily Colonel Hogan (Bob Crane).

Not all military sitcoms were US imports. ITV had produced its own military sitcom in the late 1950s: set during peace time in the rural backwater of Nether Hopping, *The Army Game* ran for fifteen series between 1957 and 1966. As its long life suggests, this situation comedy was extremely popular in its day, though Lewisohn remarks that surviving episodes 'do not seem anywhere near as funny now as they once were', a fact he attributes to the series' original proximity to the Second World War and to the era of National Service.[8] *The Army Game* was populated with a host of comic actors, several of whom would continue to appear in television series, sitcoms and the *Carry On* films: Alfie Bass, Bill Fraser, Michael Medwin, Charles Hawtrey, Bernard Bresslaw, Dick Emery and Frank Williams (*Dad's Army*'s Reverend Farthing). Like their other military compeers, the characters devoted their time to finding ways to avoid responsibility, inevitably pitting themselves against their superiors – the archetypal Sergeant Majors Bullimore (William Hartnell) and Snudge (Bill Fraser). As with *McHale's Navy* and *The Phil Silvers Show*, too, the series' military setting was often quite incidental to the episode's plots.

All of these series were precursors to *Dad's Army*, and even if they had no direct influence on Perry and Croft's first sitcom (though it is difficult to imagine that *The Army Game* didn't), they certainly created the context in which the series was received, and the standard to which it was necessarily compared. *The Army Game* and *The Phil Silvers Show* have important characteristics in common; since they are far removed from sites of military conflict (in peace time Staffordshire and Kansas, respectively), opportunities for interaction with the 'enemy' are removed from the situation, and the stability of the 'inside', to use Eaton's terms from the last chapter, is threatened by conflicts within the existing military hierarchy instead. *Hogan's Heroes* and *McHale's Navy*, by contrast, are situated in the thick of war time action, and in territory held or threatened by an aggressive enemy force. In the latter sitcom, this context is deliberately suppressed, however, in favour of a hierarchical dynamic like that of *The Phil Silvers Show*. It is this elision that Lewisohn proposes as the reason for the 'lukewarm' response of its British audience; 'the series made light of a war that had been experienced very differently in the UK' from how it had been experienced in the US, and this affected the UK reception of *McHale's Navy*.[9] Despite its popularity, *Hogan's Heroes* can be similarly criticised; laughing at the circumstances of the twentieth century's darkest period of history is, arguably, one way of confronting its horror, but reducing the privations of the POW camp to a private holiday resort complete with sauna and gourmet French cuisine seems genuinely tasteless.

Dad's Army treads a more careful path through this potentially awkward territory. As improbable as it seems now, though, especially given its often-cited gentleness and whimsy, the series' production and the response to its initial broadcast were nevertheless beset with controversy. Although the potentially controversial nature of *Dad's Army* might be difficult to appreciate from the perspective of the new millennium, almost sixty years after the end of the Second World War, the nation's sensitivity to the situation represented can be discerned in newspaper reviews of the first broadcast. *The Times*'s Michael Billington suggested that the blend of humour and sentiment was awkward, 'as if afraid of making too much fun of a hallowed wartime institution', and, most famously, in *The Daily Telegraph* Sean Day-Lewis referred to it as a 'satire on the Dunkirk spirit' – again identifying a 'nervous sense of humour' in the broadcast.[10] The series' opening credits were a particular source of sensitivity during production. 'The show's original concept', reports Koseluk, 'called for the opening and closing sequences to include actual war footage, illustrating the bleak horror of war'.[11] This proposed opening hardly seems the stuff of comedy and, while it was certainly more sensitive than *Hogan's Heroes*, there was some concern that the use of war footage might seem disrespectful to the British war effort. In an interview with Tim Devlin in *The Times* in 1973, David Croft remembers that '[t]here was a lot of opposition ... We were sending up Britain's finest hour. Paul Fox, then Controller of Programmes, thought it would be a psychological mistake'. The compromise that was found to avert this potential difficulty was to frame the opening sequence of the first episode with a scene that clearly established what followed as a retrospective look from a contemporary (i.e. 1968) perspective. It is worth, I think, looking in more detail at the opening and closing sequences of the first episode, to observe how this compromise was achieved in visual terms, and to assess how *Dad's Army*'s subject matter was accommodated ideologically.

The opening sequence has a tripartite structure, of which Croft didn't approve but which was part of the compromise required to have the show aired. It begins with Wilson's introduction of Alderman George

Mainwaring, the camera panning slowly from left to right, zooming in on a suitably aged Godfrey, Pike, Walker and Frazer as it passes, then coming to rest briefly on Mainwaring himself, before framing both Mainwaring and Wilson in the shot. Jones is absent; as the oldest member of the original platoon, he has presumably not survived until 1968. It is difficult to reconstruct how this opening originally operated, since much of its effect lies in our own retrospection: we can only note Jones's absence if we were aware of his presence in the platoon in the first place. Even though the movements of the camera might suggest to us which actors on screen will play an important role, we have no knowledge of their identities or their characters. The sequence does establish Mainwaring as the central character and, despite two brief cuts to the reactions of a cigar-smoking Walker and a querulous Frazer, the remainder of the scene consists of a close-up of Mainwaring's face against a background of the Union Flag. As I see it, this latter element seems to be the key to the compromise – the cast, significant only when we know who they are, provide an enigmatic context for the episode that follows, but the flag provides a visual anchor for the substance of Mainwaring's speech. Alderman Mainwaring, we hear, has been asked to preside at Walmington-on-Sea's 'I'm Backing Britain' campaign, a responsibility that he's glad to undertake, since, he claims, he's been backing Britain since 1940. But, he adds:

> Then we all backed Britain. It was the darkest hour in our history. The odds were absurdly against us, but, young and old, we stood there, defiant, determined to survive, to recover, and finally to win. The news was desperate. Our spirits were always high.[12]

Mainwaring's speech makes clear for its audience the retrospective nature of what is to follow, but it is positioned squarely within the discourses of war time British nationalism. The speech is without satire, there is no lampooning of the 'Dunkirk spirit', and it demands that we take the efforts of Mainwaring and his cohorts seriously.

The cut from Mainwaring's speech to the next section of the sequence is abrupt, not least because of the switch from live action to animation. Apart from the fact that it is filmed in black and white, this section of the opening sequence is identical to what would become the sitcom's entire opening sequence in future series: Bud Flanagan sings *Dad's Army*'s theme ('Who do you Think you are Kidding, Mr Hitler?', a pastiche of Second World War songs, written for the series by Jimmy Perry) as British and German forces, represented by the traditional blocks and arrows of battle schematics, manoeuvre across a map of Europe. It's familiar enough to regular viewers of the series, but the reactions of its original audience are interesting. The initial, tentative movement of the British arrows as they makes their conservative advance from the French coast generates a laugh, followed by another as the Nazi arrows make a smooth, serpentine advance, one coiling sinuously beneath another, and force a British retreat across the English Channel. The British arrow, trapped in south-east England, makes a few vain gestures towards advancing, generating another round of laughter. It is impossible, of course, to diagnose the source of this laughter at thirty-five years' remove. Nervousness, perhaps, following the clearly serious, patriotic opening scene? A received reaction to animation? Amusement at the Nazi occupation of France? The cartoon's arrows, though, offer a gentle satire on national stereotypes: the British arrows are cautious and diminutive, but remain plucky even in retreat; the Nazi arrows slither appropriately.

The opening credits continue, with the battle schematic announcing the show's title, its writers, its principal actors, and finally the episode's title. At this point, however, the third sequence begins, with the use of old newsreel footage of the war. As the voice-over discusses the Nazi advance across Europe, we see tanks crawling across a war-torn terrain, heavy artillery strikes, and the forbidding might of the German army. Against this is pitted the common British soldier, mounted on a bicycle and rallied by Churchill. Particularly insidious, the voice-over claims, is the German use of parachutists over Britain, dropping enemy saboteurs and fifth columnists into our midst, to combat which a new force – the LDV – has been formed. At this point the authentic newsreel footage is cut with pastiche: a volunteer whom we later come to know as Lance Corporal Jones rotates a road sign with two direction markers, 'To the Town' and 'To the Sea', and succeeds in confusing, not an enemy saboteur but one of Britain's own troops, who takes the wrong road despite Jones's helpless gesticulations. The next cut is to Frazer, sharpening the end of a stake buried in the ground; he tests the keenness of its point, and looks up with expectancy, evidently relishing the arrival of enemy parachutists. This is a nicely played sight gag that foreshadows *Dad's Army*'s ongoing amusement at the prospect of penetration ('They don't like it up 'em, sir' became one of Jones's catchphrases, and was taken, Perry reports, from one of his own commanding officers during the war).

Despite Croft's view that this opening sequence was a 'dog's dinner', I think that the credits provide very useful context for the rest of the episode, and for the series itself.[13] They succeed in communicating the fine balance in the series between satire and patriotism, and between reality and pastiche. Backing Britain in 1940, and in 1968, Mainwaring's commitment to the Home Guard's cause never becomes the object of satire. Neither does Jones's – the spirit of his attempt to confuse enemy parachutists is not mocked so much as his over-enthusiasm in its pursuit. The concluding scenes of the first episode make this dynamic clear: after a farcical enactment in the church hall of a method of disabling enemy tanks using a burning blanket, Mainwaring delivers a serious coda:

> But remember, men, we have one invaluable weapon on our side: we have an unbreakable spirit to win! A bulldog tenacity that will help us hang on while there's breath left in our bodies. You don't get that with gestapos and jackboots! You get that by being British! So come on, Adolf: we're ready for you![14]

Thus, the incompetence demonstrated during the course of the episode is neatly contained between Mainwaring's opening and closing speeches, which are complete with all the trappings of the British patriotic spirit. This structure is reinforced by the closing credits, which were likewise a replacement for the original use of wartime footage. A still image of the rolling landscape of the British countryside becomes the backdrop for successive superimposed images of the cast, marching resolutely to protect their country (figure 2). As in the early days of the Home Guard, they are not armed and do not have uniforms, but are arrayed in a motley collection of iconically British clothing: cloth caps, a First World War uniform, even a cricket sweater.

Despite these accommodations, the BBC was still apprehensive about the reception that *Dad's Army* would receive, and so three test screenings on consecutive evenings were conducted. Jimmy Perry reports that the test audiences' reactions were not positive overall; he quotes one individual as saying 'Well, I think it's a rotten show. There's nothing to it. Haven't we had enough of this old wartime rubbish?'[15] This seemed to be a common reaction – rather than the expected offence, *Dad's Army* provoked an attitude of weariness toward its subject matter. David Croft craftily suppressed the market research ('he made arrangements for the report to come into his office, where he put it to the bottom of the pile in his in-tray'), and Perry believes that this was the only reason that the series ever aired.

As with all of Perry and Croft's sitcoms, the relationship of 'real' experience to the series' fictional narratives and characterisations needs to be addressed. Jimmy Perry was, of course, a member of his own local Home Guard, a fifteen-year-old recruit in the 19th Hertfordshire Battalion, and his characterisation of Pike bears some resemblance to himself. His mother, he reports, 'was fearful of me being out at night and catching cold, but I loved it!'[16] Characters and events in *Dad's Army* mirror historical accounts and situations; as Perry states, '*Dad's Army* was based firmly on fact and the truth of the situation'.[17] McCann cites an example that bears a passing resemblance to Lance Corporal Jones: Alexander Taylor, a 'sprightly octagenarian' and a veteran of the Sudan, South Africa and Flanders, who enlisted with the Home Guard despite its sixty-five year upper age limit. While the farcical antics of Walmington-on-Sea's Home Guard might seem to descend into absurdism, historical accounts of such well-meaning incompetence proliferate. Famously, the 1st Berkshire Battalion 'mistook a distant cow's swishing tail for some kind of inscrutable "dot-dash movement of a flag"'.[18] And if the disguised manoeuvres of Mainwaring's platoon in 'Don't Forget the Diver' (which necessitate Frazer's wearing of a deep-sea diving suit, Jones's disguise in a pantomime tree costume, and Godfrey's placing helmets on a flock of sheep to confuse their rivals in a training exercise), seem ridiculous, one might reflect on the photographic documentation of a Home Guard training exercise in Ross in 1941, in which a man posing as a 'fifth columnist' attempted to ambush a platoon of Home Guard volunteers while disguised as a nursemaid. The image of a man dressed in a woman's tweed suit and pulling a gun on an unprepared soldier is positively Pythonic.[19] In an interview with Graham McCann, Jimmy Perry claims that he undertook research into the Home Guard beyond his own personal experience, though he found little available except some Home Guard training pamphlets and memoirs, even in the Imperial War Museum.[20] It is only recently, in fact, that historians have written comprehensively about the 'real Dad's Army'. Home Guard training manuals, often represented as the source of Mainwaring's inspiration within the series, themselves read like handbooks for *Dad's Army*'s comic plotlines. Anti-tank exercises, for example, call for the construction of a simulated German tank from wood and sacking mounted on a car.[21]

One cannot argue with Jimmy Perry for his insistence on realism or with its centrality to the show's success, and one cannot deny the often improbable likeness of even the most absurd plotlines to historically documented accounts of Home Guard activities; but the problematic of realist representation nevertheless returns from the last chapter. Gregory Koseluk quotes Perry's words from an unspecified newspaper interview from 1973: the secret of *Dad's Army*'s success is that 'it is based on real situations, with real people who are reacting the way we know they are going to react'.[22] But while producing a believable 'reality' is important to encouraging audience identification with the characters and their narratives, it is also necessary to acknowledge the 'constructedness' of this reality. The series makes use of pastiche, blurring divisions between fiction and reality, from the very beginning: the theme tune, 'Who do you Think you are Kidding, Mr Hitler?', was written by Perry for the show, but performed by Bud Flanagan, who was responsible for popular wartime songs, and the genuine newsreel footage that opens the first episodes of Dad's Army is intercut with mock footage of Walmington-on-Sea's platoon, narrated by E. V. H. Emmett, who was the original voice of wartime Gaumont-British newsreels. This makes the modified opening and closing sequences of the first episode even more enigmatic as a compromise acceptable to Paul Fox, BBC1's controller, who asserted that he was 'very much against this mixing of fact and fiction; film of actuality belongs to factual programmes and should not be used mischievously in comedy programmes'.[23] It is worth returning, I think, to the relationships between comedy and realism sketched by Cook and Lovell in the last chapter, since both models can elucidate the use of realism in Dad's Army.

Jim Cook distinguishes between two levels of narrative, the content and the structure. The latter element – how the narrative is put together – is identified by Cook as counter-realist in the comic narrative of the sitcom. It is potentially interruptive of the realist strategy of the narrative content, which would otherwise attempt to elide the process of its construction and present the narrative as plausible, believable or 'real'. In the case of Dad's Army, the emphasis on 'real situations, with real people who are reacting the way we know they are going to react' is interrupted by the intentional narrative strategy of creating comic elements that might appear implausible or even absurd. Thus, in the episode 'Don't Forget the Diver', which I mentioned above, the obvious narrative content – the platoon's participation in a strategic exercise against their rivals, the Eastgate Home Guard – is plausible enough, as are this particular exercise's parameters (the deposition of a 'bomb', represented by an alarm clock, in the enemy base, represented by a windmill, without being spotted and repelled by the enemy). The element of rivalry between the platoons, and between their respective commanding officers, adds a further, familiar narrative tension.

The comedy resides in the way in which this narrative is structured, which involves the introduction of highly implausible elements. Frazer's use of a deep-sea diving suit to remain hidden beneath the surface of a river is at best unlikely; Jones's disguise in a pantomime tree costume and Godfrey's diversionary tactics are both highly implausible. These elements are carefully integrated into the episode, however, in ways that prevent them from destroying the realist narrative. As in many episodes of Dad's Army the platoon performs a 'dry run' of its activity in the church hall, during which a suitable rationale for some absurd elements is provided – Frazer, we learn, inherited the deep-sea diving suit from a 'doomed' friend. Perry and Croft very carefully ration their interruptions of the realist narrative. The 'dry run' involves, as usual, several abortive attempts, but the writers reserve further implausibilities for the actual exercise: the window in Jones's costume is stuck and, temporarily blinded, he crashes into the river; the alarm clock, slung between Jones's legs for no good reason besides Jones's own befuddled planning, is unreachable at the appropriate moment; and, finally, Jones's awkwardness results in his getting caught on the moving sails of the windmill.

Part of the way this functions is through the naturalisation of the comic intrusion, through what Terry Lovell calls the 'found comedy' of 'human frailty'. Jones is the oldest member of the platoon and its most eager to volunteer, which rationalises both his position at the forefront of the action, and the inevitable incapability that he demonstrates (a clever combination of elements made possible by Clive Dunn's ability to play a character much older than himself, and thus perform the physical comedy necessary for the role). The extent to which the realism of the narrative is not undermined by the deliberate introduction of the counter-realist comic structure is dependent, to some degree, on the audience's perspective. But Perry and Croft's writing works hard to efface structural interruptions and implausibilities by naturalising them within the internally coherent reality of the series' narrative content.

Another way of reading *Dad's Army*'s realism is through Terry Lovell's work with social realist comedy, discussed in the last chapter. Unlike Cook, Lovell does not find that comedy is necessarily counter-realist in tendency; for Lovell, the important distinction in social realist texts is between the discourses of the normative order (the 'ideal') and the typical (the 'real'), or, as she glosses her terminology, between the way things 'ought to be' and what is 'usually the case'.[24] Many comedies of this type effect a reversal of the typical and normative orders, often with respect to sex and gender roles or age, and Lovell specifically cites *Dad's Army* as an example. This is perhaps best exemplified by the episode 'Big Guns', in which Mainwaring conducts a 'tute' in his office, explaining the drill the platoon will follow in the event of seaborne invasion. As the platoon construct the model of Walmington-on-Sea on which they will plan the drill, the exercise degenerates into petty arguments over who will be represented by which toy soldier, and, by the end of the scene, it has been reduced to a group of older men playing with toy soldiers and cars in a sandpit (figure 3). Old men, normative discourses tell us, should behave like old men, and not like boys. In Lovell's model, comedy is generated in the disjunction between normative and typical discourses. So, *ideally* the Home Guard ought to be able to conduct itself with a degree of competence, but *realistically* (and this references, to some degree, a reality beyond the internal discourses of the series) it is largely incompetent because most of its volunteers are 'past it'. *Ideally* old men should comport themselves with a dignity befitting their age, but *realistically* they behave like children. The assumptions that motivate these discourses form around a familiar stereotype – that old people are childish and useless. But if it appears that I am accusing Perry and Croft of an unpleasantly 'ageist' representation, it must be recognised that they often reverse this trend at an episode's denouement. If, after a long, slapstick pursuit of an untethered barrage balloon in 'The Day the Balloon Went Up', the platoon releases it, inadvertently, by simultaneously saluting an officer, or if Mainwaring's heroic attempts to deal with a live grenade are thwarted by a dog repeatedly retrieving it in 'Fallen Idol', conversely, in 'The Test', the physically frail Godfrey saves the day by winning a cricket match, and, in 'The Two and a Half Feathers', Jones retains his dignity and reputation by revealing that he has kept a lifelong secret, now discharged by the death of both parties involved.

Exploring comedy's relationship to reality in *Dad's Army* – effectively critiquing or problematising an uncritical evocation of the 'real' as a foundation for comedy – certainly does not diminish the quality of Perry and Croft's writing. In fact, as I hope this analysis has begun to reveal, *Dad's Army* does not appear absurd or cliched, like some of its contemporaries, precisely because of Perry and Croft's carefully constructed narratives, which draw on a broad lexicon of established comic traditions as well as on their own lived experiences. In the remainder of this chapter, I will continue to subject the formal structures of *Dad's Army* to critical analysis, making particular use of the dichotomy of 'inside' and 'outside' that I outlined in Chapter One.

Dad's Army and the dynamics of work

As Stephen Wagg has noted, situation comedies about work relations were not uncommon in Britain during the 1960s.[25] *The Rag Trade* (1963–65) is a good example of a work-based sitcom roughly contemporaneous with *Dad's Army*. This series takes place on the shop floor of Fenner Fashions, with episodes driven by conflicts between the management, Harold Fenner (Peter Jones), and the workers, led by shop steward Paddy (Miriam Karlin), with the foreman, Reg (Reg Varney), occupying a conflicted middle position. *Dad's Army*'s classification as a 'work-situated' comedy is a little more complex, however, since there are two overlapping dynamics of work in the series: as a platoon of Home Guard (the series' central organising principle) the characters operate in a non-domestic environment of work (they have a job to do, after all) but there are also fairly frequent representations of the characters in their own regular occupational environments. Sometimes the occupational relationships are replicated in the Home Guard – the hierarchy of Mainwaring, Wilson and Pike in Swallow's Bank as branch manager, chief clerk, and clerk is mirrored in their roles as Captain, Sergeant and Private – and sometimes they are inverted. In 'The Two and a Half Feathers', for example, the civilian Joe Walker informs *Mr* Mainwaring that, as an account holder at Mainwaring's bank and as a private citizen, he is not obliged to follow Mainwaring's orders when off duty. Jones the butcher often uses his dispensation of contraband meat products as a strategy of power, negotiating his rank as Lance Corporal in 'The Man and the Hour' with a couple of pounds of steak.

According to Mick Eaton, 'work' is one of the two dominant situations used in sitcom, as we saw in the last chapter. As with the use of 'home' or 'family', the 'work' situation is advantageous, not because of the audience's 'predominant ideological concerns', but because the parameters of the work environment provide an ideal paradigm for situation comedy: '[t]he situation demands a stability of character and problematic, a clearly defined boundary ... [and] allows for the representation of class differences through the treatment of the different hierarchical grades, ranks, of the running characters'.[26] As Steve Neale and Frank Krutnik develop Eaton's ideas about the 'inside' and 'outside' dichotomy, they focus mostly on the paradigm of 'home' in relation to British sitcom; when they discuss the use of the work environment, they look at US sitcoms of the 1970s and 1980s, such as *Taxi* or *Cheers*. Their conclusions, however, are entirely applicable to the work-based British sitcom: just as the domestic sitcom uses the structure of the bourgeois family to define a clear boundary between an 'inside' and an 'outside' that must be maintained from episode to episode, the work-based comedy uses 'principles of unity, allegiance, and obligation [that] are structured in a "surrogate" family network'.[27] Thus, as in the US examples discussed by Neale and Krutnik, in *Dad's Army* disruptive 'outside' forces are often seen to threaten the platoon's unity or sense of common obligation and loyalty.

Frances Gray, in *Women and Laughter*, takes a different view, however. She cites 'innumerable sitcoms in which female absence is the condition that permits male individuality by liberating them from the confines of the family "norm"', mentioning *Dad's Army* specifically in this context.[28] 'Far from being the site of the alternative family', she adds, 'the workplace in much British sitcom is precisely the place of male freedom from domesticity ... because there are no women around to "spoil things" with common sense'.[29] Of course, it is easy to rationalise the absence of women in sitcoms like *Dad's Army* or *It Ain't Half Hot, Mum* – their environments are by definition male-dominated, especially in the latter case. Gray's point, however, is well taken when one considers that the introduction of female characters or domestic situations into *Dad's Army* functions largely as a threat from the 'outside' placed in opposition to the unity and stability of the platoon's 'inside'. In this section of the chapter, I would like to investigate the dynamics of the 'surrogate family' structure of *Dad's Army*'s platoon, by considering the ways in which the series defines an ideological 'outside' against its 'inside'. What are the threats to Walmington-on-Sea's Home Guard, and how do they impinge upon the group's unity and stability? Though there may be others, four 'threats' proliferate in the series: the influence of the 'regular army' on the Home Guard platoon, interaction with the civilian population, the possibility of German invasion, and the intrusion of women into an otherwise male environment.

The principal threat to the internal stability of Walmington-on-Sea's platoon in the series' first season is interference from the regular army. It is important to note that although the hierarchical structure of the Home Guard mirrored that of the British army, its members were volunteers only, and officers in the Home Guard remained subordinate to their military counterparts. Thus, units of Home Guard, who did not always have cordial relationships with each other, were often found in struggles for authority with the armed forces. Some British generals doubted the efficacy of the Home Guard, for example, and 'some Home Guard commanders were clearly unwilling to accept the limitations on their security duties or accept orders with which they did not agree'.[30] The last three episodes of the first season, 'The Enemy within the Gates', 'The Showing Up of Corporal Jones' and 'Shooting Pains', all introduce representatives of the enlisted army as an external threat to the platoon's stable internal environment. In the first of these, a Polish army officer attached to GHQ, Captain Winogrodzki, chastises Jones, Walker and Pike for the laxity of their patrol duty and, subsequently, chastises Mainwaring for the laxity of his security measures (the German parachutists captured by Jones's patrol are allowed to escape by Godfrey and are recaptured by Winogrodzki). The other two episodes see another threat from GHQ in the form of Major Regan, who first attempts to have Jones dropped from the platoon unless he can demonstrate his fitness by completing an assault course, and then takes away the platoon's assignment as an honour guard to the Prime Minister unless its members can win a shooting contest against the Eastgate platoon. Perhaps because these episodes are successive, they appear rather formulaic: an external source of authority, represented by a 'real' army officer, threatens to destabilise the platoon's sense of unity and identity by calling into question its internal systems of authority and integrity, and even its physical composition. The accusations made against the platoon are fair enough – Godfrey *isn't* a competent guard, Jones's age and over-enthusiasm *do* contribute to his ineptitude, the platoon *hasn't* performed competently at the shooting range – but these are clearly not the issues at stake in these episodes. The platoon's internal stability is maintained in the face of external interference by a combination of guile, team spirit and well-hidden talent: Winogrodzki's authority is undermined when, because of his accent, he is arrested as a German invader by the military police who have come to collect the parachutists – a mistake facilitated by Walker, who receives an additional £10 bounty for his arrest; Regan's attempt to expel Jones is thwarted by the collective effort of the platoon, which helps him pass the assault course; and Frazer saves the platoon's reputation by turning out, *deus ex machina*, to be a veteran marksman from his naval career in the First World War. However unsympathetically represented, in all these cases the challenge from the 'outside' is one of competence or efficiency, and the 'inside' values that are celebrated and upheld are those of individual craft and cunning marshalled or revealed in service and loyalty to the group. This 'communalizing' function of situation comedy, to use Neale and Krutnik's term, imbricates the audience in a value system that prefers the flawed whimsy of 'human nature' to the humourlessness of efficient systems of authority; it is a celebration of amateurism seen at its best over professionalism represented at its worst.[31]

Perry and Croft didn't pursue this particular external threat in subsequent series, perhaps because of its predictability as a plotline. Gregory Koseluk doesn't care for it, certainly, and suggests that with this construction *Dad's Army* ran the risk of 'devolving into a British version of *McHale's Navy*'.[32] Increasingly in later series of *Dad's Army* the principal antagonisms come from the conflicted relationships between members of the platoon (particularly Captain Mainwaring) and the 'civilians' with whom they interact: the Vicar, the Verger, and, most significantly, ARP Warden Hodges. Again, Perry and Croft can be seen to exploit the historical tensions between Home Guard members and the public they volunteered to defend. The *Home Guard Training Manual* cautions against abuse of power: 'the worst fault you can show is to give the impression that you regard your job as a splendid opportunity for bullying and ordering people about' it says, and, concerning the inspection of identity cards, 'you should not do it in a dictatorial manner. We want no little Hitlers or Gestapo imitators in the Home Guard.'[33] Despite the warning, volunteers were notorious for challenging the identity of civilians, including air raid wardens and other civil defence workers. On one occasion, cited by Mackenzie, a rector in Lancashire was 'taken into custody by the local LDV for refusing to hand over the keys to an empty church school the commander wanted to investigate'.[34] The Walmington-on-Sea platoon has requisitioned the church hall for its meetings, with Mainwaring using the Vicar's office in his absence. The arrangement is not without its tensions: the Vicar and Mainwaring squabble over possession of the office in 'A Soldier's Farewell', performing a childish routine of musical chairs with each playing of the national anthem; and the Verger hovers protectively around the church hall, attempting to instruct Mainwaring on what he can and can't do. The Verger is especially poisonous in 'Don't Forget the Diver', in which he operates as the Eastgate Platoon's 'mole', listening in on Mainwaring's briefing in the church hall, and reporting to Captain Square during the manoeuvres via a telephone improbably secreted in a funerary urn. Mainwaring's particular adversary, however, is ARP Warden Hodges. Hodges provides a steady stream of mockery and invective in the later series, pointing to the platoon's follies and inabilities, and challenging Mainwaring's authority at every turn. His nickname for Mainwaring (Napoleon) attacks the Captain's diminutive size, his grand military aspirations and his dictatorial manner. Despite the fact that Hodges, the Vicar and the Verger (a trio which is occasionally allied against the platoon) offer challenges to Mainwaring's authority, however, their threats are hardly as serious as those brought to bear by the regular army – largely because, of course, these individuals possess very little power over the Home Guard. While most of Hodges' mocking remarks score palpable hits on Mainwaring's pomposity, their efficacy is rarely more than momentary, since Hodges is often proven wrong or otherwise disgraced by the episode's events. He is quick to pour scorn on Mainwaring's abilities in 'The Deadly Attachment', for example, but is put in his place when held hostage by the Germans and saved by Mainwaring's surrender. His attempts to disgrace the platoon in a cricket match in 'The Test' are thwarted by Godfrey's unlikely success at the wicket. What Hodges, the Vicar and the Verger all share is a common ineffectuality, especially in the face of action, when they are often revealed to be craven or otherwise inadequate. In 'The Recruit', for example, the Vicar and the Verger are allowed to join the platoon in Mainwaring's absence, and their own inability to perform adequately the duties about which they criticise the platoon's regular membership is made all too apparent. Undeniably pompous, Mainwaring is willing to shoulder responsibility and face the prospect of dangerous action, while Hodges – full of scorn and mockery of the efforts of others – is himself found lacking at the crucial moment. As his external challenge to the platoon's authority and dignity is pushed aside – often physically, and by the platoon's communal effort – the internal values of solidarity and of genuine commitment are reinforced.

Perhaps the most obvious adversarial influence available to Perry and Croft is the ever-present threat of German invasion – the Home Guard's *raison d'être*. The lack of any historical invasion or occupation of England during the Second World War is one of the factors that allows *Dad's Army* to function as a successful situation comedy, without the charges of tastelessness that other sitcoms set in the same period have often drawn, and it is also one proposed reason why the history of the Home Guard itself fell into obscurity and silence.[35] German troops, however, show up in episodes as early as the first series, again offering an external threat to the stability of the 'inside'; *Dad's Army*'s representation of German invaders is worth considering in some detail, since it departs from a tradition of easy stereotyping popular elsewhere in the British media.

Werner Klemperer's Colonel Klink, from the US sitcom *Hogan's Heroes*, was mentioned earlier in this chapter as a caricature embodying several stereotypical German traits, and who is set up to be Hogan's cowardly, inept stooge. We can find a more useful comparison closer to home: although David Croft and Jeremy Lloyd's *'Allo 'Allo!* ran from 1982–92, and is a contemporary of other later Perry and Croft sitcoms (*Hi-de-Hi!* [1980–88] and *You Rang, M'Lord?* [1988–93]), its situation – occupied France during the Second World War – provides an obviously shared territory with *Dad's Army*. Several commentators have compared the two, with *'Allo 'Allo!* usually suffering as a consequence. Bruce Crowther and Mike Pinfold are the most outspoken about the latter series' shortcomings. Citing its historical context, they assert that '[e]ven after making allowances for the passage of time and present-day acceptance of jokes about almost anything, it is hard to find any saving grace in *'Allo 'Allo!*'.[36] Crowther and Pinfold find the series 'wearisome' and tasteless in ways never approached by *Dad's Army*, though I suspect they overlook the fact that *'Allo 'Allo!* functions, on some level at least, as a parody of another popular BBC television series, *Secret Army*. The series relies heavily on obvious sexual innuendo, and, as Jürgen Kamm points out in his essay '"Oh What a Funny War": Representations of World War II in British TV comedy', it 'focuses on getting as much mileage as possible out of farcical constellations without ever touching upon the serious aspects' of wartime experience.[37]

The representation of Germans in the series is particularly reductive. The principal 'villain' is Herr Flick, who, like Colonel Klink, is an absurd caricature of a Gestapo officer, with a sinister limp, a black leather overcoat and a ridiculous accent. If a little jingoistic (or, as some television critics felt at the time, 'nervous') in its early episodes, *Dad's Army* never descends to this level of caricature; in fact, several episodes work in precisely the opposite fashion. In 'If the Cap Fits', Mainwaring's lecture on the identification of German soldiers is used to attack the reliance on such stereotypical markers. The slides that accompany the lecture are designed to educate the platoon on the distinguishing marks of German uniforms, but Mainwaring's remarks ignore them in favour of a critique of the facial features and emotional dispositions of the line drawings projected on the screen. When he declares that the Germans' lack of earlobes indicates criminality, all eyes turn towards Walker's ears. As Mainwaring denounces German uniforms as 'ersatz rubbish' that 'would probably fall to pieces in a matter of weeks' (unlike their British counterparts that are 'strong, sturdy, last forever, made by British craftsmen'), the camera cuts to Frazer scratching uncomfortably in his ill-fitting uniform. And when Mainwaring remarks on the German soldier's 'dozy expression' which is 'quite different, you see, from the British – keen, alert ...' he is compelled to interrupt his declaration to wake up Godfrey ('I must have dropped off'). Although one function of the 'inside/outside' model is to emphasise the otherness of an external threat to the internal normative unit, this example resists such a dynamic: the characteristics identified by Mainwaring as 'typically Nazi' turn out to be rather familiar after all.

The platoon's most famous encounter with the enemy occurs in 'The Deadly Attachment', in which Mainwaring is asked to watch the crew of a U-boat overnight in the church hall.[38] In this episode, Philip Madoc's U-boat captain is relatively understated: mildly sinister, characteristically cool perhaps, he successfully outwits Mainwaring and takes hostage, first ARP Warden Hodges and then Jones – the latter kept in check with a hand grenade hidden in his trousers, ready to be detonated in the event of trouble. Mainwaring's characteristic patriotic xenophobia is deconstructed in a similar fashion to that described above in 'If the Cap Fits'. When the German U-boat men stand to attention, Wilson's apparently accurate observation that 'they're awfully well disciplined, aren't they sir?' is met with Mainwaring's absurdly jingoistic response: 'Nothing of the sort. Slavish, blind obedience ... a nation of automatons'. A cut to Wilson's amused reaction underscores the point. The Home Guard appear ridiculous compared to their adversaries, as Jones becomes over excited, Pike taunts them with a childish rhyme (the famous 'Whistle while you work, Hitler is a twerp'), and Mainwaring is drawn into petty bickering (figure 4). Ultimately, of course, it is not the discipline or superior initiative of the British that saves the day. As the platoon and their 'prisoners' march through the streets of Walmington-on-Sea, they encounter the Colonel, who notices that something is afoot, which results in the U-boat captain pulling the pin on the grenade. As Clive Dunn gives a classic performance as the panicked Corporal Jones, Wilson coolly disarms the German prisoners. As he and the audience know from a scene at the episode's beginning, the grenade is not live – Wilson's unease about using live ammunition led him to prime the grenades with dummy detonators, against Mainwaring's direct orders. Had Wilson acted 'professionally', the German threat to the platoon would, indeed, have been substantial (and explosively fatal); once again, amateurishness wins the day. And rather like Wilson's grenades, the threats offered by *Dad's Army*'s Germans are defused by Perry and Croft's representation of them. Functioning neither as an absurd comic butt nor as a sinister, deadly force, the German invader reminds the audience of the real threat of Nazi occupation during the Second World War, even as his portrayal in *Dad's Army* critiques simplistic national stereotypes like those seen in *'Allo 'Allo!* As with Perry and Croft's use of the regular army as a threat to the stability of the situation's 'inside', the representation of Germans in *Dad's Army* works largely to reinforce the primacy of the amateur over the professional, and – in the example of 'The Deadly Attachment' – the primacy of common sense over following orders.

The last example of an external intrusion into the stability of the 'surrogate family' that comprises the work environment of *Dad's Army* is the series' representation of women. Earlier, I quoted from Frances Gray's *Women and Laughter*, whose chapter 'British Sitcom: a Rather Sad Story' considers woman-as-writer, woman-as-performer, and, most immediately relevant to *Dad's Army*, the ways in which women's roles are 'constructed by men in predominantly male discourse'.[39] The range of opportunities for female character-types, claims Gray, is very restricted – draconian wife, or sex object, for example – though, she adds that there is nevertheless 'an undeniable pleasure ... in the comic skill with which these thankless stereotypes are portrayed'.[40] She sums up the role of women in situation comedy in these terms: '[w]omen, then, are important in British sitcom as a backdrop; their absence is existentially liberating, their presence a reminder of the 'norms' which help the viewer identify the source of comic incongruity'.[41] Put in these terms, it is easy to accommodate Gray's assertions about women within Neale and Krutnik's formulation of 'inside/outside' in situation comedy – the intrusion of women into the male environment of *Dad's Army*, for example, threatens to disrupt its unity, and their subsequent expulsion reinscribes the ideological values that constitute the sitcom's surrogate family.

There are several recurring female characters who fulfill this function – most significantly Mrs Pike (Janet Davies), the over-protective mother of Private Pike and the mistress of Sergeant Wilson. Mrs Pike's appearance in an episode inevitably undermines the systems of authority or the dignity of the platoon. She worries about her son catching cold or coming to some other harm during training exercises, and she often uses her influence over Wilson as a means of effectively countermanding Mainwaring's orders. In this she is fulfilling two stereotypes at once – the infantilising mother-figure and the manipulative object of sexual attention. In one extreme example from *Dad's Army*'s first series, 'The Showing Up of Corporal Jones', she equips Mainwaring, Wilson and Pike with pink 'bunny ears', left-over costuming from a local pantomime which she believes will serve as makeshift balaklavas. As they bend over to have the ears cut off, Major Regan enters the office and Mainwaring's authority is duly compromised. Other women perform similar roles: Godfrey's sisters, for example, or Mrs Fox in the series' final episode, 'Never Too Old'. When Jones reveals to Mainwaring that 'I have fallen in love, Captain Mainwaring. With a woman', Mainwaring assumes necessarily negative consequences: 'I can't be expected to face a Nazi invasion with a woolly-headed corporal'. In these examples the introduction of women operates to debilitate the members of the platoon, rendering them ridiculous, effete or unmasculine. There are several references, too, to the realm of the domestic, which are rarely particularly positive. A glimpse of family life at the Pikes' in 'Boots, Boots, Boots' shows Mrs Pike pandering to her son's every request (even to fetching to his bedside a glass of water from the kitchen after a nightmare), in a way that is clearly ridiculous given his age. Even though the series suggests strongly that Wilson is Pike's father, Wilson's presence is illicit and invisible. Mainwaring's home life is represented in strictly negative terms, and his relationship with the unseen Elizabeth is painted in an unfavourable light. In 'A Soldier's Farewell', for example, Mainwaring's attempt to surprise his wife with a black-market toasted-cheese treat for supper is scorned in a telephone conversation, and Mainwaring is compelled to share the meal with Wilson and Jones. His work relationships are thus revealed to have a degree of intimacy absent from his domestic relationships. When Mainwaring does return home in this episode, we see him in the bottom half of a bunk bed, with Mrs Mainwaring's presence in the upper bunk signified by a bulge that impinges physically on Mainwaring's own sleeping space. A similar image appears in 'The Two and a Half Feathers'.

Mainwaring's unhappy domestic life becomes the basis for the events of 'Mum's Army', in which the platoon opens its ranks to women volunteers. Most of the 'Magnificent Seven' escort recruits – inevitably female friends on whom they have some romantic design: Jones brings Mrs Fox; Wilson, Mrs Pike; Walker, his girlfriend Edith Parish (Wendy Richards, later Miss Brahms in *Are You Being Served?*); Pike, Ivy Samways, the inaudible assistant at the sweet shop; and Frazer, Miss Ironside, a woman he admires for her 'saucy' character and her strong thighs. Godfrey is a notable exception, of course, as is Mainwaring – despite the fact that he is the only principal character who is married. At the end of the brief recruitment drive, however, Mainwaring is approached by a widow, Fiona Gray, who embodies all the values for which he stands – punctuality, British spirit, the 'old standards' – and with whom he shares an immediately intimate bond – she admires the warmth in his eyes when he removes his glasses, for example, and brings him dahlias. For Mainwaring, her statement of patriotism is the 'sort of talk I like to hear', while he confides to Wilson that Edith Parish, is 'not the class of girl we want here'. None of the women besides Mrs Gray seem acceptable, and, despite the absence of scenes that demonstrate any real inadequacy, Mainwaring decides to disband his female recruits. They are seen, certainly, to disrupt normal relations during drill, provoking obsessive editorialising about women's thighs from Frazer and a string of lewd jokes from Walker (for which he is sent home). More obviously threatening to the dynamic of the platoon is Mrs Gray. Before parade, the men and their female recruits sit in the church hall discussing Mainwaring, who is generally believed to be making a fool of himself. Mrs Gray recognises this herself, and leaves for London to spare Mainwaring the scandal. In a scene at the railway station reminiscent of David Lean's *Brief Encounter*, Mainwaring begs Mrs Gray to stay, and his behaviour indicates the extent to which her presence has disrupted the status quo. He is humble, pleading, heedless of the social and professional consequences of an affair, even uncharacteristically colloquial: 'Damn the bloody bank!', he says. But, as with all externally disruptive influences, Mrs Gray must leave the situation at the episode's end, which literally happens with the departure of the train. A final close-up of Mainwaring's face before the closing credits strikes an unusual note of pathos.

The 'outside' elements which tend to threaten the series' 'inside' do so in similar ways, then, by challenging the authority of the platoon as an autonomous body and threatening to disrupt its stability as a unit, both in terms of its relationships and of its physical composition. What makes the Home Guard an effective setting for a situation comedy, as Perry and Croft clearly understood, is the historically precarious nature of the volunteer force, which occupied a conflicted position, caught between the regular army and the civilians they volunteered to protect. Mainwaring's pomposity is a character trait at which we laugh along with members of the platoon, but when the challenge to his authority originates from the outside, he invariably 'comes through', supported loyally by his men. The ideological composition of the 'inside' is not difficult to derive from this analysis: threats to the platoon's stability come from the regular army, from aggressive German invaders, and from well-meaning women, and all of these threats are overcome so as to uphold the pre-eminence of the ordinary, amateurish British male.[42] Hodges, the Vicar and the Verger work to refine this category further: it is only acceptable to be an ordinary amateur if one is willing to live up to the spirit of one's volunteerism. The 'boundary' that defines the interior interests of *Dad's Army* is easily identified, vulnerable to attack, but defended by ordinary men.

Dad's Army and the dynamics of class

One significantly recurring disruption to *Dad's Army*'s working environment that was not considered in the last section was the contestation of authority within the platoon itself. The threat to the unity of work environment as surrogate family is not external to the situation; it is very much a part of the dynamic of the 'inside', and, as such, cannot provoke the sort of collective effort marshalled to defend the 'inside' against threats from the 'outside'. It is one of the characteristics of the work-situated sitcom, which as Eaton claims, 'allows for the representation of class differences through its treatment of the different hierarchical grades, ranks, of the running characters'.[43]

It is hardly an exaggeration to suggest that class is a dominant, if not *the* dominant, structuring principle in British culture. There is no space in this book to justify this received truism at great length, but while many readers might consider their own identities structured by ideologies of gender, race or sexuality, none of us can escape the defining hierarchy of class difference that permeates British life. Sitcoms before *Dad's Army* struggled with the issue: Hancock aspires to a class position higher than the one he occupies, as does Harold Steptoe, in a relentless search for the comfortable world of upper-middle-class respectability. They never succeed, of course. The endlessly repeatable structure of situation comedy ensures that the characters can never change the limited parameters of their situations. These constantly thwarted attempts at social elevation seem to represent a gloomily deterministic class ideology in which aspiring to a higher class is a vain endeavour. But it might be argued, conversely, that merely to represent aspiring working-class individuals was a radical gesture in the 1950s and 1960s, and that the sitcoms themselves effectively critique the class ideology that they seem repeatedly to reproduce.

While *Dad's Army* does not make radical statements about class ideology (as, for example, *Till Death Us Do Part* does), class is nevertheless an intrinsic part of the series. Graham McCann writes that 'most of all' *Dad's Army* was 'about our [British] chronic consciousness of class', and he quotes Dennis Potter's remarks in *Sunday Times* about the series:

> *Dad's Army* is made possible by the extended joke which allows the British, or more specifically the English, to turn every possible encounter into a subtle joust about status. There is as much drama swilling about in our casual 'good mornings' as in the whole of *Il Trovatore*, and more armour-plating on a foot of suburban privet than in the latest Nato tanks.[44]

The structure of the British class system is so familiar that it takes Perry and Croft very little time to establish the series' particular terrain through dress, mannerism, affectation and accent. At one end of the class spectrum we find Sergeant Wilson, a product of the upper-middle classes, on the fringe of the aristocracy (he becomes the Hon. Arthur Wilson in 'The Honourable Man'), and at the other, most of the platoon's privates – a butcher (Jones), an undertaker (Frazer) and a 'spiv' (Walker). It is interesting to note that the character Bracewell (John Ringham), an upper-class socialite, didn't make it beyond the first episode. In an interview with McCann, David Croft suggests that this was because 'Bracewell was too similar in personality to Godfrey', but the class distinction between Bracewell and his fellow platoon members would seem to have been potentially disruptive of an otherwise well-structured class dynamic.[45] Mainwaring sits squarely in the centre of *Dad's Army*'s class hierarchy: his bowler hat, his pinstripe suit and his appointment as a bank manager mark him as a stolid member of the respectable middle classes. One of *Dad's Army*'s particular strokes of genius, it is often claimed, is the reversal of the expected class hierarchy between Mainwaring and Wilson; in their relationship both at the bank and in the platoon, Wilson, the 'social superior', is Mainwaring's subordinate. In *The Achievement of Television*, Huw Wheldon describes his confusion on visiting rehearsals for the pilot episode because he had 'taken it for granted that John le Mesurier, elegant, intelligent, sardonic

and rather weary, was the officer; and that Arthur Lowe, brisk, belligerent and bustling, was the sergeant'.[46] Even their physical statures are
used as class markers. Wilson is tall, languid, permanently at ease and
Mainwaring is short, solidly built and physically pushy, which creates
an image quite at odds with the systems of authority in the series
represented by military rank.

A viewer would have to work hard not to notice the markers of class
that run throughout the nine seasons of *Dad's Army*. They occur as
much in throwaway lines and brief physical gags as they do in extended
narratives and comic sequences. In 'The Test', for example, the platoon
is pitted against the ARP cricket squad, and we observe them arrive for
the match. Mainwaring wears nondescript cricket whites and carries his
equipment in a brown paper bag, but when Wilson shows up in a
garishly striped blazer, carrying a proper cricket bag, Mainwaring is
clearly put out. 'It's a club I used to belong to', Wilson explains (figure
5). In 'The Soldier's Farewell', after a supper of toasted cheese, fried
kidneys and stout, Wilson remarks that this illicit, black-market meal
recalls his school days:

> WILSON: Reminds me of the time I was at school and we used to have
> midnight feasts in the dorm.
> MAINWARING: (Resentfully) Really? At the school I went to we didn't
> have any midnight feasts. We had to manage with a few aniseed balls in
> a corner of the playground.
> JONES: At the school I went to we didn't even have a playground.

The sequence works well, stratifying the class backgrounds of the three
men even in this moment of camaraderie, and bringing to life Wilson's
easy assumptions and Mainwaring's class anxieties with great comic
economy. Elsewhere, the series makes very effective use of the close-up
reaction shot to capture Mainwaring's resentment of Wilson's class
position, as with his reaction to Wilson's using a monocle to read the
slide notes in 'If the Cap Fits'.

The 'map' of class structure and internal hierarchy is so clearly
demarcated in *Dad's Army* that it allows Perry and Croft to draw upon it
directly for comic effect, as, for example, in 'The Two and a Half
Feathers'. In this episode's denouement, Jones recounts the events surrounding the scandal of disloyalty and desertion that has dogged him
during the episode. The sequence is presented as a flashback, with the
personalities of Jones's story represented by the characters in the series.
I make a distinction between *actors* and *characters* here, because the
sequence's comedy depends entirely on the audience observing the
frisson between the role each character plays in the Home Guard platoon,

and its translation into the context of Omdurman and the Sudan. This translation is not consistent from case to case: Hodges and Frazer are cast in the role of hostile dervishes, replicating their roles within the series as outsiders or 'others' (ARP and Scot respectively), and Wilson maintains his upper-class status as the Colonel. If the pleasure here lies in observing how character-types transfer to a different context, then, in other cases, the comedy arises from their unlikely or inappropriate reversal: the polite and gentle Godfrey is cast as a belligerent old fakir (pronounced in Jones's narration as 'old farker') who curses the detachment, and, most significantly, a foul-mouthed sergeant is represented by the ordinarily controlled and respectable Mainwaring, his bad language 'bleeped' with a sequence of loudly-blown raspberries. Similarly, in 'A Soldier's Farewell', Mainwaring's cheese-induced dream that he is Napoleon after Waterloo is brought to life by the regular cast, with the English and the French represented respectively by those members of the *Dad's Army* cast who threaten Mainwaring's authority (Wilson, Frazer, Hodges), and those whom he perceives to be loyal (Jones, Pike, Walker and Godfrey). That Perry and Croft can carry off these comic sequences is dependent, certainly, on their strong characterisations, which, by this point in *Dad's Army*'s run, were familiar to a regular audience. But part of each character's delineation lies in his easy accommodation within an all too familiar hierarchy of class relations.

Mainwaring's middle-class identity is the lynchpin of *Dad's Army*'s internal hierarchy. Threats to his authority can come from below or from above in the situation Perry and Croft have created, and other class positions are rendered as largely stable or comfortable when compared with Mainwaring's own. Wilson's status as a minor member of the aristocracy (at least after 'The Honourable Man') is a source of faint embarrassment to him, perhaps, but it is something he treats with the same insouciance that characterises his behaviour generally, while most of the working-class members of the platoon seem little concerned with any sort of social climbing. Mainwaring's class position, however, is fraught with anxiety. In the series' final episode, he admits that his wife's family (her father was the 'suffragan Bishop of Clagthorpe') consider that the marriage was 'beneath' her, and his career seems replete with this sort of frustrated class aspiration. Though it is revealed that he struggled to make it to his local grammar school in Eastbourne, and that he fought his way up through the ranks of the Swallow Bank from office boy to bank manager, his ambitions have been thwarted by his lower-middle-class origins: 'I ought to have gone on to better things years ago. Yet every time I've gone for an interview for a promotion it's always been the same thing – "What school did you go to?".'[47] Wilson's effortless passage though Meadowbridge public school needles Mainwaring, as does his election to the golf club when he inherits his title – something Mainwaring has aspired to for years without success.

If Mainwaring's social trajectory has been one of frustrated ascent, he nevertheless polices the boundaries of class beneath him with repeated assessments of what constitutes appropriate behaviour. Thus, he becomes the arbiter of jokes (particularly of Walker's off-colour witticisms), of good taste, even of the acceptability of people and relationships. Hodges the greengrocer is often stigmatised by Mainwaring on the grounds of his 'commonness', and Walker's girlfriend Edith is 'not the class of girl we want [in the platoon]', as I mentioned earlier. Even marital relationships are measured by his class standards. In 'Never Too Old', he suggests that Jones's proposed marriage to Mrs Fox might work because 'they're both the same class'. If Hancock and Harold Steptoe are outsiders looking in (or perhaps looking *up*) to what they perceive to be a superior bourgeois position, then Mainwaring becomes the realisation of their efforts: a man still limited by his class origins, but whose position is predicated on an emphatic separation from those origins. By constructing Mainwaring as a social aspirant, a man whose bourgeois status is both hard won and aggressively maintained, Perry and Croft have created an ideal situation for hierarchical struggle. Because Mainwaring's world-view is constructed by distinctions in class and rank, the dynamic between the men in *Dad's Army*'s platoon is necessarily worked out through this hierarchy. Rank is *always* at stake; even though social opposites like Wilson and Jones can overlook their differences on occasion (referring affectionately to each other as 'Jonesie' or 'Wilsie'), Mainwaring is always addressed directly by his men as 'Captain' or 'Mister'. In the final section of this chapter I will consider two episodes of *Dad's Army* in which challenges to rank and authority within the platoon take centre stage: 'If the Cap Fits' and 'The Honourable Man'.

The central conflict in 'If the Cap Fits' is Frazer's challenge to Mainwaring's authority over the Walmington-on-Sea platoon. There are minor intrusions from the 'outside', such as the Verger lurking officiously at Jones's shoulder during Mainwaring's slideshow, and Hodges' accusation that Mainwaring is showing 'funny photos' to his men; but the real threat to authority in this episode is from within and, given Private Frazer's position in the platoon, from below. Frazer is the voice of dissent in many episodes of *Dad's Army*, and in this episode the camera establishes his centrality to the conflict early on. As Mainwaring, Wilson and Jones prepare for the slideshow on identification of German uniforms, the scene cuts to long shots of the platoon seated in rows in the church hall, waiting impatiently for the show to begin.

Frazer speaks first – 'It's a perfect disgrace' – and he also occupies the centre of the shot, between Pike and Godfrey and in the row in front of Walker. He is the ringleader of the platoon's discontent, leading them in a chorus of 'Why are we waiting?' in another long shot of the hall – this time from the back, with Frazer standing in front of the screen to direct the singing. When Mainwaring intervenes – 'We'll come out when we're ready and not before' – the camera again dramatises the relationship in conflict: another long shot of the platoon places Mainwaring and Frazer standing at opposite ends of the hall, with the platoon sitting between them. Frazer's location in the foreground dominates Mainwaring's smaller appearance at the back of the hall. Thus within a short sequence of shots Frazer's centrality to the episode is established, he is presented as a challenge to authority, and in particular as an adversarial opposite to Mainwaring.

Frazer's direct challenge to Mainwaring's authority occurs in the next scene, in which he confronts his superior over his use of time: 'I'll come straight to the point. During the period we've been together you've wasted far too many hours of our precious time and tonight's lecture was the last straw.' Mainwaring is outraged by this challenge, but his response ('Now look here Frazer ...') is interrupted by Frazer, who is determined to make his point about wasted time: 438 hours in total wasted on 'useless blather'. Mainwaring consults his Home Guard training manual, and suggests to Wilson an exercise – a 'temporary exchange of rank'. He reads: '[t]here is a sure cure for this form of unnecessary grousing. Let the grumbler have a free hand to run the section or platoon and learn for himself it is not so easy.' This restructuring of the internal dynamic of relationships is acceptable, of course, because it is voluntary on Mainwaring's part and it is only temporary, a 'licensed' reversal of hierarchy that won't last the duration of the episode. Mainwaring's decision to give Frazer 'enough rope to hang himself' seems, on one level at least, to work. Frazer exerts his new rank with some force, 'busting' Wilson and Jones down from their ranks with a severe, authoritarian manner. If these actions can be seen as abusive of his newly acquired power, they can also be seen as incompetent. Wilson is busted because of a discrepancy in the stores account, but is replaced with Walker, a known black-marketeer. Jones is accused of being a 'woolly minded auld ditherer', and is replaced with the 'stupid boy', Pike, in whom Frazer discerns qualities of leadership. At the same time, however, Frazer's behaviour shows no contrition, and he continues to challenge Mainwaring's authority. Initally, when Mainwaring smugly proposes the 'temporary exchange of rank', Frazer calls his bluff with 'Give me your pips!'; the sound of Mainwaring's swagger stick clattering to the floor communicates his overthrow. Similarly, when Mainwaring upholds Frazer's authoritarian directives in the face of his other men's displeasure, Frazer's request – 'Can he have your stick and gloves?' – scores another hit on Mainwaring's threatened position in the hierarchy. At the episode's midpoint, the contest over authority remains unsettled. In the scene that marks the return to *Dad's Army*'s usual hierarchy – signalled by Wilson entering Mainwaring's office with his sergeant's stripes once more in place – Wilson suggests that the platoon are 'all very pleased to be back to normal'. Mainwaring underscores the purpose of his exercise – 'I should think Frazer's learned his lesson, wouldn't you?' – but Wilson's response leaves the struggle unresolved: 'Oh, I think he would sir, yes, yes. I hope we all have'. A close-up of Mainwaring's disapproving reaction emphasises Wilson's point, and underscores that Mainwaring has yet to learn *his* lesson.

Perry and Croft complicate the situation further by introducing an external factor during the period of Frazer's temporary command; as Frazer addresses Godfrey, Major General Menzies enters the office. He recognises Frazer as a fellow Scot, and invites him to play the pipes at a 'wee Highland get-together at the officer's mess'; Frazer gratefully accepts. As Menzies leaves the office he says, 'Good day to you, Captain Mainwaring', and as Frazer ominously intones 'Mainwaring? Oh dear ...' the audience becomes aware of the potentially ruinous threat to Mainwaring's authority: it is *Mainwaring*, not Frazer, who has been invited to pipe in the haggis before Area Command. When Mainwaring attempts to communicate forcefully the lesson learned from the exercise during drill, Frazer makes several attempts to explain the case of mistaken identity, before Mainwaring, exerting his authority, silences him. 'Upon your own head be it' concludes Frazer, with a knowing smile to which the audience is a party. At this point in the episode, Frazer's 'lesson' remains unlearned, and Mainwaring's restatement of his authority against Frazer's challenge looks set to result only in humiliation – this time in a public forum rather than within the platoon's internal hierarchy. Perry and Croft maintain this expectation up to episode's final moments. When they arrive at the dinner, the platoon are greeted by the Colonel (Menzies is, conveniently for the scenario, recalled to HQ for a briefing), and duties and places are assigned; Mainwaring is finally presented with the bagpipes as the challenge comes to its climactic point, John le Mesurier providing Wilson with an outburst of laughter and pure, unfettered delight. Frazer neatly summarises what's at stake:

> Now will you let me speak? It was *me* the General invited. *Me.* Because of the way I handled the platoon ... So now you're sunk, Captain Mainwaring,

and there's only one thing you can do – let me go in there at the head of my platoon playing the pipes and let me take the credit I deserve.

Frazer's speech, of course, still emphasises his authority in the platoon's hierarchy as he insists that it is 'my platoon'. Mainwaring remains foolishly obdurate, it seems (as Wilson puts it, 'Are you absolutely sure you're doing the right thing, sir?'), and, once again, asserts his own authority over Frazer's: 'Get back in your place Private Frazer'. But at the moment when his authority seems set finally to unravel, Mainwaring reveals, *deus ex machina*, that he *can* play the bagpipes after all – 'I spent my honeymoon at a place called Invergeekie ... The nights were long, there was nothing else to do' – and he proceeds to pipe in the haggis. As the platoon enters the mess hall, Frazer furiously prostrates himself: 'I never doubted ye could do it, sir, never for a moment, never for a single moment'. The episode's final image is a long shot of Frazer, alone, his hand over his eyes. 'God forgive me' he says, before running into the mess hall, to join the platoon again and return to his 'place'. The internal structure of the 'surrogate family' of *Dad's Army* is thus maintained; despite Mainwaring's persistent flaws, challenges to his authority must be overturned, even, in this particular case, at the expense of narrative credibility. The inevitable stability of rank in *Dad's Army* is entirely explicable by Eaton's assertions about the production constraints on sitcom. But it also sustains the ideology of a fixed and knowable hierarchy necessary for the successful working environment.

Because Mainwaring is the highest-ranking officer in the platoon, threats to his authority in terms of rank must always originate from below. Internal threats from above are allowed by Perry and Croft's elevation of Wilson over Mainwaring in terms of social class, although his rank is immediately beneath Mainwaring in both the platoon (Sergeant) and the bank (Chief Clerk). In this case the dynamics of class are not represented symbolically by military rank, nor do they align with the occupational seniority. In 'The Honourable Man' the antagonism between Wilson's and Mainwaring's respective class positions is brought to the forefront of the episode when Wilson becomes the Honourable Arthur Wilson after the death of a childless uncle: 'My side of the family moved up one place, so to speak, and so now I'm "the Honourable"'.

Just as 'If the Cap Fits' was complicated by the external intrusion of Major General Menzies, so the discussion of class in 'The Honourable Man' is made more complicated by the impending visit to Walmington-on-Sea of a Soviet hero – not a soldier, as Mainwaring asserts, but a manufacturer of tanks. At a meeting of the General Purposes Committee in the church hall, Mainwaring is elected to 'coordinate and mastermind our arrangements' by almost unanimous assent, the only dissenting voice emanating from what is established in *Dad's Army* as its lowest class position: ARP Warden Hodges, the local greengrocer. Hodges' complaint, though entirely self-serving, is couched in terms of class – 'Russians don't want officers and bank managers and all that snobbish rubbish', but would prefer an 'ordinary bloke ... a greengrocer or somebody like that'. Despite his objections, Mainwaring's position is upheld, and the committee continues (with necessary comic diversions) to make suitable arrangements, which are to culminate in the presentation of a wooden key, symbolising the 'freedom of Walmington'.

Wilson's elevation to 'the Honourable' is met with almost universal excitement (Frazer, of course, remains unimpressed), despite his typically casual protestations ('It's rather silly, isn't it?'). Pike and his mother fawn over his nobility, the Verger bows and refers to him as 'M'lord' and the Vicar asks him to approve a crest for his own private pew. He also gains access to the golf club, much to Mainwaring's chagrin. It is Mainwaring who is threatened by Wilson's class position. He has 'been trying for years' to get into the golf club, has dined on a 'snook fish-cake' rather than the smoked salmon to which Wilson has been treated, and consequently he becomes newly preoccupied with the ambitions that are forever frustrated by his origins. When Wilson protests that his new title is becoming a burden, Mainwaring responds: 'Don't give me all that soft soap. You're revelling in it. Who wouldn't? If I had a title I'd be on the board of directors of the bank not manager of some tin-pot branch.' He tempers this desire for social elevation, inherent in the aspiring middle classes, with a disgust for the aristocracy – 'being a member ... explains quite a lot about your character', he says to Wilson, 'they're an ambling, muddle-headed lot' – and he insists upon his higher rank to maintain his superiority and security. 'I'm still the manager and you're the chief clerk', he tells Wilson, 'I'm still the officer and you're the sergeant'.

Wilson's elevation threatens Mainwaring in a more overt manner, however: during drill, the Town Clerk arrives to ask Mainwaring to step aside from the role of presenting the visiting Russian with the freedom of Walmington in favour of Wilson, whose title makes him more appropriate for the job. Similar suggestions are made by some members of the platoon, and by Hodges, telephoning from his place of work. Mainwaring refuses to give ground to Wilson, and finds a confused ally in Jones. As Jones puts it to Mainwaring, there are 'three stripes on [Wilson's] honourable arm' and 'three pips on your common shoulder', which is 'one up to you', because 'although you're more common than he is, you've got better insigniature [sic] and that's the way it should be because that is the status quo'. Jones seems to be insisting that rank or professional position, which is earned, counts for more in the 'status quo' than a class position in which one was placed by accident of birth. At its best, Jones's wisdom is confused and convoluted; in this case, however, it doesn't seem to be borne out by the episode's conclusion. Mainwaring clings to his role, and insists, because he is the Captain, that Wilson ride the platoon's motorcycle, despite Wilson's inability and lack of enthusiasm. 'It's time he learned to fend for himself' he says, as Wilson proves clearly inept, pronouncing a middle-class critique of the apparently effortless maintenance of upper-class privilege. But Mainwaring's plans backfire. At the ceremony to present the key, the Russian visitor denounces the delegation: 'I represent the workers of the Soviet Union. You who are sitting here are not workers. You have soft faces. Your hands are soft. You are bourgeois middle class. You are giving me honours. You should honour your own workers'. He retreats to the staff car in which he arrived to produce Wilson, wearing a boilersuit and covered in grime from his attempts to operate the motorcycle. Here, he claims, 'is a man in a uniform not of an officer, not of an imperialist, but a slave worker', and he presents the key to Wilson. The Russian's error is a classic 'mistaken identity' gag, of course, but its operation refutes Jones's assertion that Mainwaring's pips count for more than Wilson's stripes. What the episode's final scene suggests is that the 'status quo' is, in fact, a traditional hierarchy of class: the outspoken representative of the working class (albeit of the Soviet Union) denounces the bourgeois middle class, and the representative of the aristocracy ends up acquiring the episode's prize. Does Wilson deserve the freedom of Walmington-on-Sea in the sense that the Soviet visitor intends? Certainly not. But the episode upholds an established order of class despite the bourgeois ideology of hard work and desert embodied by Mainwaring.

Although 'If the Cap Fits' and 'The Honourable Man' seem to pull in opposite directions (in the former, Mainwaring triumphs over Frazer's challenge to his authority, but in the latter, the threats offered to Mainwaring's middle-class identity are maintained by the persistent ease of Wilson's success), both episodes evince a similar ideology of class. The series makes clear that Mainwaring is the key figure in its class dynamics; he has worked his way up to his position through sheer determination, and, as a product of upward social mobility, he is well aware of both the upper and lower boundaries of his own position. The narrative expression of this class anxiety is to be found in the restless dynamics of the platoon's internal relationships, but, exemplifying what Stephen Wagg refers to as the 'reassurance' of sitcoms, 'rooted in a social structure of the past', *Dad's Army* never seeks to challenge what it treats as the 'natural order' of the British class system.[48]

Notes

1 Although most of the products of fan-writing about *Dad's Army* and Perry and Croft are celebratory and largely uncritical in their responses, several do reveal significant and very useful research on which I have drawn for this chapter. Gregory Koseluk's *Great Brit-Coms: British Television Situation Comedy* is perhaps the least critical of these major sources, but offers useful summaries of all of *Dad's Army*'s episodes; more significant in scope are Richard Webber's *Dad's Army: A Celebration*, and particularly, Graham McCann's *Dad's Army: The Story of a Classic Television Show*.

2 Lewisohn, *Radio Times Guide to TV Comedy*, p. 176.

3 *Ibid.*, p. 748. Lewisohn's statistics are complete only until the end of 1997. It's perhaps worth mentioning a few other statistics for comparative purposes – the most prolific British sitcom is *Last of the Summer Wine* (162), and other 1960s' 'classics' manage 109 (*Till Death Us Do Part*), and 59 (*Steptoe and Son*).

4 *Ibid.*, p. 177.

5 Cited in Koseluk, *Great Brit-Coms*, p. 67.

6 Perry, *A Stupid Boy*, p. 100.

7 Crowther and Pinfold, *Bring Me Laughter*, p. 110.

8 Lewisohn, *Radio Times Guide to TV Comedy*, p. 44.

9 *Ibid.*, p. 428.

10 Both Billington's and Day-Lewis's reviews appeared on 1 August 1968, the day after *Dad's Army*'s first broadcast.

11 Koseluk, *Great Brit-Coms*, p. 67.

12 'The Man and the Hour'.

13 David Croft, interview with Graham McCann, in McCann, *Dad's Army*, p. 81.

14 'The Man and the Hour'

15 Perry, *A Stupid Boy*, p. 107.

16 Jimmy Perry, in Pertwee, *Dad's Army*, p. 13.

17 Perry, *A Stupid Boy*, pp. 91–92.

18 McCann, *Dad's Army*, p. 30.

19 Mackenzie, *The Home Guard*, plate 9.

20 Perry, *A Stupid Boy*, p. 101.

21 Langdon-Davies (ed.), *Home Guard Training Manual*, p. 137.

22 Koseluk, *Great Brit-Coms*, p. 74.

23 Paul Fox, interview with McCann, in McCann, *Dad's Army*, p. 78.

24 Lovell, 'A Genre of Social Disruption?', p. 22.

25 Wagg, 'Social Class and Situation Comedy', pp. 8–9.

26 Eaton, 'Television Situation Comedy', pp. 70, 73–74.

27 Neale and Krutnik, *Popular Film and Television Comedy*, p. 241.

28 Gray, *Women and Laughter*, p. 84.

29 *Ibid.*

30 Mackenzie, *Home Guard*, p. 63.

31 Neale and Krutnik, *Popular Film and Television Comedy*, pp. 241–242.

32 Koseluk, *Great Brit-Coms*, p. 81.

33 Langdon-Davies (ed.), *Home Guard Training Manual*, p. 166.

34 Mackenzie, *Home Guard*, p. 58.

35 *Ibid.*, p. 2. Mackenzie suggests, in fact, that *Dad's Army* may have had no small effect on resurrecting historians' interest in the Home Guard.

36 Crowther and Pinfold, *Bring Me Laughter*, p. 115.

37 Kamm, '"Oh What a Funny War"', p. 277.

38 Transmitted 31 October 1973. Koseluk states that this episode is Jimmy Perry's favourite (Koseluk, *Great Brit-Coms*, p. 124), and, according to a survey conducted

by *Classic Television* magazine in June 1999, it contains the funniest moment in the history of British television: Mainwaring's outburst of 'Don't tell him, Pike!'. Oddly enough the third 'funniest moment' also involves Germans – Basil Fawlty's 'Don't mention the war!' sequence in *Fawlty Towers* (McCann, *Dad's Army*, p. 249).

39 Gray, *Women and Laughter*, p. 82.

40 *Ibid.*, p. 86.

41 *Ibid.*, p. 89.

42 Some recent assessments of the English national character, such as Jeremy Paxman's *The English* and Roger Scruton's *England: An Elegy*, have dwelt on the celebration of amateurism as a distinctive feature. Scruton suggests that 'English society was the creation of amateur initiatives', and the 'when it came to leisure, every village was a centre of spontaneous institution-building, with its football club and cricket club, its Boy Scouts and Girl Guides, its Women's Institute and its circles of amateurs devoted to needlework, music, photography, theatricals, brass bands, jam-making and ballroom dancing' (Scruton, *England*, pp. 57–58).

43 Eaton, 'Television Situation Comedy', p. 74.

44 McCann, *Dad's Army*, p. 7; Potter, 'Where Comedy is King', p. 37.

45 McCann, *Dad's Army*, p. 75. Godfrey himself seems rather genteel, though he was still, effectively, a sales assistant – a gentleman's outfitter in the Army and Navy Stores.

46 Wheldon, *Achievement of Television*, p. 11.

47 'A. Wilson, Manager'.

48 Wagg, 'Social Class and Situation Comedy', p. 14.

It Ain' t Half Hot, Mum

3

If the 1960s are generally associated with cultural revolution and an increased permissiveness in society, the 1970s became in popular opinion a decade of comparative sobriety: a time of political upheaval that ultimately heralded the rise of Thatcherism. The 1970s saw an increase in terrorist activity, an energy crisis that resulted in the imposition of the three-day working week and the 50mph speed limit, and numerous strikes and other industrial action. The nation's economic gloom necessarily affected television, since, as Andrew Crisell points out, the 'BBC's economic state was a microcosm of the nation's. Inflation devoured its licence fee, necessitating cuts in transmission hours and new programme projects.'[1] Strikes also affected transmission and were particularly damaging to ITV, notably during its eleven-week blackout between August and October 1979. Despite this pervasive gloom – or perhaps even in response to it – the 1970s saw an increased output of situation comedies: Stephen Wagg counts 175 (compared with the 100 in the 1960s). And while he characterises the 1960s as a decade of diversity in sitcom (in the representation of both social class and setting), he finds the output of the 1970s to reveal 'a more central concern with the personal and domestic problems of middle and lower middle class life', with few series dealing 'focally with working class life', and '[c]omparatively few [involving] the direct subversion of authority'.[2] The decade nevertheless produced sitcoms that have entered the established canon of 'classics' – *Are You Being Served?*, *Fawlty Towers*, *Porridge*, *Rising Damp* and *Last of the Summer Wine* – as well as the 'least respectable texts' of the 1970s reconsidered by Leon Hunt in *British Low Culture*, like *On the Buses* or *Man About the House*. These were products of what Hunt calls 'permissive populism': 'the popular appropriation of elitist "liberationist" sexual discourses, the trickle-down of [1960s] permissiveness into [1970s] commodity culture'.[3]

Although *Dad's Army* first appeared in 1968 and is often grouped in reviews and surveys of situation comedy with the innovative or 'revolutionary' sitcoms of the 1960s, it ran throughout the early 1970s (though it always remained faithful to its original situational concept), as did a couple of its contemporaries, *Till Death Us Do Part* and *Steptoe and Son*. *Dad's Army* also overlapped with several of Jimmy Perry and David Croft's other contributions to situation comedy. Perry worked on several solo projects, the first of which was *The Gnomes of Dulwich* (BBC, 1969), a sitcom starring Terry Scott and Hugh Lloyd as garden gnomes, which worked as a satire on human nature according to Perry and on the common market according to Mark Lewisohn.[4] Perry pronounces it a 'comparative success', but his two other contributions to 1970s sitcom fared less well. *Lollipop Loves Mr Mole* (ITV, 1971–72), Perry's only domestic comedy, is declared to be 'rubbish' by Perry, and *Room Service* (ITV, 1979), undertaken 'just for the money', was a source of embarrassment even during the period of its production: 'I used to hide behind the cameras', he admits.[5] David Croft co-authored two series in the 1970s with Jeremy Lloyd – the long-running *Are You Being Served?* (1972–83) and the short-lived *Come Back, Mrs Noah* (1977–78). The latter, starring Mollie Sugden and several other Perry and Croft ensemble performers (Ian Lavender, Michael Knowles and Donald Hewlett) ran for only one series; set in 2050, the sitcom was located on a renegade space station called Britannia Seven, and '[n]ot without good reason', claims Mark Lewisohn, '[it] has been cited in some quarters as one of the worst British sitcoms of all time'. This is a rather grand assertion given the competition, and one with which David Croft would not agree: 'Jeremy and I still think of it as one of the funniest things we have ever done'.[6] Clearly not winning popular acclaim, *Come Back, Mrs Noah* nevertheless lives on in Mick Eaton's extended analysis of one episode in 'Television Situation Comedy'. Eaton explicates the sitcom's subject in terms of its title:

> The title itself defines the parameters of the show: *Come Back, Mrs Noah*, referring not only to the attempts to get the module back to earth again, but also, through the use of the imperative, suggesting a calling-back, an interpellation back to the terms of our comprehension of the present/past, away from the fear of the technological excesses of the future, whose terms are continually being lampooned.[7]

Are You Being Served?, as I mentioned in my preface, needs considerably less explanation, having come to stand almost as the archetype of British situation comedy before 1990, but it is worth emphasising the similarities with Perry and Croft's collaborative work: the large ensemble of actors, often shared across other Perry/Croft and Croft/Lloyd series, the non-domestic environment, and the complex internal hierarchy of literal or metaphorical class relations.

In addition to these other ventures in sitcom writing, Perry and Croft also collaborated on the second of their co-authored series, *It Ain't Half Hot, Mum*, which overlaped *Dad's Army* by three years, running for eight series between 1974 and 1981. Of all of Perry and Croft's sitcoms, *It Ain't Half Hot, Mum* is the most difficult to write about from the vantage point of the new millennium. 'It ain't half a hot potato' suggested a friend of mine recently, with its representations of sexuality (in the effeminate, cross-dressing Gunner 'Gloria' Beaumont) and race (in Michael Bates's 'blacking up' as Rangi Ram). Some critics have addressed these representations directly: Andy Medhurst and Lucy Tuck in 'The Gender Game' discuss Gloria in the context of stereotyping in sitcom, and Leon Hunt groups *It Ain't Half Hot, Mum* with other comedies representing race in the 1970s. Although the BFI's contribution to the Campaign Against Racism in the Media (CARM) – *It Ain't Half Racist Mum* considers a broad spectrum of media representations, it nevertheless implicitly critiques *It Ain't Half Hot, Mum*'s presentation of race by its parodic title. These two issues are sufficiently important to warrant extended discussion (not least because they are the points of origin of some of the only published critical work on the series), and I shall return to them later in this chapter.

A further difficulty offered by *It Ain't Half Hot, Mum* is a personal one – a problem faced by every writer who was once an original audience member with no critical distance from the text. The series ran from my late childhood through my adolescence – I was eight years old in the year it began and fifteen when it ended – and I was an avid, appreciative viewer. In this sense, *It Ain't Half Hot, Mum* spans the development of my own understanding of television comedy, from the early days of being allowed to enter the communalising influence of television's laughter, to the separation of own my tastes and interests from those of my parents, which necessitated my sloping off upstairs to watch sitcoms targeted specifically at the 'youth culture' to which I belonged, such as *The Young Ones* and *Blackadder*, on the fuzzy, black and white, portable television. Revisiting the series after an absence of twenty years has been a perplexing experience, then, as I placed comic sequences or performances from which I had derived pleasure within new personal or critical contexts, finding that what was once transparently and naturally comical has now become entirely more complicated and ideologically debatable.

In the chapter that follows I will first consider the contexts and structures of *It Ain't Half Hot, Mum*, particularly in comparison with the mechanisms, relationships and situations at work in *Dad's Army*. In doing so, I will return to some of the structural and ideological models of sitcom I introduced in Chapter 1. The remainder of this chapter will consider *It Ain't Half Hot, Mum*'s representation of gender and sexuality, and of race, in more depth, using some of the strategies employed by earlier critical work on the series.

It Ain't Half Hot, Mum: text and context

Like the historical context of *Dad's Army* (the activities of Britain's Home Guard during the Second World War), *It Ain't Half Hot, Mum*'s background (the work of concert parties, gang shows and the Entertainments National Service Association (or ENSA)) has receded in popular memory. As with the Home Guard, too, there is very little historical documentation of these institutions beyond individual memoirs or collections of anecdotes; and, increasingly, the actors and comedians who worked to entertain the troops during the Second World War have died or no longer figure in the public eye – performers as diverse as Sir Lawrence Olivier and Sir Ralph Richardson, George Formby, Terry-Thomas, Tommy Cooper and *Dad's Army*'s Arthur Lowe.[8] Thus, despite Jimmy Perry's insistence that the activities of *It Ain't Half Hot, Mum*'s concert party mirror closely his own experience of serving as part of a similar troupe in India during the Second World War, and Croft's experience as an Entertainments Officer in Poona, the series has lacked a meaningful context for many viewers, whether in the 1970s when it was originally broadcast, or in the 2000s for readers of this book.

The formation of ENSA was initially proposed by Basil Dean, the Director of Entertainments for the NAAFI (the Navy, Army and Air Force Institutes). A theatrical producer and director, who worked entertaining the troops during the First World War, Dean, according to Richard Fawkes, 'remembered with horror the endless rounds of children from dancing academies and troupes of talentless amateurs who had tried to cheer up the unfortunate soldiers, most of them in hospital beds from which there was no escape'.[9] So, in 1938 Dean proposed the formation of an organisation of professional performers, an idea which met initially with little interest from individuals or the War Office. '[I]f actors wanted to do their bit', one officer apparently stated, 'they should join the army and fight'.[10] Nevertheless, Dean persevered and ultimately persuaded the NAAFI to support and finance ENSA. As Fawkes points out, membership of ENSA was strictly voluntary, and despite the adoption of an army-style uniform popularly dubbed 'Basil dress', members were still classified as civilians. By the end of 1944 the organisation employed 4,000 artists, cost £14 million to operate, and 'played in every

theatre of war under conditions that were always difficult and sometimes dangerous'.[11] Despite occasional assertions to the contrary, *It
Ain't Half Hot, Mum*'s concert party is not a part of ENSA, but, as the
series makes clear through the relationships between ranks in every
episode, a group of enlisted soldiers assigned to entertainment duties.[12]
In 'Cabaret Time', for example, the concert party almost falls foul of the
military police for performing in the out-of-bounds Karma Sutra Club.
They evade arrest only by disguising themselves as military policemen;
because there is no costume available for the Sergeant Major, however,
they dress him in a clown costume and attempt to pass him off as a
member of ENSA, to whom, of course, the military ban would not apply.
Despite Dean's hope for a more professional wartime entertainment
industry, the formation of concert parties by regiments and divisions of
the armed forces was quite common, especially among those that had
had concert parties during the First World War – like *The Balmorals*, the
concert party of the 51st Highland division, which 'had been the main-
stay of entertainment for men in France'.[13] Fawkes cites several examples
of groups of this sort and the shows that they produced, many of which
sound as if they might indeed have been invented by Perry and Croft.
Another similar institution described by Fawkes which mirrors the
Royal Artillery concert party in *It Ain't Half Hot, Mum* is the RAF gang
show, formed by Ralph Reader from RAF concert parties with some
additional amateur talent. Images of gang show units reproduced by
Fawkes seem to have been direct influences on Perry and Croft: a
picture of Gang Show Unit 10, which included Peter Sellers among its
members and which toured India and Burma, shows the unit kneeling
on stage dressed exactly as *It Ain't Half Hot, Mum*'s concert party
appears in the show's opening and closing credits. Several other gang
show pictures include cross-dressed entertainers. Dick Emery, for example,
was noted for his female impersonations, and originated many of his
popular television characters during his time in RAF gang shows.

The concert party in *It Ain't Half Hot, Mum* is stationed in the Royal
Artillery depot in Deolali, India, in 1945. The location of the depot is a
historical actuality; pronounced in the series as 'Do-Lally', it is, in fact,
the origin of the well-known colloquial English term. 'Do-Lally Tap',
mentioned several times during the series, was the name given to the
supposed malady that afflicted troops stationed at the depot for long
periods of time. Although there are occasional excursions to exterior
locations and incidental settings (such as the Thuggee temple in 'The
Night of the Thugs'), most of the episodes take place in a limited range
of studio-sets: the parade ground, the platoon's *basha* (or barracks), and
the Colonel's office. In *You Have Been Watching*, Croft reveals that the

available studio space was instrumental in the structure of the sitcom's setting. Confronted with limited space (90′ × 60′), budgetary restrictions that dictated both a 'main set' and that '20 out of the 30 minutes needs to be shot in front of the audience', and the needs of a live studio audience ('Building an extra set in front of the audience can't be done in less than 10 to 15 minutes and must be avoided at all costs because the audience get bored'), Perry and Croft devised *It Ain't Half Hot, Mum*'s tripartite structure, anchored in the three locations described above with another small space 'squeezed round the back'.[14] Croft's remarks about the sitcom's dependence on the physical space of the studio certainly supports Mick Eaton's argument that a sitcom's 'situation' is dictated by production limitations. The series' rather obscure title comes from a line in the first episode: Gunner Parkins, writing home to his mother, concocts the line as a less unpleasant alternative to his true feelings, which the audience hears in a voice-over as he writes the letter. It is perhaps worth establishing some nomenclature at this point: because the members of the concert party are enlisted in the Royal Artillery, their ranks are different from the more familiar Private, Corporal and Sergeant Major, with Gunner, Bombardier and Battery Sergeant Major (or BSM) representing their equivalents.

As with *Dad's Army*, *It Ain't Half Hot, Mum*'s military situation affords a recognisable, ready-made hierarchical structure around which to build its characters' relationships. But while the series shares a range of external threats to its stability with Perry and Croft's first collaborative project, the concert party's internal structure is more complex than that of Walmington-on-Sea's Home Guard. Three distinct groups form this series' stable core, with BSM Williams (Windsor Davies) moving between them – the concert party itself, the unit's two commissioned officers, and a trio of local Indian employees. Although these groups necessarily interact, some episodes of *It Ain't Half Hot, Mum* might pursue a couple of apparently separate narratives; the officers, Captain Ashwood and Colonel Reynolds, performed by Michael Knowles and Donald Hewlett, are often largely unengaged with the activities of the concert party – a running gag about the vagueness, self-absorption and detachment of the commissioned ranks. The concert party itself consists of eight members: Gunner Graham (John Clegg), the pianist and Oxford-educated intellectual, variously referred to as 'Paderewski', 'Professor', and, by the anti-intellectual BSM Williams, as 'Mr Lah-di-Dah Gunner Graham'; Gunner 'Lofty' Sugden (Don Estelle), the diminutive opera singer; Gunner 'Atlas' Mackintosh (Stuart McGugan); Gunner 'Nobby' Clark (Kenneth MacDonald); Gunner 'Nosher' Evans (Mike Kinsey); Gunner 'Parky' Parkins (Christopher Mitchell), whom BSM Williams concludes is his own illegitimate son, and is therefore his favourite; Gunner (and later Bombardier) 'Gloria' Beaumont (Melvyn Hayes), the Party's principal female impersonator; and, for the first two series, Bombardier 'Solly' Solomons (George Layton), the Jewish impresario and wily front man of the concert party. The third group, the Indians employed in the depot, include the concert party's bearer, Rangi Ram (Michael Bates); Char-Wallah Muhammed (Dino Shafeek) with his ubiquitous tea urn; and Punkah-Wallah Rumzan (Babar Bhatti), the largely non-English speaking operator of Ashwood and Reynold's 'punkah', or fan. This latter group saw the most change in its membership during the course of the series; Michael Bates died in 1978 and so from the sixth series Dino Shafeek's role increased to compensate for his absence, and the Punkah-Wallah was replaced for series 7 and 8 by another Asian stereotype, the Chinese cook Ah Syn (Andy Ho).

In common with many sitcoms, *It Ain't Half Hot, Mum* contains a number of recurrent comic set-pieces. Lewisohn remarks on 'the writers' dogged attempts to give most of the characters their own catch-phrases', though he doubts their efficacy – '[u]nlike [those in *Dad's Army*] few of them stuck this time around'.[15] I am not sure I agree with this assessment. Certain characters' catch phrases are more memorable than others – Williams's 'Shut Up!', of course, and his sarcastic, deadpan delivery of 'Oh dear, what a pity, how sad', stand as strong examples, as does Ashwood's 'Absolutely First Class!'. Perry and Croft's achievement in *It Ain't Half Hot, Mum*, functioning in similar ways to the catch phrase, is the extensive use of stock interactions – reminiscent, in some ways, of the *lazzi* of the *commedia dell'arte* tradition. There are too many to list fully. At least once an episode, often during parade, BSM Williams will move behind Lofty, slowly bending his knees until their faces are on a level and fill the camera's frame. Lofty blinks and stammers nervously as Williams leers and mugs to the camera, inevitably cracking a joke about Lofty's height or inabilities as a soldier. At least once an episode, Nosher delivers a line with his mouth full, rendering what he says unintelligible and spraying his colleagues with half-chewed food. And at least once an episode, Gunner Graham makes a well-expressed remark which Williams mocks by turning towards Graham and repeating the final few words of the statement in a camp mimicry of an upper-class accent, with the set piece usually completed by a cut to a close-up of Graham's face as he winces at Williams's crass behaviour. Enumerated in this way, these sequences might seem overly formulaic, especially if one is inclined to be suspicious of comedy's dependence on repetitive devices.[16] As a member of *It Ain't Half Hot, Mum*'s original audience, however, I remember that this particular strategy formed part of the series' appeal: I watched specifically to see the enactment of my favourite routines ('Mr Lah-Di-Dah Gunner Graham!' and the idiotic interactions of Ashwood and Reynolds) and the pleasure of seeing them performed never seemed to wear thin. This is not indicative of some sort of character flaw, I suspect, but an intrinsic part of the way sitcoms imbricate the audience in their situations, something which is particularly important in the case of *It Ain't Half Hot, Mum*, the situation of which is quite beyond the experience of the majority of its viewers.

Michael Bates receives top billing in *It Ain't Half Hot, Mum*, and Rangi Ram certainly occupies a unique place in the series; he is often the means by which the episode's events are introduced or the narrative is advanced, and many episodes conclude with his direct address to the audience, breaking the fictional frame and establishing a relationship with the audience that no other character enjoys. But the central tension that drives the series is the antagonistic relationship between BSM Williams and the concert party. Nicknamed 'Sergeant-Major Shut-Up!' for his celebrated catch phrase, Williams is the only character in *It Ain't Half Hot, Mum* who truly belongs in the situation. All of the other non-Indian characters are enlisted servicemen, of course, but none of them display any particular aptitude or ability in military business. The officers, Ashwood and Reynolds, are entirely ineffective – locked in their own world of chess puzzles, amateur horticulturalism and society events, they seem poorly suited to military life and function as a familiar (but effective) satire on the upper-middle classes. The members of the concert party are similarly lacking in military prowess, and it is here that the distinction between them and ENSA becomes important. ENSA members did not belong to the armed forces, and therefore were not expected to behave like soldiers; thus, Gloria's often-repeated line of complaint in the face of Williams's orders – 'Anyone would think we were soldiers' – works as comedy because they *are* soldiers, even though they spend most of their time acting in other ways. Almost all of Williams's energy is devoted either to making 'real soldiers' – and, by implication, 'real men' – of them through a series of training exercises (as in 'The Jungle Patrol' or 'Showing the Flag') and punitive gestures (moonlight parades or the ever-present 'jankers'), or by scheming to have them posted 'up the jungle'.

Williams's position in the narrative structure of the sitcom is complicated in other ways. Just as he is the character who most 'belongs' in the series' situation, and who drives many of the episodes' plots, he is also the character to whose interior thoughts we have most access. *It Ain't Half Hot, Mum* uses voice-over narrative on several occasions (such as Parky's letter home to his mother in the opening episode, or Ashwood and Reynolds' lust-fuelled letters in 'Forbidden Fruits'), but most frequently it is used to externalise Williams's thoughts and plans for the concert party. In 'The Inspector Calls', for example, Colonel Reynolds has forbidden Williams to drill the party because they do not have the correct uniforms, and these cannot be requisitioned for troops not being posted for jungle warefare. Williams formulates a plan to have the concert party perform a military 'number', necessitating matching military costumes. The shot reveals a close-up of Williams's face, with the voice-over of his machinations animated by Windsor Davies' rolling eyes, twitching waxed moustache and pursing lips. In 'Cabaret Time', as he plans to set up the concert party for an illegal appearance at the Kama Sutra Club, he even articulates a brief moment of conscience: 'Am I being rotten?' he asks himself. Ordinarily this access to the interior thoughts of a character signals an intimate relationship between her or him and the audience. In Williams's case, however, this intimacy is made problematic, since he is a largely unsympathetic character, generally bigoted, but in particular racist, imperialist, anti-intellectual, homophobic and, according to Perry and Croft, an entirely accurate representation of some of the NCOs encountered during their own service. Examples of his prejudices are numerous: he excoriates the 'slant-eyed Japanese' and their 'dirty yellow hands', and he rails against the ingratitude of the native Indian population. At least once an episode he mocks the speech patterns of 'Mr Lah-di-Dah Gunner Graham', with his 'university heducation' and he endlessly denounces the concert party as a 'bunch of poofs', even mouthing 'poofs!' silently in the iconic dumbshow he performs during the closing credit sequence. In 'The Gender Game', Andy Medhurst and Lucy Tuck suggest a parallel between Williams and *Till Death Us Do Part*'s Alf Garnett:

> To read homosexuality as intrinsically funny is aided, indeed directed, in *It Ain't Half Hot Mum* by the figure of the Sargeant [sic] Major, with his insulting Alf Garnett-like shouts of 'poofs!'. Unlike Garnett, however, there is no suggestion in the text that the Sergeant Major is an intentionally ridiculous figurehead of prejudice.[17]

Although I will return to Medhurst and Tuck's discussion of homosexuality in *It Ain't Half Hot, Mum* later in this chapter, I have to call this particular assertion into question. It seems to me that Williams's bigotry is often mocked at the very moment of its utterance. As he derides Gunner Graham's Oxford education, for example, he reveals his own ignorance. During his inspection of the concert party's reading material in 'Forbidden Fruits', Williams mispronounces the title of James Joyce's *Ulysses*, first as 'Useless', then as 'Usilees', and finally searches unsuccessfully for the word 'mythology' as he attempts to assert his own knowledge. Perry and Croft also make him a veritable master of malapropism, especially at those moments when he attempts to affirm his authority.

Williams's authority is consistently undermined throughout the series. He is often thwarted in his short-term conflicts with the concert party by the officers, who favour them – Colonel Reynolds, for example, is forever undermining Williams's decisions to put men on 'jankers' as a means of blocking rehearsal – and Williams is usually outwitted by the combined guile of the party and the local Indian population. This mechanism constitutes *It Ain't Half Hot, Mum*'s most enduring structure or formula: in 'The Jungle Patrol', to choose one example, Williams's attempts 'to make men' of the concert party by teaching them wilderness survival techniques is undermined by Solly's counterplan to bring along Rangi Ram, Char-Wallah Muhammed and Punkah-Wallah Rumzan. As Williams struggles with his own thirst and chews inedible roots to survive, the men slip away in pairs to be served egg and chips by Rangi Ram, and an unending supply of cups of tea from the Char-Wallah's urn. When the party, lost because of Williams's inadequate map-reading skills, blunder into Ashwood and Reynolds sitting in dinner jackets on a local administrator's verandah, they all appear fresh and only too happy to perform an impromptu concert. Williams, however, is close to collapse, belying his earlier statement about the expedition's comparative abilities to survive on patrol: 'I am used to it because I am a soldier. And you are not because you are a bunch of poofs'. In another episode, 'The Curse of the Sadhu', Williams is duped into believing that he is the victim of a holy man's curse, the cure for which is public humiliation: daubed clownishly with paint and covered in dried cow dung, Williams is made to repeat a sequence of nonsensical syllables (supposedly words in Urdu) that inevitably add up to a coherent statement in English: 'Oh what an ass I am'.

Although BSM Williams's victories over the men are short-lived and few, his point of view is occasionally aligned with that of the audience by satire on the officer class. In 'The Curse of the Sadhu', Ashwood and Reynolds are leaving for a party in Bombay. When Ashwood learns that Emily Creighton-Dunhowerd will be attending, he is quite taken aback. 'We had a bit of thing', he confesses, when, at a 'coming out' party, '[w]e both took our meringues into the conservatory'. In this scene the camera cuts between Ashwood and Reynolds as their absurd conversation unfolds, but it also cuts to Williams, who underscores the satire by rolling his eyes and barely concealing his own laughter in accord with the audience response. This is not an isolated occurrence; Williams's responses to the concert party's commanding officers are often used to anticipate or to reinforce audience reaction to the satire.

Sexuality and masculinity in *It Ain't Half Hot, Mum*

Although *It Ain't Half Hot, Mum* has attracted little serious critical attention compared to *Dad's Army*, one of its characters has drawn a great deal of scrutiny: Gunner (later Bombardier) 'Gloria' Beaumont played by Melvyn Hayes. Most of the other characters dress as women at some point in the series – even BSM Williams is compelled to stand in for Gloria in one episode – but Gloria is almost always understood by viewers as homosexual – the only member of the party to be read in this way despite Williams's assertion that they are all 'poofs'. Bruce Crowther and Mike Pinfold's *Bring Me Laughter* includes a brief discussion of Gloria in its account of the representation of homosexuality in situation comedy. Crowther and Pinfold suggest that Beaumont 'in uniform is only slightly camp' but is transformed into the 'epitome of the typical female star of a Hollywood musical' as Gloria: '[a]lthough ... [Hayes] took his Gloria character well over the edge, he managed to retain a considerable degree of believability and pathos. If Gloria remained a stereotype, it was by no means an unsympathetic one.'[18] In their essay, 'The Gender Game', Andy Medhurst and Lucy Tuck disagree. They acknowledge the necessity of stereotype in the thirty-minute situation comedy in order to provoke immediate audience recognition and response, and they discuss Richard Dyer's re-evaluation of stereotyping as a necessarily pejorative tendency, specifically in response to homosexual stereotypes (the 'sitcom queen, all wrists and sibilants').[19] But Medhurst and Tuck believe that '[s]ome sitcom stereotypes ... make ... judiciousness difficult to maintain', and they offer Gloria as a 'test case'.[20] They play with the possibility of a 'positive appraisal' of Gloria (who, they concede, is a fine performance on Hayes's part): 'should one feel in a generous mood', they suggest, and setting '[s]exuality aside', Gloria can be seen to follow in the footsteps of Hancock, Harold Steptoe and the grand tradition of frustrated ambition in British sitcom, as he attempts to recreate spectacular MGM musicals in the dismal surroundings of a Royal Artillery depot. Setting 'sexuality aside' is impossible, however, 'since the immediate reaction of any mass "family" audience is to see him as homosexual, and funny for that reason alone'. He is coded as such by immediately recognisable signifiers: 'his "unnatural" behaviour, his visible difference, [and] his campness'. The use of homosexuality as the butt of comedy is reinforced, claim Medhurst and Tuck, by BSM Williams, when he constantly berates the concert party as a 'bunch of poofs'. As I discussed earlier, Medhurst and Tuck find no suggestion that Williams is 'an intentionally ridiculous figurehead of prejudice'; in fact, his inability to distinguish between the sexualities of the men in his platoon 'serves to reinforce the idea of homosexuality as an insult'. Jimmy Perry's and David Croft's autobiographies are silent on the topic of Gloria's sexuality, but in my interview with Croft, he responded to the suggestion of *It Ain't Half Hot, Mum*'s homophobia with the insistence that Gloria was 'definitely not a homosexual' – 'he never expressed any interest in any other male ... he was a transvestite, not a homosexual'.[21] The conflation of these two categories of identity is 'a mistake that everybody makes' according to Croft – audience members, academics and NCOs in the Royal Artillery alike. Thus, taking *It Ain't Half Hot, Mum*'s writers' intentions at face value, BSM Williams's inability to distinguish transvestism (or simple theatricality) from homosexuality exemplifies his own homophobia and, by extension, that of the institution he embodies.

In order to explore this issue further, I think it is worth beginning with the recurring depiction of cross-dressing or female impersonation that is a central theme in *It Ain't Half Hot, Mum*. There are several types of cross-dressing represented in this series, including other gender impersonations and impersonations of race, as we will see later in this chapter, but the most obvious example – the performance of female identity by Gloria and some other members of the concert party – is a useful starting point. As Roger Baker points out in *Drag: A History of Female Impersonation in the Performing Arts*, there is a long history of female impersonation in both Eastern and Western cultural traditions, and the British theatrical tradition is certainly no exception.[22] Although female impersonation was a staple ingredient of RAF gang shows and concert parties during the early part of the century (allowing Perry and Croft legitimation via *It Ain't Half Hot, Mum*'s 'historical accuracy'), Baker suggests that drag acts did not begin to make a revival on stage until the 1960s, and cites Danny La Rue – himself a veteran of naval concert parties during the Second World War – as an early significant figure. Although initially making appearances in cabaret and club acts, female impersonators quickly transferred to television – from the innumerable, two-dimensional caricatures of women in Monty Python sketches, to the well-considered personae of Barry Humphries' Dame Edna Everage and Fyfe and Logan's Dr Evadne Hinge and Dame Hilda Bracket. Even Steptoe and son get to dress as 'Mrs Steptoe and daughter' in a 1972 episode, 'Live Now, P.A.Y.E. later'. Surprisingly,

Albert makes (in Gregory Koseluk's words) 'a rather convincing little old lady', certainly in comparison with the grotesque impersonation offered by Harold as his own fictional sister, Muriel.[23]

The ease with which Albert is able to portray his own wife causes Harold to reflect on a potential slippage in his father's sexual identity, and it is here that popular representations of female impersonation mark the boundaries of acceptability or domestication. Baker cites Danny La Rue's remarks about his own impersonation: 'My act is playing a woman, knowing that everybody knows it's a fella. That's the point of the joke. If I played a woman's role from beginning to end, where would Danny La Rue have got to?'[24] What makes the female impersonation in *It Ain't Half Hot, Mum* entirely safe for mass audience consumption is the series' deliberate avoidance of verisimilitude – witness Gunner Mackintosh's impression of Marlene Dietrich in 'Forbidden Fruits', for example (figure 6). Gloria is a more complex case, however. What separates his character from the concert party's other performers is his unshakeable belief in his ability to produce a convincing impersonation of femininity. Even though most of the party appears in drag during the course of the series, Gloria is uniquely concerned with the verisimilitude of his performance as a woman – plucking his eyebrows, worrying about wearing underwear that matches his dress, and, in 'The Curse of the Sadhu', balking at Williams's orders for a parade because 'I've just put my hair in curlers'. Beside him, Mackintosh's Esther Williams is a 'travesty', and this seems to be an opinion upheld within *It Ain't Half Hot, Mum*'s narratives: Captain Ashwood seems relatively convinced by Gloria's impersonations, as I will discuss later, and in 'The Road to Bannu' (one of the few episodes in which Williams has the last laugh) the Indian tribal chief is entirely convinced by Gloria's Dorothy Lamour, and wants 'her' in exchange for a rug. But if this fiction of the authenticity of Gloria's female impersonation can mark his sexuality as beyond the boundaries of the normative for an audience, the character is ultimately 'domesticated' by Melvyn Hayes's performance, which is, to paraphrase Danny La Rue, 'to play a man playing a woman, knowing that everybody knows it's a fella'. Despite Gloria's claims to authenticity, Hayes renders Gloria's impersonations in ways that are no more convincing than those of the other performers, pushing his cross-dressing firmly back into the safe circle of theatrical drag.

Croft's assertion that there is no textual evidence for Gloria's identification as a homosexual is borne out on a literal level, at least, by Medhurst and Tuck: as they point out, Gloria's homosexuality is entirely 'undeclared' in *It Ain't Half Hot, Mum*. They argue, however, that

Gloria's sexuality is indicated through innuendo, associations and 'signs', all of which are eminently legible to a mass (or heteronormative) audience. Medhurst and Tuck contrast Gloria's characterisation with the sophisticated and multilayered approach to sexuality in the radio show *Round the Horne*, in which Julian and Sandy signify their homosexuality for a mass audience by 'absurdly theatricalised male femininity', but also use *parlare*, a gay slang which communicates to a gay audience.[25] Gloria, in other words, is a gay stereotype presented only for heterosexual mass consumption. The signs of Gloria's sexual difference are too familiar in popular representation to require elucidation: his lisp, his effeminacy, his propensity for emotional outbursts and 'turns'. But, it might be argued that there are other lines to read between. Gloria is never granted an opportunity for the expression of homosexual desire; indeed he rarely expresses desire at all, since this would necessarily declare a sexual preference. In 'Down in the Jungle', the concert party have to link arms in the plane because there are no seats (or seatbelts), and when Gloria links arms with Williams he exclaims, 'Ooh! Aren't your muscles hard!', which is perhaps about as close as Gloria ever gets to a physical relationship. Elsewhere, the objectification of the male body by other characters is read in homoerotic terms by Gloria. Williams, convinced that Gunner Parkins is his illegitimate son, takes paternal pride in Parky's physique ('A fine set of shoulders, boy. Show 'em off! Show 'em off!'), and in early episodes, before the exact nature of this relationship is known to the platoon, Williams's interest in Parky casts doubts upon the Sergeant Major's sexuality: in 'The Mutiny of the Punkah-Wallahs', for example, Gloria and Solly exchange a 'look' at Williams's admiration of Parky's shoulders, and in 'The Jungle Patrol', even Gloria remarks to Solly, 'If I hadn't seen him down at the bazaar with that bint of his, I'd have my doubts'. Signs of Gloria's sexuality proliferate elsewhere, often in the unspoken. A common sequence of shots in *It Ain't Half Hot, Mum* is for a character to make a statement that identifies Gloria as homosexual, followed by a close-up of Gloria's reaction. This begins early in the series with Williams's endlessly repeated assertions that the concert party are all 'poofs' (which apparently offends none of them besides Gloria), but another early example is Ashwood's unwitting innuendo in 'My Lovely Boy': complimenting Gloria on his portrayal of Ginger Rogers, Ashwood remarks 'he's rather good at being Ginger'. The gag depends on Cockney rhyming slang (ginger beer = queer) and is pointed, as usual, by a close-up of Gloria's reaction – his cheeks sucked in with indignation or outrage (figure 7). Even on those rare occasions when his sexuality seems about to be revealed, it remains obscured or anchored firmly in the realm of fiction. To escape a posting 'up the jungle' in 'Showing the Flag', Gloria applies, in the words of Williams, to the 'trick cyclist' (psychiatrist) on the grounds that he is psychologically unfit for military service. But, Williams delights in recounting, 'rumour has it that the trick cyclist is also psychologically unfit for military service', a dynamic which Williams sums up as 'it takes one to know one'.

Within the structures of *It Ain't Half Hot, Mum*, however, Williams's claim is patently untrue. As far as he is concerned, homosexuality is entirely 'knowable' to a heterosexual audience (i.e. himself), and not just to other homosexuals, by reading the signs of sexual difference; *It Ain't Half Hot, Mum* seems to suggest that the same is true for its viewers – that despite Gloria's sexuality remaining unspoken, it can be known as 'other' by a heteronormative audience through an appropriately interpreted sexual semiotic. To a present-day television audience, accustomed to the US sitcom *Will and Grace* and Graham Norton, this type of simultaneously prurient and repressive representation of homosexuality – rendering 'it' visible only through the unspoken and the obscure – might seem at best ridiculous, or at worst little short of (in Medhurst and Tuck's words) an 'indelibly inscribed homophobia'.[26] And if we accept Croft's claim that Gloria is not scripted as a homosexual but simply as a transvestite, then we might at least suggest that he and Perry are guilty of an opportunism common enough in other media products of the 1970s. In *Up Pompeii!* (1969–70), for example, the senator's son, Nauseus, fruitlessly inscribes odes replete with double entendres to a different woman each week, always foundering on a suitable rhyme. But when Lurkio (Frankie Howerd) rolls his eyes, pushes his tongue into his cheek and confides to the audience that Nauseus is a 'funny boy', are we supposed to understand that his sexual difference is indelibly marked for our benefit?[27] The issue has been debated more extensively with respect to another of David Croft's sitcoms, this time co-written with Jeremy Lloyd. John Inman's portrayal of Mr Humphries in *Are You Being Served?* depends entirely on the types of gestures and linguistic signs that mark Gloria, though Inman is quick to point out that Humphries' sexuality, like Gloria's, remains undeclared. 'It has never been mentioned one way or the other' Inman says, and he also claims that he doesn't understand why '[O]ne or two people did think I was playing a stereotype gay person ... If you play a stereotype lorry driver, you wear big boots and jeans. Does that mean because you wear a neat little suit and a tie you must be gay?'[28] Inman's remarks seem somewhat disingenuous, but again Croft is adamant: 'we never wrote Mr Humphries as a homosexual ... he was always a mother's boy'.[29] Despite these testimonies, Mr Humphries was seen by his original audience as a homophobic stereotype, generating letters of complaint to the BBC from angry gay viewers and sensationalised coverage in the popular press, to the extent that he was almost cut from the series. Croft reports that Bill Cotton's attitude to Mr Humphries' inclusion in the sitcom was not positive: 'do we have to have the pouf?'.[30] At least one BBC television executive, then, (mis)read the signs. If homosexuality is never openly acknowledged or intended in these examples, one might argue that an audience is hardly discouraged from 'reading the signs' that are kept, in David Croft's own words about Mr Humphries, forever 'doubtful'.[31]

It is important, I think, to position the characterisations of Gloria and Mr Humphries within their cultural context. The decriminalisation of homosexuality was established by the Sexual Offences Act of 1967, only five years before the beginning of *Are You Being Served?*, and then only in England, extending to Northern Ireland in 1979 and to Scotland in 1980. One might argue that the historical location of *It Ain't Half Hot, Mum* in 1945 – at a time when homosexual activities were still considered criminal offences – attempts to circumvent contemporary politics by reverting to a period in which homosexuality was not openly discussed.[32] But just as Gloria signifies to an early 1970s mass cultural audience as visibly 'other', he is also necessarily located within the then current discourses about homosexuality as a threat to the bourgeois family unit or as a source of general moral panic. In their book on *Are You Being Served?*, Rigelsford, Brown and Tibballs rescue Mr Humphries from the impropriety of homophobia by calling a number of gay witnesses to testify that the distress in the gay community about the character's representation was a storm in teacup, and that these days Mr Humphries is regarded as a gay icon 'up there with Judy Garland and Barbra Streisand'.[33] No such claims have been made about Gloria, perhaps because contemporary television audiences are much less familiar with *It Ain't Half Hot, Mum* than the perennially repeated *Are You Being Served?* Medhurst and Tuck, at any event, acknowledge at least one personal response to *It Ain't Half Hot, Mum* – 'a programme which, one of us can testify from personal experience, was hardly conducive to the growth of a positive self-image of at least one gay schoolboy'.[34] If nothing else, recognising the political and historical contexts of *It Ain't Half Hot, Mum* explains how it has been caught up in its cultural moment's prurient interest in homosexuality, even while it lacks the discourses to express or represent openly a sexual otherness which is excluded from the 'inside' of the bourgeois audience's interests by functioning as a butt of comedy.

Another way to think through the issues of sexuality represented in *It Ain't Half Hot, Mum*, beyond discussions of stereotyping and homophobia, is to consider the series in terms of broader concepts of masculinity. The struggle for a clearly defined masculine identity, and the 'naturalness' of gendered categories are surely central issues for *It Ain't Half Hot, Mum* – the series' principal tension, after all, comes from BSM Williams's Sisyphean struggle to make 'real men' and 'real soldiers' out of a group of individuals who are, by his definitions, neither. As I remarked earlier, this theme runs throughout most episodes and drives many of the narratives, as the concert party is drilled, punished and sent on training and survival missions. The physicalities of the actors play a significant role in the discourses of masculinity; Deolali, of course, is much less temperate than Walmington-on-Sea, and so the bodies of the members of the concert party are much more visible than those of the *Dad's Army* platoon. In uniform, the members of the party are never without a profusion of sweat stains, lovingly recreated by spraying the actors with glycerine, and they are often without uniforms, displaying a range of variously unathletic physiques.[35] Part of *It Ain't Half Hot, Mum*'s physical comedy depends on the bodies of its characters – the willowy, balding (and therefore cerebral) Graham; the stick-like, awkward Ashwood; even Gloria, who, despite his protestations that all the other presentations of drag are a 'travesty' besides his own, is costumed to emphasise his small, wiry physique, comically at odds with the illusion of femininity he purports to create. Most significantly, though, the physique of Lofty operates as a recurring comic motif in the series; his shortness of stature and ubiquitous short trousers create an infantilised body which is mocked physically and verbally by Williams, and visually by the camera. On several occasions Lofty is chosen to undertake dangerous solo missions – such as his search for help in 'The Road to Bannu', in which we are given long and wide-angled shots of his child-like, diminutive figure trudging incongruously through the inhospitable terrain. None of the concert party's members represent what might be considered as conventionally perfect specimens of masculinity by the standards of the 1970s – even Gunner Mackintosh, nicknamed 'Atlas' by the platoon, is played by an actor of average physique. Set against them, however, is BSM Williams, to whom Windsor Davies brings a superbly exaggerated articulation of masculine physicality, with his clenched buttocks, his stomach sucked into concavity, and his chest thrust outward and upward. This caricature of masculinity is often framed by the soft, unathletic or childish bodies of the party, to create a comic juxtaposition of opposites, but also a visual structure that does little to establish a normative masculinity. As the scenes when Williams is alone, relaxed and shirtless in his *basha* make clear, this image of hyper-masculinity is BSM Williams's (as distinct from Windsor Davies') own performance, as much an impersonation of gender as Gloria's presentation of Ginger Rogers. This is succinctly demonstrated in the 'video' for Windsor Davies and Don Estelle's chart-topping hit, 'Whispering Grass'. While Estelle, as Lofty, sings in his fine operatic voice, Davies, in character as Williams, struts and swaggers, thrusts out his chest, twitches his moustache, alternately purses his lips and flashes his large, widely spaced teeth, winks and mugs to an implied audience, in what can only be described as a genuinely grotesque masquerade (figure 8). The video makes clear that Lofty is present only for his voice and Williams for his physical performance – he adds very little to the vocal performance, certainly. Seen here in its most exaggerated form, perhaps because it depends on dumbshow, Williams's performance of masculinity collapses in on itself; making eyes at members of the video's fictional audience, strutting his hyper-masculinised body, and even wiggling his backside in time to the music, Williams makes himself the object of spectatorship, becoming precisely the theatricalised spectacle that he identifies in the series with homosexuality. Davies's performance seems to recognise this: at one point, Williams catches sight of someone looking at him and he becomes momentarily hostile, looking the implied spectator up and down with disgust (figure 9).

Williams is keen, then, to distinguish himself from the men under his command specifically in terms of his masculinity – as he tells the concert party in 'The Jungle Patrol', 'I am used to [the jungle] because I am a soldier. And you are not because you are a bunch of poofs'. He insists repeatedly on his own strength of will and criticises the members of the party for having none. Thus, in 'The Mutiny of the Punkah-Wallahs' Williams refers to his 'iron control', and in 'Forbidden Fruits', when the dietary additive used to suppress sexual appetite has run short, he expresses concern about the party's ability to resist sexual urges because 'them boys haven't got my iron control'. Even as he insists on his ability to discipline his own body, however, it rebels; in 'The Jungle Patrol' he demonstrates how to find water in vines, though he adds, after drinking, that it doesn't taste very nice and will no doubt upset the delicate stomachs of the undisciplined members of the party. He barely gets the words out of his mouth before turning to vomit. A similar sequence occurs in 'Monsoon Madness', in which he follows up a boast to demonstrate his self-discipline by taking a large number of salt tablets, resulting in his exit from the scene followed by a bout of loud, off-camera retching. In both these cases, the immediate response of the concert party (and the audience) is laughter. Williams's insistence, then, that his self-discipline and 'iron control' separate his body – the body of a 'real man' and a 'soldier' – from the soft, undisciplined bodies of a 'bunch of poofs' is repeatedly undermined by his body itself, which is revealed to have no more discipline (and sometimes less) than the 'unmasculine' bodies that surround him.

It is perhaps not surprising, in the context of It Ain't Half Hot, Mum's emphasis on the performance of gendered identities, that BSM Williams is a strong proponent of the 'naturalness' of gendered behaviour and relationships – though it is certainly going too far to suggest that Perry and Croft sought to articulate a consistent critical debate about essentialised and socially constructed identities. Nevertheless, Williams's pronouncements about what he considers to be 'natural' – like his other statements or performances of masculinity – are inevitably called into question. For Williams, almost any type of theatrical endeavour is effeminating. He rails against cross-dressing particularly, but also against 'face-painting', theatrical costuming, even education: he remarks repreatedly that Gunner Graham's degree in a typically unmasculine discipline (English Literature) makes him unfit or unprepared for military service. In 'The Mutiny of the Punkah-Wallahs' he asserts to the Colonel that he 'cannot bear to see men dressed up as women' because 'It's not natural, sir'; and in 'The Night of the Thugs' he is unappreciative of a musical number in which Solly and Gloria, dressed in yellow, feathered bird-suits, court each other and produce an egg. 'I don't like to see two men making up to each other', he complains, 'It's not natural'. In both these cases the Colonel responds in ways that offer an alternative definition of the 'natural'. In this latter example, he responds directly to Williams's complaint – 'They're supposed to be birds', he replies, insisting on the performance itself as the paradigm for judging the 'naturalness' of their behaviour. That identity is *performed* takes precedence over the essentialised notions of gender assumed by BSM Williams. Similarly, in the former example from 'The Mutiny of the Punkah-Wallahs', the Colonel finds only Gunner Parkins's female impersonation to be unnatural compared with those of the concert party's other performers; Parkins, the Colonel complains, 'had his lady's things hanging right down ... most unnatural'. Once more, the Colonel's definition of what constitutes the 'natural' upholds the primacy of performance – it hardly seems to matter that the women on stage are actually cross-dressed men, so long as the illusion of their femininity is sufficiently convincing to pass.

As the representative of highest authority within the 'work family' of It Ain't Half Hot, Mum's situation, Colonel Reynolds often has the last –

and most definitive – word. Another key figure in undermining BSM Williams's insistence on the essentialised naturalness of gendered identities is the series' other commissioned officer. Perry and Croft mark Captain Ashwood as heterosexual in several episodes; from his 'bit of a thing' with Emily Creighton-Dunhowerd to numerous mentions of his wife, there are frequent references to his heterosexual desires. But while Ashwood occupies a safely heterosexualised identity, he is also the character who is most enthusiastically apologetic for the illusion of femininity created by the concert party's performances. In the series' opening episode, he maintains, in the face of Williams's insistence that the cross-dressed performers are 'not real girls', that they 'don't look too bad at all, really' and that they are the 'nearest thing we're going to get to women'. He is particularly impressed by Gloria, whom he thinks 'makes an absolutely first-class girl', and is thrilled to hear about his new outfits; 'Oh good show!' he declares with much enthusiasm, when he hears about Gloria's new dress in flame-coloured taffeta 'with a split right up to here'.[36] Ashwood, of course, ranks above Williams, and his opinions about female impersonation are frequently validated by Colonel Reynolds ('I quite agree, Ashwood'; 'Good point!') even though some of his far-fetched plans and ideas are regularly dismissed ('Don't be a fool, Ashwood'). Although neither Reynolds nor Ashwood are characters with whom the audience is supposed to feel a strong personal association (residing squarely in the stereotype of the British 'upper-class twit'), within *It Ain't Half Hot, Mum*'s situation the two officers inevitably represent a voice of higher authority than the Sergeant-Major's. Thus, while Williams can insist on essentialised notions of gender and sexuality, and can attempt to force these natural-ised categories on the men in his party, the opinions of the officers and, to some extent, the fluidity of Ashwood's own desire, work to under-mine Williams's authority.

An episode that usefully brings together a number of the ideas about gender and sexuality discussed in this chapter is 'Forbidden Fruits'. Sex is the episode's principal theme, and it concludes with a self-conscious 'bedroom farce' motif; the premise is that supply of desire-dampening 'white powder' given to the Char-Wallah to put in the tea by the depot's Medical Officer has run short, and the men – including BSM Williams and the two officers – are no longer having their sexual appetites sup-pressed. 'Forbidden Fruits' opens with a dress rehearsal for the concert party's new show, 'A Night in Montmartre'. Gunner Mackintosh, unflatteringly decked out as Marlene Dietrich in a slip, women's under-wear, stockings, and a matching hat and heels, occupies the centre of the medium shot, singing 'Falling in Love Again' in a flat Scotsaccented monotone. He is flanked by Nobby and Nosher, both attired as singularly unconvincing prostitutes and striking awkward, though apparently provocative, poses. The image underscores the pantomimic nature of their female impersonation, and a cut to the 'more authentic' Gloria reveals a similar image; overdressed as a member of the underground, Gloria wears a purple beret and low-cut blouse, a black mini-skirt slit to the waist, stockings and silver heels – an outfit that reveals the male body beneath the drag more than it creates any illusion of female identity. Gloria's statement that he 'fancies' himself wearing a sari, is met with Solly's retort – 'I don't!' – and a sequence of expositions that anchor most of the party's desire in heterosexual expression: Solly remarks that 'blokes' dressing as women is no substitute for the real thing; Atlas can't stop thinking about 'big girls'; Lofty thinks about 'small girls'; and Parky thinks about girls of 'any size'. Ordinarily denied sexual desire by the doctored tea, most of the party turn out to be reassuringly heterosexual after all. The full survey of the party is completed in a subsequent scene in which Williams looks over their reading material – the only member of the platoon to be denied an expression of desire or a 'dirty book' is, of course, Gloria, maintaining his 'doubtful' status.

Despite the officers' presumption that it is the undisciplined members of the concert party who will be overcome by their desire, it is, in fact, the officers themselves who cannot control their bodies. Other than the scenes I mentioned above, the episode doesn't revisit the issue of the concert party's sexual desire, but focuses instead on Williams's pursuit of his 'Chinese bit' and Reynolds's infatuation with Mrs Daphne Waddilove-Evans. Ashwood tortures himself with thoughts of his wife, and becomes embroiled in the final scene's bedroom farce. In all cases, the bodies of the 'real man' or of the upper-class 'real soldier' are those that collapse in the face of desire. Williams's scene with Ling Su (Mrs Waddilove-Evans's maid, to whom Rangi Ram plays pander) leaves him contorted with frustrated desire in medium close-up. Ashwood dashes water in his face to keep control, and Reynolds loses it when Mrs Waddilove-Evans visits him in his office ('Bite my neck, Charles, bite my neck!'). This surrender to desire is mocked in the episode's closing scene, in which a sequence of confusions place Reynolds with Ling Su, Ashwood – having been slapped – hiding behind the curtains, and Williams bursting shirtless into Mrs Waddilove-Evans's bedroom just as her husband returns home unexpectedly. The situation is salvaged by Solly, of course, who is on hand with the rest of the party to capture the spectacle with a borrowed camera. He concocts the improbable story that the concert party is simply rehearsing a farce. What 'Forbidden

Fruits' mocks principally is the weakness of the heterosexual body; the disciplined body of heterosexual masculinity, with its purported 'iron control' or superior authority, is seen to be subject to collapse in the face of desire. Set against these images are the normative bodies of the concert party (excepting Gloria) – the men without authority in class or military hierarchies, without particular anxieties about their sexuality (they dress as women, but acknowledge that it is no 'substitute' for the real thing), but also apparently without any need to act on their stated heterosexual desire. In the last chapter, I concluded that the ideological 'inside' of *Dad's Army*'s structure was defined by the lower-middle-class British amateur. *It Ain't Half Hot, Mum*, expanding into the anxious territory of 1970s' male sexuality, defines a similar figure – the normative identity, the 'us' of mass audience spectatorship, turns out to be that of the lower- or middle-class, unathletic and sexually apathetic man, itself another stereotype of British male sexuality.[37]

That *It Ain't Half Hot, Mum* functions in this way is hardly surprising. It is, after all, a piece of mass cultural entertainment from the early 1970s, of the sort popular at 8pm on a weekday night on BBC1, and perhaps it is unfair to expect it to articulate a radical politics of identity – although Murray Healy at least entertains the possibility that '[Perry] and Croft could be accused of coming to comedy with an explicit agenda of sexual politics', since, among other things, their final collaboration, *You Rang M'Lord?*, 'was the first British series ever to have a regular lesbian character'.[38] 'To have *any* explicitly homosexual representation at all in family entertainment was problematic in the early 1970s', he adds – citing the demand from BBC Light Entertainment's Bill Cotton that 'the poof' be excised from *Are You Being Served?* – and so the inclusion of the (in)visible homosexual figure of Gloria might be seen as a radical gesture. Since '[Perry] and Croft comedies present a conventional structure which decentres the dominant ideology of the family' by being set in work environments, Healy sees the possibility of a space for the sitcom 'queer': the homosexual character is placed 'outside' the family, but, as in *It Ain't Half Hot, Mum* for example, the ideological centre of the series is 'beyond the family too, making this a potentially ambivalent space'. While the comic, or ludic, ambivalence may be subject to closure by the dominance of the bourgeois family as the normative social organisation, the possibility exists for resistance. As Healy points out, '[t]he dominant may assume' the primacy of the bourgeois family, 'but the "unfinalizedness" [of comedy] does allow for' other readings.[39] In *It Ain't Half Hot, Mum* it is possible to assume the position of the dominant, and therefore to read homophobia into the representation of Gloria and into the collapse of other heterosexual identities into the comic butts of homosexual subversion (Ashwood's slippage of sexuality as he finds Gloria too convincing as a woman, for example, or BSM Williams's slide into a grotesquely camp spectacle as he performs as an object of spectatorship in 'Whispering Grass'). But it is equally feasible, I think, to read the series as the product of a cultural moment in which anxieties about what constitutes masculinity conspired to leave normative masculine identity as a range of uncongenial stereotypes exhibiting a significant degree of instability and fluidity.

'It is making me feel so proud to be British': *It Ain't Half Hot, Mum* and race

As I remarked earlier in this chapter, the representation of race in *It Ain't Half Hot, Mum* has also attracted some critical attention. The series has a fairly stable core of Indian characters (Rangi Ram, Char-Wallah Muhammed and Punkah-Wallah Rumzan) for most of its episodes, and there are many other cameo appearances besides: assorted wallahs, gamekeepers, police officers, stationmasters, and tribesmen, with the occasional incidence of Chinese or Japanese characters. That Rangi Ram was played by a white actor (Michael Bates) in 'blackface' seems scarcely credible from our contemporary perspective, and, indeed, Bates's performance has drawn criticism on these grounds. Even moderate apologists Bruce Crowther and Mike Pinfold mention that the 'practice of blacking up' that persisted into the 1970s 'was later realized to be unacceptably offensive', though the popular variety show, *The Black and White Minstrel Show*, continued to linger until 1978.[40] In the final part of the chapter, then, I would like to evaluate the representation of race in *It Ain't Half Hot, Mum*, by attempting to contextualise the series in terms of British cultural history as well as in its own immediate televisual context.

In *British Low Culture*, Leon Hunt suggests that it would be 'misleading to omit considerations of race from any discussion of 1970s comedy', let alone from an investigation of a series that fundamentally explores race.[41] Hunt traces light entertainment's consideration of race to two sources – an older 'stand-up' tradition of comedy with 'unreflexive racist jokes' told by figures like Bernard Manning, and a newer televisual tradition typified by *Till Death Us Do Part*, which Hunt describes as a 'crucial permissive text of the 1960s'.[42] Discussions of Alf Garnett and his 'ideological complexities' are common enough in critical analyses of British sitcom, and Andy Medhurst, in his introduction to the section on situation comedy in Therese Daniels and Jane Gerson's *The Colour Black*, most succinctly captures the nature of the problem:

> The key question about Garnett, and it's a crucial one for the politics of comedy as a whole, is whether we are invited to laugh at him or with him. Johnny Speight has always claimed that he wrote Garnett as a monster so as to expose his bigotry to ridicule ... The problem is that Warren Mitchell's performance as Garnett completely overshadows those of [his daughter and son-in-law].[43]

Medhurst's point underscores the inability of any writer to control completely her or his text's reception; with the very best of liberal intentions, Speight could not guarantee that his audience only enjoyed *Till Death Us Do Part* because of its mockery of bigotry. Hunt sees the paradigm of the 'race sitcom' that *Till Death Us Do Part* establishes 'trickling down' into two 'modernising initiatives – an attempt to "naturalise" and broaden the range of representations of black characters in sitcom ... and to follow Johnny Speight's pioneering attempt to turn racism itself into a subject for humour on television'.[44]

Nevertheless, even in its more radical or liberal incarnations, Hunt claims that British 'race humour' prioritises Afro-Caribbean Britons over its more recent Asian citizenship. He cites examples of the 'comparatively non-stereotypical [Afro-Caribbean] characters' from *Porridge* and *Rising Damp* in contrast to the 'grossly caricatured Asians (some of them "blacked up") in *Curry and Chips*, *It Ain't Half Hot, Mum* and *Mind Your Language*'.[45] Hunt certainly highlights the fact that *It Ain't Half Hot, Mum* was not the only British comedy of the 1960s and 1970s that included Asian characters, and not the only piece of British visual culture that involved 'blacking up'. *Carry On up the Khyber* (Rank, 1968), for example, featured several members of the *Carry On* cast impersonating Indians. In this particular example of the film series, set in Northern India in the late 19th century, the 3rd Foot and Mouth hold the native population in abeyance with the fearsome prospect that they wear nothing beneath their kilts; but when the Indians capture the effete sentry, Private Widdle (Charles Hawtrey), and discover that the 'Devils in Skirts' do wear underclothing after all, they foment a rebellion, which is only overthrown in the final scene when the regiment 'present arms': they raise their kilts on command and, *sans* underpants, rout the rebellious horde. Despite the fact that *Carry On up the Khyber* made it into a 'Top 100 British films' list published by the British Film Institute (ostensibly because it almost manages a critique of British imperialism), the film upholds a number of unpalatable

Indian stereotypes. Even the characters' names betray a high/low cultural division between British and Indian: with the exception of the infantilised, un-self-controlled Private Widdle, the British characters' names (Sir Sidney Ruff-Diamond, or Captain Keene) contrast strongly with those of the native population, which use bodily functions and physical objectification to parody historical figures and peoples. Thus, Kenneth Williams plays the Khasi of Kalabar, his daughter is Princess Jelhi, and the leader of the hostile local tribesmen, the Burpas, is none other than Bungdit Din (Bernard Bresslaw). We find similar configurations on television. Whatever Johnny Speight's intentions in creating Alf Garnett, it is somewhat more difficult to rescue his other 1960s sitcom, *Curry and Chips* (LWT, 1969). Set in the canteen of a manufacturer of seaside novelties, this sitcom starred Spike Milligan blacked up as Kevin O'Grady, a half-Pakistani, half-Irish character known as the 'Paki Paddy' – two stereotypes for the price of one. Kenny Lynch played 'Kenny', an anti-Pakistani, Afro-Caribbean Briton, who neatly displaced the burden of racist remarks onto a non-white character – ably demonstrating Hunt's point about priority and hierarchy in British 'race humour'. Perhaps the worst of these representations, however, didn't arrive until the late 1970s with *Mind Your Language* (LWT, 1977–79 and 1986). Despite Medhurst's assertion that '[t]o label a text as "racist", nothing more nothing less, is not to open it up to productive analysis', he is content to suggest that '[i]f any sitcom does deserve the dismissive rubber-stamping of "racist", it must be *Mind Your Language*'.[46] Set in an English language school, the series depended on a gallery of xenophobic and racist stereotypes (Indian, Italian, Greek, Japanese, German, Pakistani, Chinese ...) and revolved, as Medhurst puts it, around a single joke: 'these-foreigners-are-hilarious-because-they-talk-funny-don't-they'.[47]

If *It Ain't Half Hot, Mum* makes use of *Mind Your Language*'s one and only gag, it certainly has a larger repertoire of jokes, and its Indian characters are more complex than the two-dimensional representations promoted by some of its contemporaries. Jimmy Perry discusses the accusations of racism against *It Ain't Half Hot, Mum*, including that of a BBC executive who claimed 'they wouldn't repeat the series "because it's racist"'.[48] Perry states that his and Croft's intentions were entirely in the spirit of multicultural awareness: '[w]hat David and I were trying to do was to explain why we had so many Asians living in the UK and how we became a multiracial society; it was the effect of the aftermath of Empire'. The dismissal of the series as racist, then, 'filled [Perry] with despair', and was 'purely based upon ignorance' articulated by an 'all British' critical audience. In fact, claims Perry, 'British Asians loved it –

and still do – they call it "our programme"'. From a contemporary
vantage point – following the broadcast of sitcoms like Farrukh
Dhondy's *No Problem!* (C4, 1983–85), *Tandoori Nights* (C4, 1985, 1987),
and, more recently, the sketch comedy show *Goodness Gracious Me!* –
this claim might seem a little unlikely. But given *It Ain't Half Hot,
Mum*'s historical moment and the absence of other qualified contenders,
it is possible to see how a sitcom that regularly cast Asian actors in
Indian roles, and that occasionally saw the Indian characters with the
upper hand at an episode's conclusion, might have offered an Asian
audience its best chance at sympathy and identification. The casting of a
white actor, Michael Bates, as the leading Indian character was not, as
we have seen, without precedent in the 1970s, and Perry and Croft both
defend this particular decision, too. In 1972, Perry states, 'there were
very few Asian actors and, sadly, not one experienced enough to play a
leading comedy role'.[49] An interview with Zia Moyheddin, in Jim
Pines's collection, *Black and White in Colour: Black People on British
Television Since 1936*, supports this suggestion in part: when asked about
the practice of blacking up white actors to play Asian roles in drama, he
admits that 'there weren't many Asian or black actors around at this
time', but he also suggests that 'producers would not take the trouble, or
even think that it was important enough to take the trouble, to find the
right (that is Asian) actor'.[50] Moyheddin acknowledges that blacking up
was a common practice but also that it was more 'hurtful' to him than
'offensive'. Michael Bates's own response to criticism is perhaps best
taken tongue-in-cheek – he proposed that since he was, in fact, born in
India and other two Indians in *It Ain't Half Hot, Mum* were Pakistani
and Bangladeshi, he was the only 'authentic' Indian in the production.[51]
Besides the Char-Wallah and the Punkah-Wallah, there are countless
cameo roles in which Asian actors appear, and, again defending himself
against claims of racism, Perry writes that '[d]uring the series David and
I were responsible for starting off, and encouraging, many Asian actors
who have since become well known'.[52] Croft adds that the unofficial
censorship of *It Ain't Half Hot, Mum* by not broadcasting repeats
effectively ensures that these early performances by Asian actors on
popular television are not seen, a state of affairs in which he sees a
distinct irony.[53]

We might approach a more detailed evaluation of *It Ain't Half Hot,
Mum*'s alleged racism by locating it in larger cultural or historical
contexts than those of early 1970s British television. Perry claims that
his intention in producing the series was to help explain Britain's
'multiracial society', and his autobiography makes clear that a lot of *It
Ain't Half Hot, Mum*'s material was based on 'fact' as he experienced it.

He gives an anecdote, for example, about the response of a dhobi-wallah (launderer) to an officer's request that he use soap flakes to clean clothes rather than beat them on rocks in the river – 'Sadly sahib, not enough soap flakes to fill river'.[54] This anecdote crops up in 'The Jungle Patrol' as a joke in a conversation between Rangi Ram and Char-Wallah Muhammed, where, without Perry's context, it might seem like any other gag taking 'native simplicity' as the butt of the comedy. This comic exchange 'actually happened', then, but even its original utterance remains ambiguous: was the dhobi-wallah's response the product of naivety, or a sly gag at the officer's expense trading on the latter's assumptions about native simple-mindedness? Facts, of course, are ideologically inflected – an issue that Stuart Hall explores specifically in response to representations of race in 'The Whites of their Eyes: Racist Ideologies and the Media'. Hall begins by establishing three important characteristics of ideology that are worth repeating here: (1) that ideologies are not 'isolated and separate concepts' but rather consist of disparate elements articulated as a 'distinctive set or chain or meanings'; (2) that even though individuals utter ideological statements, 'ideologies are not the product of individual consciousness or intention'; and (3) that ideologies function by 'constructing for their subjects ... positions of identification and knowledge that allow them to "utter" ideological truths as if they were their authentic authors'.[55] Thus, the ideologies of race articulated by the media are much larger than the individual intention, the individual author, or – in the case of our discussion here – the individual situation comedy. Hall distinguishes between two types of racism, which he refers to as 'overt' and 'inferential'.[56] He describes the former as 'the open and favourable coverage ... given to arguments, positions, and spokespersons who are in the business of elaborating an openly racist argument or advancing a racist policy or view'. Within the contexts of the sitcoms considered in this chapter, we might ascribe overt racism to Alf Garnett, or to BSM Williams's pronouncements about the Japanese – though it is important to note that these expressions of 'overt racism' are not 'favourable coverage' since they are deliberate indicators of *character*, which are subsequently critiqued by other characters or by the series' narratives. Hall uses the term 'inferential racism' to describe 'those apparently naturalised representations of events and situations relating to race, whether "factual" or "fictional", which have racist premises and propositions inscribed in them as a set of *unquestioned assumptions*'. It is here, according to Hall, that the 'good and honest liberal broadcaster' can go astray, producing a seemingly well-intentioned, liberal text which nevertheless articulates a position founded on potentially racist assumptions. Suggestions of this type of invisible, 'inferential racism' cause the most affront to the liberal broadcaster (we might remember Perry's own expression of 'despair' at the accusations of racism against *It Ain't Half Hot, Mum'*), but Hall emphasises that it is a mistake to locate the intention of racism in this case with the individual – 'an ideological discourse does *not* depend on the conscious intentions of those who formulate statements within it'.[57]

Stuart Hall writes about the racial assumptions that inform the media in terms that are particularly useful, I think, for an investigation of *It Ain't Half Hot, Mum*. He acknowledges racism's 'long and distinguished history' in British culture, 'grounded in the relations of slavery, colonial conquest, economic exploitation and imperialism in which European races have stood in relation to the "native peoples" of the colonised and exploited periphery' and identifies three particular characteristics that underlie discourses about these relations:

(1) Their imagery and themes were polarised around fixed relations of subordination and domination. (2) Their stereotypes were grouped around the poles of 'superior' and 'inferior' natural species. (3) Both were displaced from the 'language' of history into the language of Nature.[58]

Although Hall develops these characteristics with reference to the adventure narrative, he also stipulates that they are at work in comedy, albeit in more complex configurations. He identifies what he calls the 'base-images of the "grammar of race"' – the 'slave-figure', 'the native' and 'the entertainer' – through which the above discourses of racism are communicated. Are these images represented in *It Ain't Half Hot, Mum*? It is certainly possible, I think, to locate the stereotypical images that Hall discusses. Although slavery is not an immediate context, many of *It Ain't Half Hot, Mum*'s Indians occupy positions of great sub-servience to the British characters even if, technically, they are salaried workers – particularly those Indians who form part of the series' regular cast. Rangi Ram is the concert party's bearer, and he is seen in a variety of menial roles, including shaving the British characters, scrubbing tables, working as a stagehand, running errands, even polishing BSM Williams's boots. All these activities are undertaken with an irrepres-sible cheeriness, of course. Punkah-Wallah Rumzan occupies the most subservient position of all the regular Indian characters; employed to pull monotonously on a string that operates a fan to ventilate the officers' quarters, he is repeatedly kicked for slouching at his post, becoming, literally, the butt of a recurring sight gag. Another of Hall's 'base-images' – the native – is also seen in the series, in the form of aggressive tribesmen, fortune tellers and the 'sadhu'. The 'native' is also evoked as a means of hierarchical distinction, particularly by Rangi

Ram. Almost a catchphrase, Rangi's 'Don't talk to me as if I were some damn native' is used by him to separate himself from the 'uncivilised' Indian population. 'When will these damn natives learn to keep their place?', he asks at the conclusion of 'Meet the Gang'; and, in 'My Lovely Boy', during a conversation with Williams, he follows up his familiar statement with 'I am British gentleman, as you are, and know the form'. The point of the joke resides in the obvious fact that he is, in his own terms, one of these 'damn natives' after all, as is demonstrated by his linguistic and cultural misconceptions about British life, and physically embodied by the elasticated 'snake belt' with which he secures his turban. Even representations of educated Indian characters function in similar ways. In the first series, the chief of the local police force, Inspector Singh, features a couple of times, in phone conversations with Captain Ashwood. The source of the comedy in these exchanges seems to be that they speak identically ('Toodle-pip, old boy', Singh says to Ashwood as he rings off), the laugh depending on the unspoken assumption that this type of language is incongruous (and, therefore, amusing) in the mouth of an Indian. Other stereotypes of Indian or Asian cultural primitivism crop up regularly – the mention of numerous relatives involved in complex familial relationships, for example, or Rangi's 'wise Hindu sayings', which range from the authentic-seeming 'It is wise water-buffalo that knows his own spoor' to the parodic 'House with red lamp over door is not always headquarters of Communist Party'.[59] Figures of the 'clown' or 'entertainer' abound, too, not least in Rangi Ram's use of language. As in the case of Inspector Singh, Rangi is made to use comically incongruous British expressions – Solly's 'crocodile trick' in 'The Jungle Patrol', for example, is a 'top-hole wheeze' – but Rangi is also made to mangle British expressions and to speak in pidgin English. 'It is an ill wind that blows up nobody's creek', he philosophises; 'Don't be such clever dicky', he says as he chastises Rumzan; and, in a gag in the true 'Carry On' tradition, he insists that the Punkah-Wallah's ventilation system is to be replaced by an 'electric fanny'. Perry and Croft would no doubt defend these images in terms of their own authenticating experience in British India – that these are not racist stereotypes, but realistic representations of 'the way things were'. They may even be explained as 'anti-racist' on the basis of repre-sentation alone – the appearance of Indian characters (unusual enough in British situation comedies, especially of this period) arguably makes a statement, as Jimmy Perry hoped, about the multiracial nature of British culture. Hall argues that situation comedies such as *It Ain't Half Hot, Mum* step beyond the concept of inclusion, however, because 'they are *about race*':

the same old categories of racially defined characteristics and qualities, and the same relations of superior and inferior, provide the pivots on which the jokes actually turn, the tension-points which move and motivate the situations in situation comedies.[60]

There is another aspect to the representation of British India that we might consider, however: the possibility that Perry and Croft include a critique of imperialist ideology within the comic strategies of *It Ain't Half Hot, Mum*. The series' first episode opens with the national anthem, the union flag and a world map depicting the extent of the British Empire in 1945, with Donald Hewlett's voice-over about the 'heroes of India': Clive, Sleaman, Havelock. He then refers to British India's 'new generation of heroes' and the camera cuts to the opening credits, with the concert party performing their opening chorus, 'Meet the Gang'. The juxtaposition of the 'old' and the 'new' heroes of British India is a classic comic reversal, in which the image of Clive of India is replaced by that of Gunner 'Lofty' Sugden. The effect of the sequence has a couple of possibilities – is the concert party used to parody the *gravitas* of British imperial heroism (the deliberate pomposity with which the episode starts suggests parody from its outset), or is the dignity of the Empire used to indicate the ridiculously undignified nature of the Royal Artillery concert party? In other words, are we invited to laugh *at* the British Empire – or *with* the Empire *at* a 'bunch of poofs'? A similar ambivalence can be detected in other comic sequences in *It Ain't Half Hot, Mum*, often when the Indian characters discuss the idiosyncrasies of British culture. In 'The Curse of the Sadhu', for example, Rangi Ram, Char-Wallah Muhammed and Punkah-Wallah Rumzan are discussing Reynolds's and Ashwood's imminent departure for Bombay in the Colonel's 'jeepy'. Rangi Ram is instructing Muhammed in the intricacies of an officers' cocktail party, which he describes as a 'holy ceremony', with the chanting of ritualised incantations like 'Your bottom's up!' On one level, of course, this scene functions as a display of the 'base-images' of race described by Hall, since it depicts a familiar aspect of British social life interpreted by a primitive, 'native' consciousness. But, it might also be argued, the defamiliarisation of the practice by Rangi Ram's native sensibility reveals its absurdity; the officers' cocktail party in the last days of the British Raj, seen from the vantage point of the early 1970s, *is* an oddly archaic, ritualised form of social interaction. BSM Williams – the series' most vociferous proponent of empire – is made repeatedly to fetishise the 'jungle' as a source of colonial anxiety, filled with danger and hostile forces, yet his training exercises in the wilderness never seem to bear out this fantasy. In 'The Jungle Patrol', despite Williams's insistence that the party will barely survive in the wilderness 'miles from anywhere', Rangi Ram reveals to Solly and Gloria that there's a 'bus to cinema' close by if they feel like watching a movie before turning in for the night. Similarly, when the party's troop transport appears to have crashed behind enemy lines in 'Down in the Jungle', Williams leads a small squad on a reconnaissance mission and succeeds in capturing what he believes to be a group of Japanese soldiers. The episode concludes with the revelation that they are not Japanese, but rather that they are waiters in the 'Great Wall Chinese Restaurant' – the plane has, in fact, crashed just outside Calcutta. On one hand, the episode seems unable to escape a very limited range of representation, as the Asian characters slide from one stereotype (hostile Japanese soldier) to another (amiable Chinese waiter). But, one might argue, the intended butt of the joke that this misrecognition manufactures is Williams, whose colonial fantasy mistakenly constructs a threatening Other and a hostile landscape from the innocent and the mundane: the episode ends with the party ordering a takeaway.

In closing this chapter, I would like to cite one more example from *It Ain't Half Hot, Mum*. In the episode 'My Lovely Boy', the concert party's show is interrupted by the Colonel's announcement that the war is over in Europe. Despite the party's celebration, Williams insists they will be staying on in India to fight the 'slant-eyed Japanese', to 'teach them a lesson for encroaching on our Empire' with their 'dirty yellow hands'. This is certainly one of Williams's more overtly racist pronouncements in the series, shot in medium close-up with the light of British patriotism shining in his eyes. It is followed, however, by a cut to Michael Bates as Rangi Ram, singing 'Rule Britannia' via Gunner Parkins's ventriloquist's dummy, which is dressed in Royal Artillery uniform. There are several layers of images here, it seems to me; Williams's exaggerated jingoism is mocked by a travesty of an otherwise appropriately patriotic song, performed in the familiar 'gottle o' geer' convention of ventriloquism. But the 'soldier dummy' is a displacement of the song's source – as the other accent in its speech indicates, the mockery originates in Rangi Ram, the native 'British subject' whose piece of empire the Sergeant Major purports to defend. Ultimately, though, one might claim that the character of Rangi Ram is a further displacement, and that words originate in a white identity performing an Indian character performing the role of patriotic, white dummy. What is the definitive reading of this complex image (figure 10)?

In my discussions of both homophobia and racism in *It Ain't Half Hot, Mum* I have attempted to present a broad spectrum of attitudes and opinions because, as I hope I have shown, the 'polysemous' nature of televisual media makes a definitive reading of their representations as much an impossibility as an author's controlling the reception of his or her text. I certainly do not intend to operate as an apologist for homophobic or racist representations in the media, and I do believe in the sincerity of Perry and Croft's insistence that they intended no such prejudice. If we decide to read *It Ain't Half Hot, Mum* only as a 'racist text', then what happens to the voices of British Asian viewers in the early 1970s, for whom the series provided one of the few sites on television for recognition or inclusion? And if we assume only a homophobic agenda for the series, don't we also deny the potentially liberating discourses that Murray Healy finds in the work of Perry and Croft? Medhurst's assertion that 'to label as "racist" ... is not to open it up to productive analysis' might also be extended to include statements about homophobia, and I hope that my attempts to resist labelling *It Ain't Half Hot, Mum* in these ways have demonstrated that it is an interesting text and a key participant in the discourses of masculinity, sexuality and race in early 1970s British culture.[61]

Notes

1 Crisell, *An Introductory History*, p. 185.
2 Wagg (ed.), *Because I Tell a Joke or Two*, p. 15.
3 Hunt, *British Low Culture*, p. 2.
4 Perry, *A Stupid Boy*, p. 274; Lewisohn, *Radio Times Guide to TV Comedy*, p. 275.
5 Perry, *A Stupid Boy*, p. 276.
6 Lewisohn, *Radio Times Guide to TV Comedy*, p. 146; Croft, 'You Have Been Watching', p. 186. Croft explains the series' disappointing viewing figures as a result of *Come Back Mrs Noah*'s scheduling against 'the runaway success of Kenny Everett'.
7 Eaton, 'Television Situation Comedy', p. 82.
8 Perhaps the most comprehensive study of wartime entertainment is Richard Fawkes's *Fighting for a Laugh: Entertaining the British and American Armed Forces 1939–1946*. Other, more anecdotal accounts include John Graven Hughes, *The Greasepaint War*, Eric Taylor, *Showbiz Goes to War*, and Catharine Wells, *East with ENSA*.
9 Fawkes, *Fighting for a Laugh*, p. 12.
10 *Ibid.*
11 *Ibid.*, p. 13.
12 Susan Boyd-Bowman suggests that the concert party is an 'ENSA troupe' in her essay 'Back to Camp'.
13 *Ibid.*, p. 36.
14 Croft, 'You Have Been Watching', pp. 174–175.
15 Lewisohn, *Radio Times Guide to TV Comedy*, p. 352.
16 John Cleese, for example, has expressed an antipathy to comic traditions – mostly of radio humour – that depended largely on the use of easy catchphrases to generate laughter. He admits, however, that audiences find their own in spite of best efforts to avoid them. The *League of Gentlemen* decided to kill off their Local Shop's Tubbs and Edward because 'Catchphrases can limit the characters ... we are aware that it can all become stale' (*NME*, 17 March 2001, pp. 18–19).

17 Medhurst and Tuck, "The Gender Game', 50.
18 Crowther and Pinfold, *Bring Me Laughter*, p. 101.
19 Medhurst and Tuck, 'The Gender Game'. They quote Dyer's remarks from 'Stereotyping', in Dyer (ed.), *Gays and Film*.
20 Medhurst and Tuck, 'The Gender Game', p. 50.
21 Author's interview with David Croft.
22 Baker, *Drag*.
23 Koseluk, *Great Brit Coms*, p. 53.
24 Baker, *Drag*, p. 202.
25 Medhurst and Tuck, 'The Gender Game', p. 51.
26 *Ibid.*
27 David Croft produced *Up Pompeii*, as I mentioned in an earlier chapter.
28 Rigelsford, Brown, and Tibballs, *Are You Being Served?*, pp. 23, 24.
29 Author's interview with David Croft.
30 Croft, 'You Have Been Watching', p. 170.
31 Author's interview with David Croft.
32 Stephen Wagg, 'Social Class and Situation Comedy', p. 14.
33 Rigelsford, Brown, and Tibballs, *Are You Being Served?*, p. 30.
34 Medhurst and Tuck, 'The Gender Game', p. 51.
35 Croft, 'You Have Been Watching', p. 177.
36 'The Inspector Calls' and 'The Road to Bannu'.
37 Leon Hunt explores some of this territory in 'Lads and Loungers: Some 1970s masculinities', *British Low Culture*, pp. 56–73.
38 Healy, 'Were We Being Served?', pp. 255, 256. Unfortunately, Healy collapses the identities of Jeremy Lloyd (David Croft's collaborator on *Are You Being Served?*) and Jimmy Perry, crediting Lloyd and Croft with Perry and Croft's collaborations. This error does undermine the substance of his argument, and I have substituted Perry's name appropriately.
39 Healy, 'Were We Being Served?', p. 254.
40 Crowther and Pinfold, *Bring Me Laughter*, p. 141.
41 Hunt, *British Low Culture*, p. 50.
42 Ibid., p. 51.
43 Medhurst, 'Introduction', p. 17.
44 Hunt, *British Low Culture*, p. 51.
45 *Ibid.*, p. 52.
46 Medhurst, 'Introduction', pp. 17, 18.
47 *Ibid.*, p. 19. The character of Ali Nadim was played by Dino Shafeek, *It Ain't Half Hot, Mum*'s Char-Wallah Muhammed.
48 Perry, *A Stupid Boy*, p. 180.
49 *Ibid.*, p. 181.
50 Pines (ed.), *Black and White in Colour*, pp. 73, 72.
51 Lewisohn, *Radio Times Guide to TV Comedy*, p. 353.
52 Perry, *A Stupid Boy*, p. 181.
53 Author's interview with David Croft.
54 Perry, *A Stupid Boy*, p. 175.
55 Hall, 'The Whites of Their Eyes', p. 272.
56 *Ibid.*, p. 273.
57 *Ibid.*, p. 274.
58 *Ibid.*, pp. 274–275.
59 'My Lovely Boy' and 'Cabaret Time'.
60 Hall, The Whites of Their Eyes', p. 278.
61 Medhurst, 'Introduction', p. 17.

Hi-de-Hi! 4

Perry and Croft's third collaborative sitcom, *Hi-de-Hi!* (1980–88), overlapped its predecessor by a single series. In *You Have Been Watching*, Croft reports that the fact that both *Are You Being Served?* and *It Ain't Half Hot, Mum* 'were going strong' gave them the time to plan yet another series.[1] While displaying many of the characteristic devices and structures of their work, *Hi-de-Hi!* departs from their previous pre-occupation with the Second World War. Perhaps, after *Dad's Army* and *It Ain't Half Hot, Mum*, they had come to feel that the comic possibilities afforded by these series' similar situations had been thoroughly mined, or perhaps the context of the Second World War itself had receded further from popular consciousness. One governing principle remains in place with *Hi-de-Hi!*, however; the series' situation was 'historical' (though remembered with a healthy dose of nostalgia) and based once again on the real life experiences of both Perry and Croft – that of the seaside holiday camps pioneered by Billy Butlin and Fred Pontin in the late 1940s and 1950s. As I mentioned earlier, both Perry and Croft worked in holiday camps shortly after the war, and although neither remains particularly impressed by the quality of their work during that period in their careers, both have referred to the valuable experience of the entertainment industry that their time at Butlin's afforded them. In the chapter that follows, I would like to ground *Hi-de-Hi!* in its situational '1950s holiday camp' context, as well as considering its status as a product of the 1980s, before looking more closely at some of the series' ideas and motifs. As with all of Perry and Croft's work, class plays a significant role in this sitcom, though it is articulated in different ways in *Hi-de-Hi!* Without the structure of military rank against which to play the types of comic reversals and complications of class hierarchy that we have seen in *It Ain't Half Hot, Mum* and *Dad's Army*, Perry and Croft have turned to other situational devices to showcase these relationships. Furthermore, for the first time in their collaborative

career, Perry and Croft's scripts for *Hi-de-Hi!* include a regular cast of female characters, some of whom function as the series' principal figures. Although it might seem unusual that this 'innovation' was so late coming to Perry and Croft's work, I will consider their writing for women in the context of other British sitcoms and the remarks made about them by feminist critics such as Frances Gray.

'The first rule of comedy: you must have reality'

Hi-de-Hi! takes place in 1959, in the fictional Maplin's holiday camp at the equally fictional Crimpton-on-Sea. The series' situation in 1959 is deliberate and specific; as one character points out in an early episode, the characters are poised on the brink of a new decade – one that Perry and Croft's audience knows will bring irrevocable changes to the world that *Hi-de-Hi!* self-consciously invokes. This is an important strategy since it foregrounds the series' dependence on nostalgia, locating it in a time when (according to a famous campaign line used by Harold Macmillan in the 1959 general election), the people of Britain had 'never had it so good' – a stark contrast with Thatcherite 1980s of *Hi-de-Hi!*'s original broadcast. If *Dad's Army* and *It Ain't Half Hot, Mum* had found a readily appreciative audience in those members of the viewing public who had lived (and served) through the war, *Hi-de-Hi!* had the potential to appeal to subsequent generations that vacationed at holiday camps from the 1950s right up to the moment of the series' production – a much broader and generationally diverse audience. In the face of Thatcherite privatisation, the growing economic division between the prosperity of entrepreneurial individuals and the poverty of the con-siderable numbers of unemployed Britons, and Thatcher's infamous statement that 'there's no such thing as society', it is not surprising that the world evoked by Perry and Croft in *Hi-de-Hi!* was so appealing: a working-class paradise and a perpetual holiday in happier times, cele-brating good fun and collective experience.[2]

The holiday camp phenomenon began shortly after the war, when a Canadian entrepreneur, Billy Butlin, founded his eponymous chain of vacation camps; 'Butlin's' becomes synonymous with this particular holiday experience, though 'Pontin's' was a later, famous rival. The experience itself was 'cheap and cheerful', a budget holiday marketed specifically at the working classes and packed with all sorts of popular entertainments, activities and competitive events which were orches-trated by a staff of Redcoats – red-blazered entertainments staff who chivvied the campers through the unpredictability of British summer weather. Butlin's was obviously seen as working class and popularly parodied as such: in *Hi-de-Hi!*'s pilot episode, an upper-middle-class character registers a degree of horror that her son intends to take a job at Maplin's – 'Working-class people go there!' Butlin's camps still operate today, but their heyday as the vacation experience of the masses ended with the introduction of the cheap continental package holiday (though Fred Pontin – 'Book early!' – offered the hybridised 'Pontinental'). If the continental package holiday rapidly attracted formulaic parody itself (the cheap, half-finished hotels, 'dodgy' foreign food and scantily-clad girls of sitcom movies like *Steptoe and Son* and *Are You Being Served?*), Butlin's holidays remained notorious for their broad, working-class culture, and were seen as grim, cheap alternatives to their Costa del Sol rivals – rather more like prisoner-of-war camps than holiday resorts. Jimmy Perry reports that the BBC approached Butlin's about filming *Hi-de-Hi!* at their camp in Clacton, and that Butlin's threatened legal action, having 'just spent over half a million pounds trying to get rid of the very image we were about to portray'.[3] As I have already mentioned, Perry and Croft both had experience with Butlin's on which they drew for *Hi-de-Hi!*: Perry served as a Redcoat at Pwllheli, North Wales during the summers between RADA terms, organising entertainments and serving as a feed to the camp comic; and Croft worked as a producer in holiday camp revues. As with their earlier series, claims are made about *Hi-de-Hi!*'s verisimilitude, with the suggestion that the characters were drawn from real life experience and that many of the plots or schemes the series explores were routines that Perry encountered during his time as a Redcoat. Perry mentions particularly 'the birthday scam', in which one Redcoat would put up birthday cards in his chalet and invite a camper in for a drink, collecting a generous round of gifts when the information circulated through the camp; Perry and Croft use this idea as one of Ted Bovis' 'scams' in 'The Beauty Queen Affair'. As Fred Pontin himself once remarked to Perry, 'You know, Jim, I remember everyone of those characters, they all existed'.[4]

Perry and Croft's holiday camp, Maplin's, was founded by the never-seen Joe Maplin, a notoriously cheap and dictatorial magnate, whose presence is felt in the series through autocratic and badly-written memos read verbatim to the camp's staff. The fictional 'Crimpton-on-Sea' camp was actually an old Warner holiday camp in Dovercourt, which, according to Perry, 'had just the right slightly frayed at the edges look', and which provides *Hi-de-Hi!* with a wonderfully down-at-heel ambience. It also allows regular exterior locations and the crowded camper scenes, which distinguish the series' settings from the relatively closed intimacy of *Dad's Army* and *It Ain't Half Hot, Mum* – from the expanse of the 'Olympic-size' swimming pool (unheated, but which, we are told, soon warms up when it contains 500 campers) to the shabby splendour of the Hawaiian Ballroom.[5] Our introduction to the camp and its staff in *Hi-de-Hi!*'s pilot episode is carefully structured and context-ualised, and it is worth considering this first encounter in some detail. The opening credits begin with a flashing, neon-style logo and the rock'n'roll pastiche signature tune (once more written by Jimmy Perry), followed by a sequence of black and white film footage from the 1950s, featuring Harold Macmillan, Nikita Kruschev and Fidel Castro, as well as authentic 'home movies' of holiday camp fun. As with earlier Perry and Croft sitcoms, the opening titles work hard to evoke the cultural situation of the comedy through sound and image freighted with period nostalgia. The pilot episode cuts initially to an incongruous location, however: stock footage of the 'Backs' and other recognisable tourist sites are overlaid with the words, 'Cambridge, 1959'. A switch from the black and white montage of the titles to the colour shots of Cambridge signifies that we are no longer looking back to 'then' from our position in the 1980s, but have entered into the 'now' of 1959.

The first scene takes place in the stereotypical habitat of the Oxbridge don, complete with leaded-glass windows, oak panelling and shelves lined with books. We are introduced to what at first seems like our point-of-view character, Geoffrey Fairbrother (Simon Cadell), an eminent professor of archaeology who has decided to resign his position at Cambridge in favour of a job as Maplin's entertainments manager because, as he tells his incredulous mother, he feels 'boring' and 'in a rut': 'I want to meet some real people and I'm starting today'. It seems like a classic set-up; a character makes a transition from one environ-ment to another, and the 'new world' encountered is mediated through her or his naivety. The episode's next scene, however, introduces another similar set-up. Camp comic Ted Bovis (Paul Shane) and his first-time trainee, Spike Dixon (Jeffrey Holland), enter Geoffrey's train compart-ment, with Ted explaining some of the camp's routines to Spike in an animated fashion. Geoffrey occupies a seat in the background of the shot as the camera cuts between Ted and Spike, but he is again used as a point of access for audience recognition. As viewers, we discover that Ted and Spike are comics, heading for Crimpton-on-Sea to work at Maplin's, with each of these revelations acknowledged by cuts to the reaction on Geoffrey's face. Furthermore, when Ted professes to be 'bitter' about not being appointed as entertainments manager, because Joe Maplin advertised the position in *The Times* and hired a 'bloomin' university professor ... an arche-bloomin'-ologist', we found ourselves again more closely identified with Geoffrey. We know, of course, that he is the 'arche-bloomin'-ologist' that Maplin has appointed, and we know that Ted has unwittingly revealed his resentment to the individual who will shortly be his boss. These two opening scenes are important in establishing the principal comic tension between Geoffrey and Ted that drives *Hi-de-Hi!* – the tweedy, bookish Cambridge don versus the brash, northern, working-class comic. But despite the episode's initial suggestion that Geoffrey serves as the audience's point of view, *Hi-de-Hi!* quickly establishes that Ted Bovis, for all his shortcomings, is the representative of the 'inside' into which the viewer is to be initiated. In an interview with Susan Boyd-Bowman, David Croft remarked explicitly that '[t]he standpoint of comedy is important. The show is looked at through the eyes of Ted Bovis and Peggy, not Geoffrey Fairbrother and the upper middle class.'[6] Towards the end of the episode, Geoffrey decides to leave the camp because, he tells his second-in-command Gladys Pugh (Ruth Madoc), he doesn't 'fit in': 'It's not my world', 'I can't communicate with these people'. This is made especially clear physically in a short sequence of tableaux that shows the passing of his first week at Maplin's: a montage of posters announcing daily events – 'Square Dancing', 'Krazy Nite' – is intercut with a series of black and white photographs – (pastiches of original Butlin's holiday photos) that depict campers and staff in costume, gurning, roaring with laughter, all embracing the raucous fun of the camp's entertainments – except, of course, for Geoffrey Fairbrother, who stands, unsmilingly awkward, in the background of every frame (figure 11). The campers and staff have 'open' bodies, with their mouths wide and their shoulders thrown back in laughter, their eyes meeting the camera; while Geoffrey's body is 'closed', his mouth shut and his shoulders hunched, his gaze averted. Even his attempts to 'play my part to the full' result in stilted and uncomfortable performances, crippled by self-consciousness and bad comic timing, in which he becomes the 'patsy' of the gag – as with the 'pie-in-the-face' bit during campers' introduction to Maplin's entertainments staff. After his arrival at Maplin's, then, the audience's allegiance slips away from Geoffrey; while he never becomes an unsympathetic character, he remains an 'outsider' to the camp's culture, and his miscalculated attempts to participate inevitably result in his becoming the butt of the joke.

Our allegiance also shifts from Geoffrey to Ted as a result of our own imbrication in the inside world of *Hi-de-Hi!*'s 'Yellowcoats', the Maplin's equivalent of Butlin's Redcoats. This is achieved very skillfully by Perry and Croft through two separate rounds of character introductions. Initially, as Ted and Spike enter the camp we encounter the staff 'off-duty', as frankly speaking, dissatisfied employees, rather than as professional entertainers in performance. In this way we meet Fred Quilly (Felix Bowness), Maplin's riding instructor, who complains that Joe Maplin is too cheap to provide him with adequate equipment ('no $7^3/_8$ riding helmets') or decent horses ('they have to tiptoe past the glue factory'), and we also learn that he is no longer a professional jockey because of accusations of 'pulling horses'. Similarly, we encounter Mr Partridge (Leslie Dwyer), the children's entertainer, in his Punch and Judy booth, professing a hatred for his job ('I hate kids') as he beats the Baby with Mr Punch's truncheon; and dancing instructors Yvonne and Barry Stuart-Hargreaves (Diane Holland and Barry Howard), who consider themselves above the vulgarity they see inherent in Maplin's entertainment – 'It's so common', remarks Yvonne of the camp's raucous tannoy system. Rounding out the Yellowcoat staff in the pilot episode are three Yellowcoat 'girls' who have lines – Sylvia (Nikki Kelly), Betty (Rikki Howard) and Mary (Penny Irving) – and three Yellowcoat 'boys' who don't (the Webb Twins, Chris Andrews). Another staff member, Maplin's Elvis impersonator, Marty Storm (Richard Cottan) didn't make it beyond the first episode of the first series, but for the purposes of the pilot replicates the model of 'behind-the-scenes' mundanity: despite his flashy stage moniker, his real name is the singularly prosaic 'Wilf Green'.

Our first encounter with the regular characters in *Hi-de-Hi!*, then, is as members of the inside environment of Maplin's holiday camp, fixing their perspective as our point of view. This is reinforced by the second of the episode's introduction scenes, which takes place by the 'Olympic-sized' swimming pool, where the entertainments staff are presented to the week's campers. In this scene we observe the professional identities of the staff in operation, presented as the campers are allowed to see them and much at odds with the aspects of character we have already experienced. Fred Quilly gallops around the stage with an unfettered enthusiasm, in obvious contrast to his earlier gloomy complaining; and Mr Partridge as 'Uncle Willy' displays a geniality deeply at odds with his relentless misanthropy. We know that these personae are a performance because of the episode's first round of character introductions and, lest we forget, Perry and Croft provide us with reminders of the differences between the real and the performed identities of the series' characters: during his address to the campers, Fred makes a snide remark that only Ted Bovis can hear about Joe Maplin's cheapness, and Mr Partridge roughly shoulders children out the way on his way to his stage per-formance as 'Uncle Willy'. This structure communicates an important issue in *Hi-de-Hi!*: regardless of how much enjoyment the campers derive from their week at Maplin's (and they certainly appear to – one of

Perry and Croft's stated objectives with this series was to depict the tremendous fun experienced by visitors to holiday camps in the 1950s), the point that this 'fun' is the product of work done by professional entertainers is made abundantly clear. The fact that, as viewers, we are allowed to see behind the scenes – to see how the illusions are manufactured and the extent to which they are at odds with the real identities of their practitioners – places us in a position more closely allied with the staff than with the campers. So, while we might enjoy the sight of Spike, dressed as a 'funny policeman', being thrown repeatedly into the pool during the first episode in the same terms as the fictional audience of campers ('it's funny to see a man dressed as a policeman thrown into a swimming pool'), we can also enjoy it from our insiders' perspective (we know it as a scripted interlude constructed by Ted to cover dead spots in his patter, and we see Spike's growing discomfort and dismay with each ducking). I will return to the construction of *Hi-de-Hi!*'s jokes in greater detail later in this chapter, but it is important to stress here that the mechanisms which Perry and Croft establish in this episode place the viewer in a uniquely privileged position. The position of the audience continues to be emphasised in every episode. Just as *Dad's Army* and *It Ain't Half Hot, Mum* assemble the core members of their casts on the parade ground to reinforce the interactions between the groups that defines the interiority of the sitcom, so *Hi-de-Hi!* depends on a similar recurring encounter: the meeting at the start of each day when the staff plan the day's events or initiatives, to which, by necessity, we are made a party.

The issue of audience point of view is undertaken by Susan Boyd-Bowman in her essay, 'Back to Camp', which offers a modified version of Eaton's model of 'inside/outside' for Perry and Croft's sitcoms – one in which the collective 'inside' is located between 'poles of "others"'.[7] In the case of *Dad's Army*, she suggests that the Home Guard platoon is poised between the 'village establishment' and the 'enemy'; in *It Ain't Half Hot, Mum*, the concert party is located between 'high command' and the natives; and in *Hi-de-Hi!*, the camp's staff, as a 'self-contained group', is caught between Joe Maplin and the campers. For Boyd-Bowman, these poles 'define the world of the series more precisely than the family/outsiders duality of the classic [domestic] sitcom', though I am not sure her proposed model contributes much more than a particularised breakdown of the several types of external threat facing the inside interests in Perry and Croft's first two series. In the case of *Hi-de-Hi!*, however, the polarised distinction helps to articulate the series' structure in terms of what we might call a 'spectrum of fun'. Joe Maplin, the unseen dictator of Maplin's holiday camps, issues semiliterate directives that underscore his reputation in the series for ill-treatment and insensitivity; his interaction with the entertainment his camps offer is driven entirely by cost-effectivity. In 'Lift Up Your Minds', for example, Geoffrey's attempts to increase the campers' enjoyment by requiring more participation by the entertainments staff at breakfast succeeds – breakfast time becomes more popular with the campers – but Geoffrey is reprimanded by Maplin because the increased consumption of eggs and bacon has decreased his profit margin. The other pole in Boyd-Bowman's model is occupied by the campers, Joe Maplin's opposites, one might argue, in that they are involved only in the consumption of fun rather than in its production or in deriving profit from it. This 'spectrum of fun' refracts, also, through the internal structure of the entertainments staff. At one pole, Geoffrey Fairbrother wants to immerse himself in the production of Maplin's entertainment, but his engagement with its production functions on an intellectual rather than a visceral level, resulting in his awkward, embarrassed position on the periphery of *Hi-de-Hi!*'s world. Similarly, chalet maid Peggy (Su Pollard) who aspires to become a Yellowcoat, encounters entertainment almost entirely on the same level as the campers. Her naive idealisation of the entertainment industry and her irrepressible enthusiasm provide many of *Hi-de-Hi!*'s moments of pathos; her unsolicited and often preposterous ideas for activities are routinely dismissed by the rest of the staff, and, by her own admission, all she has to work with is her personality and 'lots of go'.[8] In this sense, Geoffrey and Peggy are opposites – neither of them has what *Hi-de-Hi!* licenses as an appropriate critical distance from Maplin's holiday camp fun: Geoffrey has too much distance, and Peggy not quite enough. In this way, Geoffrey and Peggy define the poles between which the series' interior structure is poised in Boyd-Bowman's terms, though neither is strictly outside it; while their peripheral positions are the source of some of the comedy in *Hi-de-Hi!*, the series nevertheless finds ways to reintegrate or accommodate these characters, such as Ted's sympathetic defence of Peggy's abilities or his strategies to save Geoffrey's dignity in the face of his miscalculations.

Just as in Perry and Croft's earlier sitcoms, *Hi-de-Hi!* has a carefully constructed interior into which the viewer is drawn. It is structured differently from their earlier sitcoms, it seems to me, because of the particular nature of its 'work family'; rather than celebrating the amateur in the face of unsympathetic professionalism, as *Dad's Army* seems to, *Hi-de-Hi!* celebrates the role of the professional, to which the television audience is allowed a limited access. This series, more than its predecessors, is about the 'show business' that has shaped its writers' careers.

'Second rule of comedy – pretty girls are not funny'

Although Perry and Croft had included some female characters in their earlier collaborations (*Dad's Army*'s Mrs Pike and *It Ain't Half Hot, Mum*'s Mrs Waddilove-Evans, for example), *Hi-de-Hi!* saw the introduction of a regular female cast, one of whom (Gladys Pugh) is identified by the opening credits as one of the series' four main characters. From our contemporary perspective, this comparatively late introduction of regular female characters by Perry and Croft seems a little surprising, but, as Frances Gray remarks in *Women and Laughter*, in the 'absence of a female tradition' in comedy writing, British sitcom has proved to be a 'rather sad story' in terms of its representation of women, who typically occupy a narrow range of roles.[9] Gray was writing (as were Perry and Croft) before the appearance of *Absolutely Fabulous*, which, Pat Kirkham and Beverley Skeggs argue in '*Absolutely Fabulous*: Absolutely Feminist?', was facilitated in the 1990s by the 'phenomenal growth of alternative comedy in Britain in the 1980s and the space created within that by and for female and feminist comics'. The appearance of such female-dominated shows was perhaps also facilitated by the beginning of Channel 4, which broadcast the first episode of *The Comic Strip Presents* on its opening night, and which subsequently broadcast other examples of progressive comedy, such as Farukh Dhondy's sitcoms mentioned in the last chapter.[10] Gray doesn't consider *Hi-de-Hi!*, because she chooses to focus mostly on domestic comedies, but Susan Boyd-Bowman's 'Back to Camp' would seem to disagree with her general thesis. According to Boyd-Bowman, *Hi-de-Hi!* operates in ideologically progressive terms. Its historical setting serves 'the progressive potentialities of television comedy' since, as she explains, if 'we find the naiveté of our former selves both funny and unthreatening, then we're inclined by the historical perspective to be more introspective' about the rigidity of the class and gender hierarchies represented.[11] Its use of 'show business' as a governing principle invokes an institution which is 'traditionally fond of those who don't fit "straight" gender roles', and which is 'used in [Perry and Croft's] series to clearly contrast with, if not subvert, the ideologies of family and nation'.[12] And the use of an ensemble 'allows the series to mobilise nuanced gender divisions' in a way that 'opens up discourses on femininity and social mobility'.[13]

I would argue, however, for a much less progressive reading of the series' representation of women. The female cast of *Hi-de-Hi!* is stratified in terms of class in a way that allows them very little opportunity for sustained solidarity. The main female character, Gladys

Pugh, is also Maplin's most senior female staff member; but she is marked distinctly in terms of class in a variety of ways. Perry and Croft's script exploits the broad comic possibilities of her strong regional accent; the other, 'posher' Yellowcoats criticise the 'grating' quality of her voice and mimic her accent; she herself remarks that 'I'm not a posh-voiced, upper-class nob'.[14] Marshalled against her in many episodes are the other female Yellowcoats, Sylvia and Betty. Although subordinate to Gladys in several ways (Gladys has occasion to remind Sylvia that she's not 'management' on a number of occasions), Sylvia and Betty are both characterised by 'posh accents'; it's interesting to note that the third female Yellowcoat from the first series, Mary, spoke with another regional (Scottish) accent, and was replaced in the second series by Val, who more obviously shared an accent (and its attendant cultural baggage) with Sylvia and Betty. Yvonne Stuart-Hargreaves certainly sees herself as a member of a high-ranking social class, but her 'double-barrelled' surname (traditionally a marker of social pretension in non-aristocratic contexts) and the fragility of her gentility and good taste (the pinning up of cabbage-rose wallpaper in her and Barry's dingy chalet) clearly locate her as no more than a pretender to such status, and as someone who sees class as a means of social demarcation and control. Peggy Ollerenshaw, the female character lowest in the hierarchy, is a chalet maid, forever aspiring to rise from her drudgery to what she perceives as the glamorous life of the Yellowcoats, from which she is forever excluded. As David Croft remarked in an interview with Boyd-Bowman, Peggy is a 'Cinderella who's never going to the ball'.[15]

The distinctions in class among the women of *Hi-de-Hi!* are exploited by Perry and Croft to create systems of conflict between them which drive the series' plots and subplots. We observed this mechanism at work in their earlier sitcoms, particularly *Dad's Army*, in which the class distinction between Mainwaring and Wilson operates in tension with the hierarchy of rank in both their civilian and military lives. It seems to me, however, that in *Dad's Army* and *It Ain't Half Hot, Mum*, as well as among the male characters in *Hi-de-Hi!* itself, while the stratification of class can never be erased, it is frequently suspended as a means of resolving an episode's conflict, unifying the characters around the recognition of a shared collective purpose. In two episodes that I will discuss in the next section of this chapter, 'Lift Up Your Minds' and 'On with the Motley', we see Ted and Geoffrey each 'bail out' the other from a difficult position in order to facilitate the return of the stability necessary for maintaining *Hi-de-Hi!*'s 'situation'. The normative state for *Hi-de-Hi!*'s female characters, by contrast, would seem to be of conflict or division.

An episode from *Hi-de-Hi!*'s second series, 'Peggy's Big Chance' explores these divisions most succinctly. In this episode, in response to Joe Maplin's directions for increased 'pool fun', Geoffrey grants Peggy her 'big chance' to perform in the entertainment, potentially in front of the visiting entertainments director, and he subsequently arranges for Peggy to be interviewed for a position as a Yellowcoat. Her role as a shark in the swimming pool fails, producing a comic rather than a threatening effect, and her interview with the entertainments director doesn't impress him. The episode's end sees Peggy back where she started, as a chalet maid, with her aspirations to be a Yellowcoat once more frustrated but reaffirmed. Responses to Peggy's chance to prove herself are divided largely along gender lines. Mr Partridge is generally contemptuous of the entertainers among whom Peggy hopes to be included, when compared to his generation of troupers, but the other male characters are inclined to be supportive of her bid for recognition. Geoffrey, for example, grants Peggy her chance and obtains her interview in the first place, and when she fails Ted pronounces the bias against Peggy to be nothing more than 'class distinction'. Spike agrees. *Hi-de-Hi!*'s women, by contrast are uniformly against her. Gladys dismisses the suggestion that Peggy could participate in the entertainments as 'Ridiculous. She's not the right class of girl at all', and, after the entertainment director's decision, she finds this opinion confirmed: 'I'm not surprised. Why, I feel sorry for the girl, but she's just not the right type.' The female Yellowcoats are similarly and stereotypically opposed to Peggy. In a scene in the camp's coffee bar, the three of them stage what they refer to as 'a council of war about Peggy':

BETTY: I just don't think Peggy's the right type to be a Yellowcoat.
SYLVIA: I quite agree. I've got nothing against her personally, but it's that awful raucous voice – it cuts right through you like a knife.
VAL: If she's the sort of Yellowcoat Joe Maplin wants, what on earth are we doing here?

Inevitably, the criteria that they discuss depend implicitly on distinctions of class; Peggy is not the 'right type', not the right 'sort', defined within the series by a particular kind of pretty, middle-class femininity. Peggy's 'raucous voice', like the 'grating' Welsh accent mimicked by Sylvia, is regional, provincial and unsophisticated. Betty reveals in this scene that she had to recite Shakespeare, in addition to showing Joe Maplin her legs, as part of her audition to be a Yellowcoat.

Another system of stratification is imposed on the female characters of *Hi-de-Hi!* by conventional standards of femininity and sexuality. In keeping with Yvonne's self-segregation from the vulgarity of the camp, she is largely removed from the competitive cycles of sexuality in which the other women are involved. She is also set apart as a result of her age, and because of her marriage to Barry (who is coded as effete and, like *It Ain't Half Hot, Mum*'s Gloria, has been read as homosexual despite Croft's assertions to the contrary) with its endless slippages of sexual dysfunction: sometimes Barry has the 'headache' and sometimes Yvonne. Perry and Croft capitalise on the self-contained, 'deadended-ness' of their sexuality by writing scenes between them that take place in the seclusion of their chalet and depend on sexual double entendre; sometimes these scenes are so short that they consist only of a single verbal exchange with little or nothing to do with the episode's plot. These have become a popular comic set-piece, often recognised by the live studio audience with sustained applause. In one of the more substantial of these scenes, in 'Peggy's Big Chance', Yvonne and Barry are caught pinning up cabbage-rose wallpaper in their chalet, with Yvonne giving direction to Barry, who is working in a floral apron, reversing their normative gender roles (figure 12). When Yvonne criticises Barry's ability to line up the pattern on the wallpaper – 'The stalk's not quite lined up with the flower' – the camera cuts to a close-up of Barry as he makes the weary rejoinder, 'It's happened before, dear, it'll happen again'. At this scene's end, Peggy innocently reiterates Yvonne's criticism, and we are given another close-up of Barry's expression – this time, his cheeks are sucked in with camp outrage, rather like Melvyn Hayes's Gloria reacting to the exposure of the 'open secret' of his sexuality. Whatever we are supposed to assume about the nature of Barry's sexuality, it is clear, as I remarked above, that the basis of his and Yvonne's relationship is not consistent, and is allowed to fluctuate for comic possibility. In this respect Yvonne's femininity and sexuality are not stable, and therefore they are non-normative.

Peggy also occupies a marginal position within *Hi-de-Hi!*'s sexual economy. Boyd-Bowman refers to her 'dizzy blonde dowdiness', exemplified by her unflattering chalet maid's uniform and glasses, though she also appears glamourously in the Hawaiian Ballroom on her nights off, where she is sometimes seen locked in an embrace with one of the campers.[16] Within the rules established by *Hi-de-Hi!*, Peggy's relationships with the campers are sanctioned in ways that those of the entertainments staff are not, precisely because she is a chalet maid and therefore beneath their professional hierarchy, answering to the unseen, draconian (and stereotypical) Miss Cathcart. Nevertheless, she is not seen as a figure of desire within the series, and her liaisons are represented as subjects of amusement, like her awkward, spasmodic attempts to become a Yellowcoat. The remainder of the female cast members articulate a more conventional sexuality than Yvonne or Peggy through the ways their characters are coded. There is considerably more emphasis on the bodies of these women: Sylvia, for example, routinely wears shorts that are shorter than the hemline of her 'yellowcoat', and her common stance with her hands in her blazer pockets often provokes the suggestion that she's only wearing a jacket. In fact, despite *Hi-de-Hi!*'s repeated reminders that the series is set in 1959, Sylvia's image – a deep tan, the collar turned up on her blazer and blouse, and her blazer sleeves pushed midway up her forearms in a manner reminiscent of Don Johnson in *Miami Vice* – introduces an anachronistic and distinctly 1980s style deliberately, it seems to me, to increase the overt sex appeal of the character. This is certainly nowhere more apparent than in 'Peggy's Big Chance', when Sylvia appears as a diver armed with a knife in order to kill 'Peggy the shark'. The quite astonishing brevity of her bikini is entirely at odds with *Hi-de-Hi!*'s historical context – particularly when one compares it to the famously scandalous swimsuit worn by Ursula Andress in *Dr No* (1962), which seems rather conservative as a result. Sylvia and Gladys's relationship is defined by their sexual interest in Geoffrey Fairbrother, beside whose unease and discomfort with sexuality they appear aggressively predatorial, and their rivalry is articulated in oppositional physical terms: Sylvia is tall, blond and 'posh', Gladys is short, dark and 'ordinary'. But while both of these characters are caricatures of femininity, their respective roles prove Ted's 'rule' of comedy correct – that 'pretty girls aren't funny'. Ruth Madoc's characterisation of Gladys Pugh is one of the butts of *Hi-de-Hi!*'s comedy; the 'cool prettiness' of Sylvia is not.[17]

Perry and Croft's representation of female characters in *Hi-de-Hi!* might appear rather bleak. Although, as Andy Medhurst and Lucy Tuck have remarked, stereotypes are a necessary component of sitcom structure, and, as Frances Gray acknowledges, there is a certain pleasure to be derived from observing these stereotypes performed well by strong female comedy actors, the writing for the women in this series indulges some unflattering representations of femininity. There is a perhaps predictable emphasis on sexuality and physicality, which is underscored by the introduction of anachronistically desirable images and by the marginalisation of characters who are unable to participate in the conventional economy of female sexuality that the series depicts. Furthermore, the absence of any sort of solidarity or community between the women makes it difficult for me to subscribe wholly to Susan Boyd-Bowman's suggestions about *Hi-de-Hi!*'s potentially progressive agenda or 'nuanced gender divisions'. Even though there are significant antagonisms between the male characters in the series, we see many moments of communal activity – such as the poker game in 'Lift Up Your Minds' between Ted, Spike and the usually antagonistic Fred Quilly and Mr Partridge – of a kind that the women, collectively, are not granted. In the 'Beauty Queen Affair', the Yellowcoats are seen to sunbathe together, but the scene is constructed to appeal to a voyeuristic television audience, as well as to generate a sequence of gags that define other characters' personalities: Fred's ribald remarks, Yvonne's expression of disgust, and Barry's sexual ambiguity. 'Doesn't do anything for me', Barry says limply, and the joke works because, in normative terms, it should – the scantily-clad Yellowcoats are offered precisely as objects of desire. It is worth, however, contextualising Perry and Croft's work with other sitcoms from the 1980s. Although I cited Kirkham and Skeggs's remarks on the rise of female and feminist comedians in the 1980s at the beginning of this chapter, the decade's other popular sitcoms are bounded by similar limitations. Even the 'alternative comedy' movement, often associated with political progressivism, makes very limited use of writing for women in its famous sitcom products of the 1980s; the *Blackadder* series and *The Young Ones* are male-dominated comedies, with the former displaying a great deal of relish in its discussions of 'totty' and women who 'go like a privy door when the plague's in town', and the latter representing what has been seen as a conventionally dysfunctional bourgeois family, but with the downtrodden, domestic mother-figure replaced by a man, the long-haired and nurturing Neil (Nigel Planer).[18]

Boyd-Bowman suggests that 'Peggy's Big Chance' raises 'discourses on femininity and social mobility', although I see its articulation of these discourses as ultimately less progressive than she does.[19] The discourses of social mobility explored in 'Peggy's Big Chance' seem to suggest that such mobility is not actually possible – at least in Peggy's case. As she is too painfully aware, she doesn't have what it takes; she says to the Yellowcoats: 'It's alright for you – you're all pretty and you've got nice figures and posh voices. The only thing I've got is me personality and lots of go.' Despite this acknowledgement of her shortcomings (rather like Harold Steptoe's 'I'm just a rag and bone man, and that's all I'll ever be' at the conclusion of the *Steptoe and Son* episode, 'A Star is Born'), Peggy is not defeated (as Harold Steptoe or Hancock often are) at the end of 'Peggy's Big Chance': 'I'll get there somehow', she adds, 'You'll see' (figure 13). But while Peggy's irrepressibility is laudable, failure is one of the defining aspects of her character. The audience knows what Croft has stated explicitly – that Peggy is a Cinderella figure who is '*never* going to the ball'.[20]

As I mentioned in Chapter One, the representation of social mobility in class aspirants like Hancock and Harold Steptoe was seen as progressive in the 1950s and 1960s merely because it appeared on television. The characters' repeated failure to rise suggested a gloomily deterministic class ideology, but their simple existence could be read as a revolutionary gesture. Similarly, while some observers see *Are You Being Served?* and *It Ain't Half Hot, Mum* as homophobic or racist in their characterisations, it has been argued that the act of representing Asian and homosexual characters on popular television in the early 1970s was itself a form of progressivism. To what extent could the presence of female characters in a work rather than a domestic environment still express a similar sense of progressivism by the early 1980s? In my interview with David Croft, he expressed an awareness that his and Perry's early work was an 'all male story', and that they were 'at pains' to find ways to introduce female characters into *Dad's Army* in meaningful ways.[21] Croft felt that a distinguishing characteristic of his writing for *Hi-de-Hi!* was the mixture of comedy and pathos given to Peggy, so that she was at once 'terribly funny but very poignant' in ways that depart from purely stereotypical representation, but he expressed no sense that he or Perry had any overtly progressive agenda regarding women: in *Hi-de-Hi!* women were 'used where it was appropriate'. Although Frances Gray finds British sitcom 'a rather sad story' for women, she does acknowledge the opening up of possibilities in the work of the 'only woman writer to have become a "name" like Galton and Simpson' – Carla Lane (whose comedies include *The Liver Birds* (1969–78), *Butterflies* (1978–83), and *The Mistress* (1985–87)). She also acknowledges a popular comic actress whose long-developed comedy persona has allowed her to 'transcend' some of the 'limits imposed by sitcom values' – Penelope Keith.[22] As I mentioned earlier, Gray largely restricts her analysis to domestic situation comedy, but it is interesting to note that the examples she chooses to express the possibilities she imagines for women in sitcom are from the late 1970s and early 1980s – contemporary with Perry and Croft's *Hi-de-Hi!* In this light, then, perhaps it is fair to read Boyd-Bowman's optimistic remarks about progressivism regarding gender roles – and particularly about the expression of the social mobility of women – as true of *Hi-di-Hi!*'s contemporaries, if not of *Hi-de-Hi!* itself. As Gray notes, '[s]itcom is slow to reflect new currents in society' and '[n]o female character in British sitcom has yet been given the dramatic licence of a Hancock or an Old Steptoe to be rude, disruptive, dirty or aggressive'.[23] Clearly, Gray is writing without access to *Absolutely Fabulous*, since Patsy Stone and Edina Monsoon transcend (*if* that is quite the word) a great many of the limiting 'sitcom values' that she explores. But accordingly it is worth remembering, I think, that *Hi-de-Hi!*'s context is the world of sitcom that Gray describes, and not that inhabited by Patsy and Edina. Likewise the sorts of progressive possibilities for women described by Boyd-Bowman in *Hi-de-Hi!* are best evaluated in the 'uneasy space' occupied by female characters in almost all British sitcoms of the 1970s and 1980s.

'A feed line like that must be said in a posh voice'

While *Hi-de-Hi!* observes the ways in which class is inflected by gender, Perry and Croft also explicitly consider the expression of class difference through high and low cultural capital. This issue was touched upon in *It Ain't Half Hot, Mum*, in the interactions between 'Mr La-di-dah Gunner Graham' and BSM Williams discussed in the last chapter. In Williams's opinion, at least, Graham's academic background renders him useless for jungle combat, and locates him within the broadly inclusive category of 'non-masculine' men. But if Graham's 'superior' comments are sometimes ridiculed, Williams's manifest ignorance generates little audience sympathy with his anti-intellectualism. In *Hi-de-Hi!*, the two main characters occupy opposite cultural poles, and so the contrast between high and low culture becomes one of the series' central themes. Geoffrey Fairbrother is an unambiguously upper-middle-class character – in *Hi-de-Hi!*'s pilot episode, his mother separates him and herself from the working classes, mentioning her husband's club and the family's 'blood'. Perry and Croft compound the incongruity of the character in his role as the entertainments manager of a holiday camp by making him an academic; if Gunner Graham's background in English literature is of little use for survival in a Burmese jungle, then Geoffrey Fairbrother's archaeological knowledge is even less use in a holiday camp. As an archaeologist, a scholar of dead cultures associated in popular consciousness (and by Ted Bovis) with the unwrapping of mummified bodies, he is incongruously placed in charge of enter-taining the living, raucous participants in contemporary mass culture. The camp's host, Ted Bovis, is Geoffrey's opposite; and the Cambridge professor's inability to communicate with the campers compared with Ted's easy rapport places audience sympathy with the practical, down-to-earth comic rather than with the awkward intellectual. As Susan Boyd-Bowman remarks,

> There is at play a populist 'common sense' which operates between the pomposity of authority and the cynicism of the philistines. The plots of many episodes of *Hi-de-Hi!* turn on the clash of 'high culture' values ...

and the knavish 'low culture' epitomised by Ted, who always knows what the campers want. We are invited to become moral as well as cultural arbiters.[24]

In the section of her essay entitled, 'Camping It Up', Boyd-Bowman refers to the licence made possible by the holiday camps on which Maplin's is modelled: '[l]ike carnival, holiday camps are sites for expressing that which is repressed from everyday life – a place of licence'.[25] Although she doesn't elaborate on this observation in the remainder of her essay, Boyd-Bowman's use of the word 'carnival' refers to ideas that originated in the work of the Russian theorist Mikhail Bakhtin. Bakhtin's theories are developed in *Rabelais and His World*, a text that examines the medieval origins of the carnival as a space in which conventional hierarchies of authority may be overturned, but more recent critics have worked with Bakhtin's ideas in a variety of historical and cultural contexts. Perhaps most immediately relevant to *Hi-de-Hi!* and its setting is Rob Shields's work on Brighton in 'Ritual Pleasures of a Seaside Resort: Liminality, Carnivalesque, and Dirty Weekends'.[26] Brighton, of course, has its own history, but Shields's analysis of its trajectory from a Regency pleasure beach to the destination of the 'dirty weekend' in the 1920s and 1930s establishes some useful discourses about the seaside as a site for a particular sort of licensed 'carnival' activity. The seaside, suggests Shields, has a 'liminal status ... *vis-à-vis* the more closely governed realms of the nation'.[27] The use of the term 'liminal' here is derived from the work of the sociologist Victor Turner, in which it is used to describe places or periods of time in which the routines of normal behaviour are suspended or reversed as a result of the 'loss of social coordinates'.[28] Seaside resorts function as liminal spaces because they blur the demarcation between the land and the sea, located, literally, at the margins of the nation; they possess what Shields refers to as the 'unterritorialised status of the beach, unincorporated into the system of controlled, civilised spaces'.[29] Although Brighton's history has specifically royal associations, Shields's charting of the shift in its status, from an aristocratic resort, initially to a middle-class one and ultimately to the popular site of the working man's holiday, is applicable to most coastal holiday resorts. The opening of the railways in the middle of the nineteenth century facilitated the mobility of the population, and contributed to the reinvention of seaside resorts in forms that still endure, as places of cafes and fish-and-chip restaurants, souvenir and novelty shops, arcades, dirty postcards and pier-end shows. Like the ritualised carnivals of earlier British culture, the working-class seaside holiday came to mark a

collective release from the rationalised regimes of industrial labour ... .
This liminal 'time-out' was partly accomplished by a movement out of
the neighbourhoods of 'everyday life' to specific resort towns along the
English coast and later to specialised holiday camps which were
designed to provide a liminal programme more efficiently.[30]

Thus, Shields sees the type of holiday camp that Maplin's represents as
the conclusion of the development of the seaside as a liminal space.

Before looking at the ways in which *Hi-de-Hi!* expresses this
liminality, it is worth elucidating briefly Bakhtin's definitions of
carnival and the grotesque body. In the introduction to *Rabelais and His
World*, Bakhtin sets out to delineate the folk culture of early modern
Europe, of which he discerns three distinct forms: 'ritual spectacles'
such as carnival pageants, 'comic verbal compositions' such as
parodies, and 'various genres of billingsgate' meaning curses and
vernacular language.[31] These types of ritualised carnival activity were
opposed to the official routines and hierarchies of everyday life – they
were 'nonofficial, extraecclestiastical and extrapolitical', as Bakhtin
remarks – and they functioned as a temporary suspension of normal life
and a departure, to quote Victor Turner, from quotidian 'social
coordinates'.[32] They articulated a collective folk humour that Bakhtin
distinguishes from the private, insular work of the satirist, for example,
and which celebrated what he calls the 'material bodily principle', an
aesthetic of 'grotesque realism'.[33] Although grotesque realism itself is
preoccupied with degradation and scatology, its overall effect is positive,
celebrating the collective, rather than the private or bourgeois individual. It can be distinguished from its opposite, the classical aesthetic,
most easily in terms of the bodily principles on which Bakhtin dwells.
The classical body is 'finished': it is closed, controlled, dominated by
rationality and by what Bakhtin refers to as 'upward topography' –
culminating in the head. The grotesque body, by contrast, is entirely
unfinished, always outgrowing or transgressing its own limits: 'the
stress is laid on those parts of the body that are open to the outside
world, that is the parts through which the world enters the body or
emerges from it, or through which the body itself goes out to meet the
world'.[34] Thus, the grotesque body is open, without control, dominated
by the 'lower bodily stratum' and 'downward topography'. Bakhtin, of
course, is writing about early modern culture, particularly in relation to
Rabelais's work, but other critics have taken up his ideas in response to
modern culture. Peter Stallybrass and Allon White's *The Politics and
Poetics of Transgression* describes the suppression of carnival in British
culture from the late seventeenth century onwards through the banning
of folk cultural events such as horse fairs, as the bourgeois subject

sought to constitute an identity through the exclusion of the 'low Other'. These carnivalesque institutions were pushed away from the centre of culture to its margins, into liminal spaces such as the seaside resort. But they also become a part of the bourgeois subject itself. As Stallybrass and White remark:

> The bourgeois subject continuously defined and re-defined itself through the exclusion of what it marked out as 'low' – as dirty, repulsive, noisy, contaminating. Yet that very act of exclusion was constitutive of its identity ... These low domains, apparently expelled as 'Other', return as the object of nostalgia, longing and fascination.[35]

It is a testament, perhaps, to the authenticity of Perry and Croft's representation of the seaside holiday camp that *Hi-de-Hi!* seems explicable in terms of the models of the carnivalesque discussed above. Certainly more than either *Dad's Army* or *It Ain't Half Hot, Mum*, this series depends on the 'lower bodily stratum' for the generation of its comedy. As in its real-life inspirations, Maplin's activities revolve tirelessly around the processes of eating and drinking, and other bodily functions. The variety of odd costumes that the staff are compelled to wear are the source of much scatological humour. In 'The Beauty Queen Affair', Spike's Olly the Octopus lifts up its tentacle to send an arc of yellowish-brown liquid (supposedly ink) reminiscent of a stream of urine onto the front of Geoffrey's white coat; in 'The Day of Reckoning', the pantomime horse 'misfires' by venting gusts of powder from its rear end rather than its nostrils; and in 'Peggy's Big Chance', Peggy's shark costume's snorkel makes a noise obviously intended to sound like a fart. Particularly in the characters of Geoffrey Fairbrother and Ted Bovis, we can observe an articulation of the open and closed bodies of the grotesque and classical aesthetics described by Bakhtin. Geoffrey is a definitively 'classical body'; his life, indeed, is defined by his training in classical history. In *Hi-de-Hi!*'s pilot episode, as a bourgeois subject he longs for the 'real people' he imagines he will meet at Maplin's, and for the restorative powers of working-class culture compared to the stifling, 'boring' high-cultural environment in which the episode begins. As entertainments manager he finds himself in a position of authority, constantly subjected to attempts at subversion from 'below' which he resists by an insistence on the rules and regulations of the camp. Geoffrey often expresses his willingness to join in the activities of the camp staff, but he remains an awkward, 'closed' body; in the montage that I described in the first section of this chapter, his tight-lipped, static expression as he stands like a statue in the frame's background isolates him from the collective fun of the grotesque campers, who are roaring with open-mouthed laughter. He is frequently unable to make himself heard over the din of camp activities; his attempts at Maplin's rallying cry of 'Hi-de-Hi!' are tentative and over-calculated; and he is unable to respond to the passionate overtures of Gladys Pugh. Ted Bovis, by contrast, embodies the superabundant qualities of the grotesque aesthetic. In physical terms his large, garishly costumed figure contrasts with Geoffrey's thin, tweedy (or navy-blazered) appearance, and he is driven by the appetites of the 'material bodily principle': he offers Spike the vision of cheese on toast, brown ale and a 'couple of birds' as the epitome of a good time. His appetites are generally satisfied by the profits generated from his proliferating attempts to subvert the rules of the camp. Unlike Geoffrey, also, Ted is very much a part of the collective body of Maplin's, united with the campers by laughter and excessive behaviour. At the end of 'On with the Motley', we see Ted in the final stages of his 'Famous People on the Karsy' routine – a splendid expression of the carnivalesque as he stands brandishing a lavatory brush, his open-mouthed face framed with a toilet seat as the audience roars its appreciation (figure 14).

To use Bakhtin's theories of carnival and grotesque realism to explain the class dynamic between Ted Bovis and Geoffrey Fairbrother might seem rather like using a sledgehammer to crack a nut. Moreover there are any number of other explanations for their exaggerated or 'carnivalised' relationship compared with, for example, the more under-played tensions between Captain Mainwaring and Sergeant Wilson in *Dad's Army*. *Hi-de-Hi!* was produced in the 1980s, a decade that licensed more scatological representation in televised media than its predecessors and, obviously enough, the series was set in an environment associated with popularly low-cultural excess. I think that the most important contribution that Bakhtin's ideas make to a consideration of *Hi-de-Hi!*, however, is as a means of foregrounding the specific dynamic between Geoffrey and Ted in terms of high and low culture, and particularly in terms of how cultural authority is challenged or subverted in the series. The contestation of cultural authority is without doubt an enduring preoccupation in British comedy, and it is perhaps nowhere more overt than in *Monty Python's Flying Circus*, in which the incongruity embodied in hybrids between high and low culture is a common source of comedy: '"Boxing Tonight" – Jack Bodell v. Sir Kenneth Clark' or the 'Housing project built by characters from nineteenth-century English literature' sketch are two of many possible examples.[36] Although not offering such moments of incongruous hybridity, Perry and Croft make extensive use of the juxtaposition between high and low culture to produce comic reversal or deflation: in

'Peggy's Big Chance', for example, when discussing potential 'Pool Wheezes', Geoffrey suggests that 'in Greek mythology there were the sirens ... beautiful women who called across the waters and lured sailors' – to which Ted responds, 'Where I come from we call them tarts'. In *Hi-de-Hi!*, authority is a contested quality in several ways; in a literal sense Geoffrey has 'authority' as the manager of the camp's entertainments staff, and he also speaks with the weight of cultural authority – a university education, the use of high-cultural references and, above all, a 'posh voice'. As Ted remarks of him in 'The Beauty Queen Affair', 'You've got the authority. You're real'. At Maplin's Holiday Camp, however, the 'world turned upside-down' also makes Ted into a figure of authority; he is the acknowledged master of comedy and, as Boyd-Bowman puts it, of 'knavish "low culture"' in its various forms.[37] Geoffrey himself confirms this (and establishes the series' dynamic) at the conclusion of *Hi-de-Hi!*'s pilot episode, when he remarks that 'I think what Ted does is absolutely marvellous'. In the remainder of this section, I will look more closely at two episodes from *Hi-de-Hi!*'s second series that conveniently bracket the relationship between high and low cultural forms: 'Lift Up Your Minds' and 'On with the Motley'.

'Lift Up Your Minds' sees the comic realisation of an idea raised in several earlier episodes: that of Geoffrey Fairbrother's urge to use the forum of the holiday camp for the process of cultural education. In 'Desire in the Mickey Mouse Grotto' he had mentioned his ambition to 'stretch the campers' horizons' with music, drama, or ballet; and in 'The Beauty Queen Affair' he continued with this agenda: 'We have a wonderful opportunity here to broaden their horizons – make them realise that there's more to music than marches ... I really do believe that given the right stimulus there are no limits to the spiritual heights to which mankind can soar'. In 'Lift Up Your Minds' he returns again to his sense that the campers' 'cultural needs' are being neglected in the process of entertainment. The ways in which Geoffrey characterises high and low cultures follows Bakhtin's trajectory of upward and downward topography: high culture belongs to 'spiritual heights', whereas low culture wallows in the lower bodily stratum. 'We're only catering to their hedonistic appetites ... eating, drinking' – and 'loving', adds Gladys. Despite its egalitarian presentation as broadening the campers' experience, this process of cultural education is also seen by Geoffrey in terms of an elevation, or an escape from the material bodily principle. He proposes to give a record recital he had formerly given at Cambridge, and Gladys' enthusiastic announcement of this exciting new event on Radio Maplin is used to perpetuate the stratification of culture. 'Discovering Shostakovich', presented by 'Geoffrey Fairbrother,

MA' is followed by a jostling scrum of competitive events – a 'spaghetti-eating competition, a nappy-changing competition, and a "Who's got the wrong trousers on?" competition' – invoking all the the functions of the lower bodily stratum: eating, defecating and (suggested by the 'wrong trousers') sex.

A cut to a card game in a staff chalet between Ted, Spike, Fred Quilly and Mr Partridge further underscores the tension between high and low culture; Fred remarks on the inappropriateness of the event, especially following the campers' lunch of 'steak and kidney pudding and rhubarb and custard'; and Ted, mispronouncing the recital's composer as 'Soskatovich', predicts that it will be a disaster. Ted, the audience knows, understands what the campers want, and so our expectation that Geoffrey's attempt at cultural improvement will fail is firmly established by this scene – and also by the brief appearance of Yvonne Stuart-Hargreaves, who endorses the project, since *Hi-de-Hi!* establishes her as a snob, quite without the cachet possessed by Geoffrey Fairbrother as the 'authentic' representation of high-cultural authority. Unsurprisingly, then, 'Discovering Shostakovich' falls entirely flat. Despite Geoffrey's protestations that he won't offer a 'clinical' analysis of Shostakovich's compositions, his introduction to the recital is still verbose, prompting mocking asides from the staff members compelled to attend. Barry's 'That's what I always say', and Ted's 'You can say that again' – both responses to Geoffrey's precise musicological vocabulary – for example, serve to undermine Geoffrey's intellectual authority. The definitive subversion, however, comes from the literal eruption of the grotesque body into the space of the classical, when one of the few attending campers belches loudly as a result of over-indulgence at lunch.

Geoffrey realises that he has failed; this defeat, coupled with another professional setback, leads a panic-stricken Gladys to believe that he will attempt to leave Maplin's. Despite Ted's resentment that an archaeologist should have taken the job for which he considered himself most eligible, he offers to help. At Gladys' urging, Geoffrey offers another recital – Rachmaninov, this time – and it appears to be a resounding success. The ballroom is packed with appreciative campers, who applaud rapturously at the recital's conclusion. Geoffrey is hurried from the hall by the staff and Ted reveals the real circumstances of the event's success: it included a prize draw for a 'Lucky Programme Number', and a prize for most enthusiastic applause – both of which turn out to be vouchers for a 'luxury cream tea', pandering precisely to the 'hedonistic appetites' that Geoffrey sought to rise above. Geoffrey is entirely fooled by Ted's ruse. 'Given the chance people do appreciate the finer things in life', he muses – though the episode suggests strongly that this is not true. Geoffrey's didactic agenda, his attempt to elevate the minds of the campers, is ultimately made dependent on the body and the appetites of the low 'Other' he sought to exclude.

The series' subsequent episode, 'On with the Motley', approaches the relationship between high and low culture from the opposite direction. Ted's agent secures him a booking at a local golf club event, following the heart attack of a fellow comic. This is an opportunity for Ted to break into the wider world of performance, since it is rumoured that a talent scout from Hughie Green's *Opportunity Knocks* will be in attendance. The episode opens with Ted performing his stand-up comedy routine in the Hawaiian Ballroom, demonstrating, as Geoffrey remarks, that he's a 'favourite of the campers'; though, with the exception of Spike and Peggy, Ted's colleagues remain unimpressed, a fact communicated visually through their stony, impassive expressions as they sit at the bar. 'Excruciating bad taste', comments Yvonne, and Mr Partridge offers a damning critique: 'He's a third-rate comic playing to a third-rate audience – wouldn't last five minutes in a decent theatre'. Although these two characters have been established for viewers of *Hi-de-Hi!* as unreliable sources of judgement (because of the snobbish Yvonne's empty social pretension and the alcoholic Partridge's unrelenting cynicism and misanthropy), 'On with the Motley' proves them correct. In a scene driven as much by pathos as low comedy, Ted reveals to Spike that 'It were a bloody disaster', and proceeds to describe his humiliation during the course of his performance at the golf club. Neither Ted nor Spike can understand why Ted's material didn't succeed, but as he elaborates the problem becomes abundantly clear to *Hi-de-Hi!*'s audience. His opening jokes, about 'the two tarts and a sailor', 'the vicar in the chemist's shop', and the 'poof and the bishop', are followed by his *pièce de resistance* – a full, five-minute rendition of his 'famous people on the toilet' routine – none of which succeed with the golf club's middle-class audience. Ted rails against the 'toffee-nosed' set, but acknowledges that he is 'back where I belong' at Maplin's, a fact underscored in a later scene by Gladys Pugh. When Peggy reveals to Geoffrey and Gladys that Ted's performance failed, Geoffrey seems relatively understanding, reflecting sympathetically on Ted's humiliation. Gladys, however, remains obdurate: 'Humiliating my foot! He's getting ideas above his station'. The stratification of culture is again made clear – as a master of low comedy, Ted Bovis has no business attempting to perform in a cultural environments higher than his own. The episode closes with Ted back safely in his own world, performing his toilet routine ('What do you mean I'm round the bend – I'm flushed with success!') to enthusiastic applause.

There are a number of ways of interpreting the structures explored by the episodes described above. In Mick Eaton's terms, for example, the play between inside and outside determines Perry and Croft's plotting of events, so that although Geoffrey occupies a position tenuously at the edge of the 'inside', his continued presence in *Hi-de-Hi!* requires Ted's recuperation of his record recitals; and, similarly, Ted's brush with the cultural expectations of the 'outside' in 'On with the Motley' confirms his membership in the internal dynamics of Maplin's. Another way of interpreting these episodes might be in more broadly social terms, so as to demonstrate the limits of cultural representation. It is only in the topsy-turvy, liminal world of Maplin's holiday camp – in the 'collective release from the rationalized regimes of ... labour' experienced by *Hi-de-Hi!*'s campers and in the temporary suspension of the realities of life in the 1980s for a BBC television audience – that carnival rules.[38] But what a Bakhtinian analysis of the opposition of high and low cultural forms in *Hi-de-Hi!* offers us is a diagnosis of the middle-class, bourgeois values of its viewership. As Stallybrass and White remark in the conclusion to their book,

> The bourgeois subject continuously defined and re-defined itself through the exclusion of what it marked out as 'low' ... These low domains apparently expelled as 'Other', return as the object of nostalgia, longing and fascination. The forest, the fair, the theatre, the slum, the circus, the seaside-resort, the 'savage': all these, placed at the limit of civil life, become the symbolic contents of bourgeois design.[39]

Hi-de-Hi! and the rules of comedy

One of the features distinguishing *Hi-de-Hi!* from the other series in the Perry and Croft canon is its extensive use of 'metacomedy' as it comments on the production of comedy itself. Several writers have remarked on this characteristic: Barry Curtis, for example, invokes *Hi-de-Hi!*'s metacomedy to talk about the role of reality in sitcom. As Curtis points out, Ted insists on the need for reality even in 'the highly contrived situations of the crudest slapstick ... For Ted, "reality" is an opportunity to create complicity with his audience, to create tension, and, in relieving it, to get a "belter" – an involuntary laugh'.[40] As I discussed early in this chapter, this has significant implications for the positioning of the audience as part of the internal world of Maplin's entertainment, and, in the last section, it contributes to the carnivalesque quality of *Hi-de-Hi!* as it elevates low comedy to the status of a high art.

Critical analysis of comedy is widely treated with considerable suspicion. In *Hi-de-Hi!*, comedy's efficacy is judged by its ability to produce, in Ted's words, a 'belter'. In his introduction to *The Colour Black*, Andy Medhurst captures popular attitudes to the criticism of comedy very succinctly: it is seen as the preserve of 'dessicated academic killjoys, a plot by the sombre and humourless to confiscate laughter', and he repeats an often-cited truism – that to analyse or explain how (or why) a joke works is 'to render the once funny unfunny'.[41] Having made a career of teaching a diverse range of comedy, from Greek Old Comedy to the *The Simpsons*, I have certainly encountered resistance from students to the explication of either centuries-old jokes or contemporary satire, which makes me feel not unlike Geoffrey Fairbrother – a humourless pedant, whose dusty, irrelevant specialism places him in a relationship with comedy antithetical to the involuntary 'belter' that should define our response. Many practitioners of comedy are themselves similarly suspicious of the critical investigation of how comedy functions; as Ken Dodd once remarked: 'the difference between Freud and me is that he never had to play the first house to the highly critical audience at the Glasgow Empire on a wet Monday night'.[42] The distinction arises, then, between the theories of comedy and its practice, between the critic and the artist. Jimmy Perry's autobiography demonstrates his deep suspicion of amateur comedians as he distinguishes between the professional producer of comedy and the talented amateur; conversely commentators on comedy sometimes cite their own affiliations with its production – as Stephen Wagg does in his introduction to *Because I Tell a Joke or Two*. Others, such as Michael Apter in '*Fawlty Towers*: A Reversal Theory Analysis of a Popular Television Comedy Series', invoke the implicit approval of the artist – in this case, John Cleese – as a validation of their own critical work. It would certainly be possible to submit any of Perry and Croft's comedy to analysis in terms of Freud's theories of the joke, or in those of other psychoanalytic theories of comedy, or in the structuralist terms mapped out, for example, by Jerry Palmer in *The Logic of the Absurd*.[43] Although I do feel that the critical investigation of the structures of comedy is a worthwhile enterprise, both as an analytical exercise and as a means of increasing one's enjoyment, I would like to resist the application of 'comic theory' to *Hi-de-Hi!*'s use of metacomedy in favour of an investigation of what the metacomedy suggests about Perry and Croft's ideas from their perspective as producers of comedy.

The principal mechanism by which we experience *Hi-de-Hi!*'s metacomedy is Ted's instruction of the novice comedian Spike. Spike mediates our response to Ted; like him, we experience a gag – initially, at least – without the polish that Ted brings to public performance. It is broken down into what Arthur Asa Berger, in *Narratives in Popular Culture, Media, and Everyday Life*, refers to as 'jokemes'. For Berger, a joke can be defined as a 'short fictional narrative, meant to amuse others, that ends with a punchline'.[44] Each joke consists of several elements – 'jokemes' – which, strung together in an appropriate sequence and capped off with a punchline, produce laughter. Anyone who has told a joke that has fallen flat because he or she has omitted an element vital to the delivery of the punchline knows the value of the jokeme. What we see repeatedly in *Hi-de-Hi!* is Perry and Croft's exposure of the jokemes that constitute Ted and Spike's comic routines.

One memorable example of this occurs in 'Peggy's Big Chance', when Ted instructs Spike in the correct manner to slip on a banana skin: 'Then I shout "Look out, mind that banana skin!", you say "What banana skin?" then you slip on it and shout "Whoops!" and you fall in the water. Do that bit.' Spike proceeds to perform the 'bit' under Ted's scrutiny, and it is judged ineffective. Ted continues to break the routine into its constituent parts:

> TED: No, no. You're anticipating it. Let me show you how to slip on a banana skin. You step on it with your heel, not your whole foot, not your toe, but your heel. Watch. You're walking along. Step, heel, slide, slide, slide, recover, trip, and you're in the pool. Do it with me.
>
> TED AND SPIKE: Step, heel, slide, slide, slide, recover, trip, in.
>
> TED: What I've taught you there, Spike, is pure gold. Practise it until you can do it in your sleep.

Slipping on a banana skin, of course, is a highly contrived, almost stereotypical piece of slapstick comedy. Like all slapstick, the act must appear involuntary or effortless in its transaction, to maintain what Ted elsewhere refers to as a 'rule of comedy': the act's realism. But as Ted points out, the 'bit' is not the product of involuntary action; it is, rather, a tightly choreographed routine, depending on precise placement of the foot, its comic climax delayed by the momentary possibility of recovery. The 'bit', then, has been deconstructed, broken down into its constituent 'jokemes' for both Spike's and our benefit. There is a delight in observing what happens backstage, as it were, and *Hi-de-Hi!* successfully defines its viewers as privileged observers of the production of comedy for the campers. But Ted's invitation to Spike to 'Do it with me', which results in the two of them performing the 'bit' flawlessly and perfectly in unison underscores their own professionalism and natural 'comic timing', both diegetically as Ted and Spike and non-diegetically as Paul Shane and Jeffrey Holland (figure 15). In *Dad's Army*, the uncoordinated movements of Corporal Jones – while a celebration of Clive Dunn's brilliance as a performer of physical comedy – invite the audience's empathy as 'fellow amateurs'; but here, in *Hi-de-Hi!*, the professional is lauded: 'Here's how it's done', Perry and Croft seem to suggest, 'but don't attempt this at home'.

The banana skin routine is not *Hi-de-Hi!*'s only such example. In 'Lift Up Your Minds' we encounter a similar construction; Ted, judging Spike's pie-in-the-face antics to be 'pathetic', reveals the secret of the 'art' of pie-throwing: 'you never chuck or throw a pie – you always place it'. We learn about the appropriate consistency of the mixture (or 'slosh') and the preferred shaving soap required for its manufacture, the 'graceful movement' with which it is placed, twisted, and allowed to fall away, and finally the necessary follow-up performed by the victim to complete the 'bit'. This, Ted insists, is the way to generate a 'belter', and, as in the earlier example, this routine gives Paul Shane and Jeffrey Holland an opportunity to demonstrate their own abilities as professional comic actors. Spike's opposite in this structure is Geoffrey Fairbrother. Ted has occasion to give Geoffrey similar instruction in performing comic routines, but, unlike Spike the budding professional, Geoffrey is the quintessential amateur. Despite the detailed instructions that Ted gives Geoffrey, including feeding him lines and gags, Geoffrey's lack of professional comic ability always disrupts the routine. In 'The Beauty Queen Affair', for example, Geoffrey sabotages his initial appearance on stage by inadvertently pulling out the microphone jack from its amplifier, by executing a 'Freudian slip' (instead of introducing a beauty contest with 'Yes folks, this is the big one', he substitutes 'Yes folks, this is *a* big one'), and by rendering Ted's easy colloquial patter in his own stilted language ('Your friend and mine' becomes 'Your friend, and, indeed, he is my friend as well'). These moments of comic inadequacy in *Hi-de-Hi!* are usually met with conspicuous silence from the audience of campers, underscoring Perry and Croft's separation of professional and amateur practitioners of comedy. *Hi-de-Hi!*'s studio audience (and, by implication, the television audience watching at home) seem to enjoy these moments very much, however, because of Simon Cadell's performance as Geoffrey Fairbrother. Cadell's ability as a comic actor enables him to perform successfully as an amateur with no comic talent; in other words, Geoffrey Fairbrother's poor comic timing is enjoyable precisely because of Simon Cadell's very good comic timing.

Contemporary critics often seize upon the presence of meta-discourses as an indicator *de facto* of postmodernism. While I think that such claims might be made for the products of the 'alternative comedy' movement of the 1980s – *Blackadder*'s self-conscious anachronisms and ruptured histories, and *The Young Ones*'s metanarratives and surreal interludes – I doubt that the more traditional structures of *Hi-de-Hi!* allow for such interpretative gestures. In this series, Perry and Croft principally display what they know best: the means by which professional performers of comedy develop the routines with which they entertain us. Perhaps more than any of their other collaborations, *Hi-de-Hi!* dramatises Perry and Croft's own experiences as practitioners of the high art of low comedy.

Notes

1 Croft, 'You Have Been Watching', p. 186.
2 Margaret Thatcher's statement, reproduced in Marwick, *A History of the Modern British Isles, 1914–1999*, p. 312, original appeared in the October 1987 edition of *Women's Own*.
3 Perry, *A Stupid Boy*, p. 266.
4 *Ibid.*, p. 271.
5 *Ibid.*, p. 266.
6 Boyd-Bowman, 'Back to Camp', p. 60.
7 *Ibid.*, p. 57.
8 'Peggy's Big Chance'.
9 Gray, *Women and Laughter*, p. 82.
10 Kirkham and Skeggs, '*Absolutely Fabulous*: Absolutely Feminist?', p. 291. Saunders' sitcom precursor to *Absolutely Fabulous*, *Girls on Top*, was broadcast on ITV in 1985–86.
11 Boyd-Bowman, 'Back to Camp', p. 56.
12 *Ibid.*
13 *Ibid.*, pp. 58, 59.
14 'Peggy's Big Chance'.
15 Boyd-Bowman, 'Back to Camp', p. 59.
16 *Ibid.*, p. 58.
17 *Ibid.*
18 Curtis, Elton, Lloyd, and Atkinson, *Blackadder*, p. 121.
19 Boyd-Bowman, 'Back to Camp', p. 59.
20 *Ibid.*, (emphasis mine).
21 Author's interview with David Croft.
22 Gray, *Women and Laughter*, pp. 89, 98.
23 *Ibid.*, pp. 109–110.
24 Boyd-Bowman, 'Back to Camp', p. 57.
25 *Ibid.*, p. 60.
26 Shields, *Places on the Margin*, pp. 73–116.
27 *Ibid.*, p. 74.
28 *Ibid.*, p. 83.
29 *Ibid.*, p. 84.
30 *Ibid.*, pp. 85–86.
31 Bakhtin, *Rabelais and His World*, p. 5.
32 *Ibid.*, p. 6.
33 *Ibid.*, p. 18.
34 *Ibid.*, p. 26.

35 Stallybrass and White, *The Poetics and Politics of Transgression*, p. 191.
36 Wilmut, (ed.), *Monty Python's Flying Circus*, pp. 194, 166
37 Boyd-Bowman, 'Back to Camp', p. 57.
38 Shields, *Places on the Margin*, p. 85.
39 Stallybrass and White, *The Poetics and Politics of Transgression*, p. 191.
40 Curtis, 'Aspects of Sitcom', p. 7.
41 Medhurst, 'Introduction', p. 15.
42 Ken Dodd, *TV Times*, 17–23 April, 1982. Cited in Curtis, 'Aspects of Sitcom', p. 5.
43 Palmer, *Logic of the Absurd*.
44 Berger, *Narratives in Popular Culture*, p. 163.

You Rang, M' Lord?

5

Perry and Croft's final collaborative effort, *You Rang, M'Lord?*, followed closely on the end of *Hi-de-Hi!*'s run and, as David Croft points out in *You Have Been Watching*, it reflected a sense that, while *Hi-de-Hi!* had run its course, they were committed to continuing to work with the talent and public popularity of its actors. In fact, as I will consider in more detail later in this chapter, Perry and Croft mined the talent of their previous series (and of Croft and Lloyd's sitcoms) much more extensively in *You Rang, M'Lord?* than in *Hi-de-Hi!* Although the series demonstrates many of the themes and structures of Perry and Croft's earlier work, it does depart from the well-established format of their situation comedies. Unlike other Perry and Croft sitcoms, *You Rang, M'Lord?* has a distinct serial structure, though it is also the most stable example of their work in terms of maintaining the original situational concept and the cast – both of major and supporting actors. The series' content, for the first time, did not come directly from their own lived experiences, though Croft remarks that both he and Perry had very distinct (and fond) memories of the period. Futhermore, the familiar thirty-minute 'time slot' was abandoned for episodes of fifty minutes, a remarkable experiment in form. Popular opinion of *You Rang, M'Lord?* has been mixed, but the concept sustained 26 episodes in four series, which surely indicates some measure of public acclaim. Perry and Croft have both suggested that *You Rang, M'Lord?* was their favourite work for television, though the series is the least remembered of their collaborations, seeing few repeated screenings and no commercially available recordings. Croft suspects that the series is rarely seen largely because of its fifty-minute episodes, which make it difficult to accommodate within repeat broadcast schedules.[1] Although *You Rang, M'Lord?*'s pilot episode begins in 1918, the series' situation is quickly established as London in 1927, in the household of Lord George Meldrum (Donald Hewlett). The situation is familiar enough – in fact, possibly more familiar to a television audience than the settings of Perry and Croft's earlier comedies, as a result of the popularity of 'below-stairs' narratives, from series like *Upstairs Downstairs* to ITV's *Jeeves and Wooster*, the latter being broadcast during the same period as *You Rang, M'Lord?* At first glance, the domestic setting of the series seems unusual for Perry and Croft, though it incorporates both the working environment of the servants and the domestic activities of the family they serve, with the latter sufficiently removed from the bourgeois ideology that dominates domestic sitcom that it seems worlds away. In keeping with their earlier work, the evocation of the series' historical setting establishes an important context for the tone of the comedy – we know that Britain was not invaded during the Second World War, that the days of the British Empire in India were numbered by 1945, that the new decade following 1959 would change British culture in significant ways, and we know, too, that by 1927 the last days of the aristocratic household were swiftly approaching.

You Rang, M'Lord? begins nine years earlier, though. In a sequence reminiscent of the beginning of *Dad's Army*'s first episode, the pilot begins with a cinema newsreel of the Great War's progress – silent footage, of course, with piano accompaniment. The scene cuts to a realistic, war-torn battlefield, identified as 'France 1918', with colour and sound fading into the scene as the cinema's piano fades away. This is a much more 'filmic' transition than is found in some of the other first scenes designed to anchor the viewer in their historical period, particularly those of *It Ain't Half Hot, Mum* and *Hi-de-Hi!* The scene follows two British privates – Alf Stokes (Paul Shane) and James Twelvetrees (Jeffrey Holland) – as they make their progress across the battlefield, before finding the body of an officer in a trench or shell crater. Although there are traditionally structured 'gags' in the sequence, the battlefield's realism, as well as much of the scripted dialogue, contributes immediately to what Mark Lewisohn has identified accurately as the series' 'darker' nature. The officer, whom Alf presumes dead and proceeds to rob of a watch and the emerald stone from his ring, turns out to be alive, and Alf proposes that his transport back to safety gives them all an opportunity to retreat from the conflict. James reluctantly agrees. The next scene reveals the hospitalised officer – Captain 'Teddy' Meldrum (Michael Knowles) – in good health and spirits, and very grateful to Alf and James for saving him. He promises to express this gratitude should either of them require a favour in the future. Alf and James part company at this point, seemingly forever; James professes disgust at Alf's dishonest nature, and wants no part of the profits generated by the stolen goods. In another well-effected transition,

James is asked by a nurse to serve Teddy his champagne ('We've got a bit of a rush on – they've just started the Battle of Amiens'), and the image of him presenting the glass to the bedridden Captain fades to that of him, dressed in his footman's uniform, serving the sleeping Teddy with his early morning tea. A subtitle locates the scene in 'London 1927'. This opening sequence, removed as it is from the situation that otherwise encompasses *You Rang, M'Lord?*, establishes the dynamics that structure the comedy for its successive four series: the attitude of distrust and antagonism that defines the relationship between the shifty, dishonest Alf and the upstanding, rather sanctimonious James; the class resentment felt by Alf towards his social 'betters' compared with James's willingness, even enthusiasm, to serve; the absurd privilege of the British aristocracy and their attitudes to the lower classes.

The pilot episode covers a little more background material before finalising the series' 'inside'. The death of the Meldrums' butler necessitates the appointment of another at the same moment at which Alf Stokes retires his music hall act and seeks to return to his career in service, and a piece of subterfuge secures the recently vacated position of parlour maid for his daughter, Ivy (Su Pollard). The Meldrum household consists of two distinct groups, which makes for a unique structure in Perry and Croft's sitcoms that sees the two populations that are opposed in their interests as often as they operate together against a defined 'outside'. The Meldrum household 'above stairs' is overseen by its patriarch, Lord George Meldrum (Donald Hewlett), a self-proclaimed Victorian aristocrat with a fortune based on rubber (and historically, it is suggested darkly, on slavery). His principal business concern, the Union Jack Rubber Company, manufactures 'motor car tyres, invalid cushions with holes in the middle, and those little bits that go on top of pencils' and, predictably and indicated largely through innuendo, condoms.[2] Despite Meldrum's much professed Victorian morality, he continues a passionate, clandestine affair with Lady Agatha Shawcross (Angela Scoular), the wife of his business and social rival, Sir Ralph Shawcross (John Horsley). His younger brother, the Honourable Teddy Meldrum, remains damaged by the Great War, a fact which manifests itself in a fetish for working class women – particularly parlour maids, the last five of whom he has 'ruined'. Teddy is a rather caustic character, especially contemptuous and careless of those he perceives as his social inferiors, and his monocle and outlandish tailoring (as well as Michael Knowles's fine performance) mark him as a stereotypical 'silly ass' in the Wodehouse tradition. Lord Meldrum has two daughters with entirely different characters: Poppy (Susie Brann) is a 'bright young thing' and Cissy (Catherine Rabett) is a cross-dresser. Poppy is vain, selfish, vacuous, often petty, and although she is given moments of pathos and drama by Perry and Croft, she makes an unsympathetic comparison with her sister Cissy, who has a social and political conscience, stands for council election (and wins) as a member of the United Workers' Party, and operates a soup kitchen. Cissy not only dresses as a man, but has the distinction of being one of the first recurring lesbian characters in British sitcom – an issue to which I will return at length later in this chapter. The aristocratic family is completed by Lady Lavender (Mavis Pugh), the elderly, alcoholic and 'batty' mother of Lord Meldrum's late wife. Largely confined to her room, Lady Lavender is the source of much surreal or erratic behaviour; as the major shareholder in the Union Jack Rubber Company, she is often found in an antagonistic relationship with her son-in-law.

The members of the cast 'below stairs' are organised in a strict hierarchy, typical of the situation-comedy workplace and, of course, representative of the minute distinctions of authority imposed upon servants in aristocratic households. At the servants' head, after the first episode, is Alf Stokes, the Meldrums' butler, a character whose shady inclinations were well established in the series' 1918 background. Paul Shane's performance has a number of nuances: sometimes Alf functions as a 'lovable rogue' figure (in his scheme steadily to drink dry the Meldrums' wine cellar, for example), but at other times his character is distinctly menacing. In 'Beg, Borrow or Steal', for example, Alf's scenes in the pawn shop are neither comical nor endearing; amidst threats of physical violence and blackmail, Alf commits criminal acts and he is only saved at the episode's conclusion as a result of his daughter's pleading with James Twelvetrees. It is this sinister quality to Alf's character that Lewisohn claims made *You Rang, M'Lord?* less popular with Perry and Croft's typical audience. One might argue, though, that the range of emotions provoked by Shane's performance is the result of the depth of characterisation that the standard thirty-minute sitcom episode would not have been able to afford. Alf is also notable for his vocal resistance to the class system in which he finds himself, which introduces a continuous, explicit discussion of class issues into *You Rang, M'Lord?*, issues which are only implicitly, sporadically, and gently insisted upon in Perry and Croft's earlier sitcoms. As I discussed earlier, Alf's foil 'below stairs' is James Twelvetrees, the footman, who is an individual committed to the idea of 'service', to his loyalty to the Meldrums specifically, and to moral rectitude. Perry and Croft complicate his character in ways that complement that of Alf Stokes – while a decent, upstanding figure, James seems often slavish in his dealings with the Meldrum family, and snobbish in his dealings with those he sees as his social inferiors. Both of these aspects confer an ambivalence on his character – again as Lewisohn is quick to point out and diagnose as a source of the series' unpopularity. Perry and Croft develop a longstanding affective relationship between James and Poppy, a relationship that is doomed to failure because of the class barriers it threatens to cross. The conflict between James's investment in the stability of the class hierarchy and his personal feelings towards Poppy provides many scenes of pathos throughout *You Rang, M'Lord?*'s duration.

Although Ivy Teasdale, the parlour maid, is hierarchically inferior to the Meldrums' cook, Mrs Lipton (Brenda Cowling), she is certainly a more important character to the workings of *You Rang, M'Lord?* As the only recurring character in the series not intimately familiar with the routines and structures of the aristocratic household in general, and of the Meldrums' specifically, she operates as a point-of-view character for the audience, a little like Geoffrey Fairbrother when he first appears in *Hi-de-Hi!*, though the audience's association with Ivy is maintained throughout *You Rang, M'Lord?*. We learn not only about the carefully monitored daily activities of domestic service, but also about the natures of the other characters through the naivety of Ivy's view of the world. While Su Pollard's Ivy Teasdale is not as gormless as Peggy Ollerenshaw, the audience is clearly expected to be a step or two ahead of her understanding: we know what the hints of the other staff about Cissy's interest in Peggy mean before she can figure it out, for example. Episodes of *You Rang, M'Lord?* often conclude with an epilogue by Ivy, in the form of a bedtime prayer, that is reminiscent of Rangi Ram's final remarks in *It Ain't Half Hot, Mum*; if Rangi's apparently simple, 'native' logic points up the folly of the episode's actions, Ivy's prayer similarly reflects on the episode's events seen from her simple and unsullied perspective. This simultaneously gives the audience a sympathetic relationship with Ivy's interiority, and allows them a suitable critical (and comical) distance from the corrupt or hypocritical activities of the series' other characters. Once again, this demonstrates Perry and Croft's careful consideration and skillful placing of audience investment.

You Rang, M'Lord?'s other characters are less nuanced than those discussed above, and more reminiscent of the stereotypical or 'catch-phrase' characters of other sitcoms. Mrs Lipton keeps a flawless kitchen, makes 'most excellent tea' and cherry cake, and serves as a suitably stable anchor around which the activities (and characters) of the servants navigate. The bootboy, Henry (Perry Benson), moons after Ivy, provides sarcastic one-liners, and suffers the same set-piece several times each episode – a 'box on the ears'. The lowly, put-upon scullery maid, Mabel (Barbara New), occupies the position at the absolute bottom of the Meldrum household, not even fit to be seen by the family. Like Henry's, her character depends largely on repeated set-pieces – her 'I can't remember the last time I had ...' when confronted with any of Mrs Lipton's cooking, followed by her mournful 'That'll be nice' when she's offered apple peelings, fish heads or cold porridge instead. The final regular cast member, Constable Wilson (Bill Pertwee) isn't strictly part of the household, but takes all his meals in Mrs Lipton's kitchen and serves as a rival to Alf in pursuit of Mrs Lipton's affections. Perry and Croft contrive to include Wilson even in episodes that take place outside the Meldrum household; in 'A Day in the Country', for example, when Lord Meldrum takes his entire household on a 'servants' picnic', Wilson gets to drive the charabanc. *You Rang, M'Lord?* also sees the greatest recurrence in Perry and Croft's work of supporting characters – 'society' figures like the Bishop (Frank Williams), Cissy's 'friend' Penelope (Sorel Johnson), Teddy's long-suffering fiancée Madge (Yvonne Marsh), and the workers at the Union Jack Rubber Company such as Barnes (Ivor Roberts) and Jock (Stuart McGugan). The consistency of characters across the four series of *You Rang, M'Lord?* contributes to the authenticity of the world that Perry and Croft create and to the serial quality of the sitcom.

The duration of *You Rang, M'Lord?*'s episodes affects its structure in a number of ways. As Croft remarks in *You Have Been Watching*, the longer episode length gave him and Perry an opportunity to develop the characters beyond the necessity for recognisable stereotypes on which most thirty-minute sitcoms must depend. I have already observed the effects of this above. But Croft also suggests that the longer format allowed a more thorough development of scenes. This doesn't mean, necessarily, that the plots of episodes are more complex than in other Perry and Croft sitcoms; although some scenes might function as stand-alone comic set-pieces, or as minor contributing narratives, most episodes of *You Rang, M'Lord?* seem to observe an almost Aristotelian consistency of location, duration and plot. Individual scenes, however, are paced differently from those in Perry and Croft's earlier work. There is much less broad physical comedy, and the frenetic activity of the 'gang show' that is common to *Dad's Army, It Ain't Half Hot, Mum* and *Hi-de-Hi!* has been replaced with a considered stateliness that contributes to the series' ethos as a period piece. Thus, telephones ring and time is taken to answer them, the camera lingers on carefully composed interior and exterior shots, and, particularly in the series' many dramatic (rather than broadly comic) scenes, the pacing allows a subtlety of performance rarely encountered in sitcom. A good example of this last occurs in an early episode, 'Love and Money'. After a birthday party thrown for Cissy, Poppy invites herself downstairs to the kitchen for a drink with James. She has been flirting with him through several episodes, and this gesture is understood by James as another aspect of her flirtation. He prepares the kitchen by lighting candles and opening a bottle of wine, creating an intimate space that the camera subsequently exploits with close up shots. Poppy continues to flirt with James – 'Do you like being a servant?', she asks him, 'Do you like my friends?' When he responds – 'Perhaps I have ideas above my station' – and kisses her, she screams and rebuffs him: 'Remember your place in future'. The scene is manifestly not funny, even though the close-up of Poppy's face as she stands outside the kitchen door, clearly more thrilled than shocked at James's behaviour, generates a brief laugh from the audience. It concludes with James clearing away the evidence of the event and beginning to pour the wine into the scullery sink. He stops himself, and says bitterly, 'Why shouldn't I drink their wine?', in an articulation of the conflict and annoyance he feels at Poppy's cruel manipulation of his emotions. This sombre, extended scene – one of many in the series – is more sustained than almost any of Perry and Croft's evocations of pathos in their earlier collaborative work, and it certainly influences the overall tone of *You Rang, M'Lord?* Along with this dramatic component, *You Rang, M'Lord?* also sees a noticeable increase in production values over most other situation comedies, with sets and costumes more in keeping with BBC costume drama than sitcom. The series' studio sets are much more extensive than those of earlier Perry and Croft productions, with bedrooms for all the residents of the Meldrum household, above and below stairs, drawing room, dining room, study, kitchen and scullery, as well as recurring locations such as the Shawcross household or the Union Jack Rubber Company. These sets were designed with an astonishing level of attention to detail that contributed to the series' considerable cost; one source reports that the antiques used to dress the set cost £750,000 to insure for each series.[3] *You Rang, M'Lord?*'s sets make for a stark comparison with those of *It Ain't Half Hot, Mum*; the limitations on studio space were contributive, as I mentioned in Chapter Three, to Perry and Croft's structuring of their second sitcom. They clearly had no such restrictive spatial limitations for *You Rang, M'Lord?*

In earlier chapters, I have located Perry and Croft's sitcoms within the context of other situation comedies, positioning *Dad's Army*, for example, both among other sitcoms of the 1960s and and among those with a 'military' situation. It was not until the 1980s, with *Hi-de-Hi!*, that Perry and Croft seemed to separate themselves from new trends in sitcom – such as the emergence of the 'alternative comedy' tradition, discussed in the last chapter – or rather, they continued to produce their trademark sitcoms in spite of the development of other sub-genres of comedy. In the case of *You Rang, M'Lord?*, it is not easy to see many connections between its ideas and those of other BBC sitcoms of the early 1990s. *Absolutely Fabulous*, of course, satirises the enterprise culture of the late 1980s and 1990s, in ways that *You Rang, M'Lord?* might recall in its representation of a collapsing social order in the 1920s, and *Blackadder Goes Forth* (perhaps *You Rang, M'Lord?*'s nearest relative in terms of historical situation) deliberately parodies the nostalgic atmosphere and the patina of authenticity that Perry and Croft's sitcoms typically produce. Both Perry and Croft cite *Upstairs, Downstairs* as an obvious precedent for the series, but I think that another very popular genre of entertainment in the 1980s – what has been referred to as 'heritage cinema' – has much to do with *You Rang, M'Lord?*'s popularity and viability in the early 1990s.

'Heritage cinema' is almost always used as a perjorative term to describe a genre of period films spanning from the mid-1970s to the early 1990s, from films like *Chariots of Fire* (1981) to *Howard's End* (1991). In Ginette Vincendeau's *Encyclopedia of European Cinema*, Richard Dyer describes the films' typical characteristics as:

> use of a canonical source from national literature, generally set within the past 150 years; conventional filmic narrative style, with the pace and tone of '(European) art cinema' but without its symbolisms and personal directorial voices; a museum aesthetic, period costumes, décor and locations carefully recreated, presented in pristine condition, brightly or artfully lit.[4]

Certainly, with its attempt to emulate a more 'filmic product', its significant budget and attention to design detail, and its move away from the broad comic characterisations of, for example, *Hi-de-Hi!*, *You Rang, M'Lord?* shares some of these characteristics. Aside from the increased diversity and quality of the series' studio sets, when compared with those of other sitcoms, *You Rang, M'Lord?*'s frequent use of exterior locations closely mirrors the idyllic representations of England we see in heritage cinema, such as *A Room With a View*'s (1995) Summer Street or the genre's countless representations of Oxbridge. By comparison, Perry and Croft's earlier exterior locations suffer in terms of their authenticity – in *You Have Been Watching*, David Croft describes the difficulties of recreating *It Ain't Half Hot, Mum*'s North West Frontier in King's Lynn with tropical potted plants and washing line – or in terms of their aesthetic idealisation – *Hi-de-Hi!*'s holiday camp

Crimpton-on-Sea is deliberately run-down. In *You Rang, M'Lord?*, however, the glorious idyll of England 'between the wars' is easily recreated, and the series takes every opportunity to emphasise the fact, in episodes such as 'A Day in the Country', which takes place on a beautiful country estate; or 'Gretna Green or Bust', which features an extended chase with antique motor vehicles through a lush countryside of hedgerows and village pubs; and in the frequent displays of the exterior of the Meldrums' house. Even within this general ambience of the heritage film, *You Rang, M'Lord?* uses particular shots that would not seem out of place in a Merchant-Ivory production: in 'A Day in the Country', for example, the camera lingers on an extreme long shot of Cissy as she sits under a tree by the bank of a river. Much of the frame is lush and green, but Cissy stands out because she's dressed entirely in brilliant white, a contrast picked up by the two swans swimming in the foreground.

You Rang, M'Lord? shares more than just these physical similarities with heritage cinema, however. In 'Re-Presenting the National Past', Andrew Higson argues that the heritage film considers, on the level of narrative, the nature of 'Englishness' and the instability of English identity in the early twentieth century, including the dissolution of social structures and the 'end of the aristocracy'. He suggests, however, that this representation of instability and flux is overpowered by heritage cinema's indulgence in the spectacle of its *mise-en-scène* – the period costume, the scrupulous attention to detail in properties and settings, the idealised representation of the English countryside. As Higson summarises in 'The Heritage Film and British Cinema', '[a]t the level of image ... we are presented with an upper-class version of the national past, secured in images of exclusive and private heritage property which no longer seem to speak of social union, and which depict England as great once more'.[5] Thus, heritage cinema considers a particularised version of a national past and its culture, heavily inflected by nostalgia. *You Rang, M'Lord?*, of course, has some important generic differences from heritage cinema, not insignificantly in its audience; Perry and Croft's sitcoms are produced for television and for a mass cultural audience, and heritage films for a literate, if somewhat conservative, middle-class intelligentsia. But it is worth recognising, I think, the extent to which the balance in *You Rang, M'Lord?* between Perry and Croft's more radical representation of the breakdown of social structures – in terms of class (Alf's working-class, 'revolutionary' animosity) and sexuality (Cissy's lesbianism) – and the increased appeal to authentic period detail mirrors that of the heritage film. Despite the difference in audiences, *You Rang, M'Lord?* and heritage cinema ultimately derive from the same historical context – that of the boom in heritage industry during the 1980s as a result of Thatcherite economic policy.

Following the trajectory established by earlier chapters, I would like to address two themes that have I have traced throughout Perry and Croft's work, and that tend to dominate British sitcom generally: the pervasive issues of class and sexuality. Both of these themes are strongly presented in *You Rang, M'Lord?* Finally, I will address one of Perry and Croft's unique particularities: their use of the same performers across different series, which is more significantly apparent in *You Rang, M'Lord?* than in their earlier work together.

'It's a topsy-turvy world'

The representation of class distinctions has been a preoccupation of Perry and Croft's sitcoms, and possibly, as I have said before, of British sitcom generally, from its beginnings with the class-consciousness of Anthony Aloysius St John Hancock. Class is of particular concern in *You Rang, M'Lord?*, however, foregrounded by the explicit statements of class antagonism put in the mouths of both aristocratic and working-class characters. Indeed, David Croft admits in his autobiography that one of the appealing characteristics of the late 1920s setting of the sitcom was that it was a time of 'great social change and saw the decline of the aristocracy and the rise in the influence of the left wing'.[6] The late 1920s were particularly turbulent; the spectre of Bolshevism prompted a re-election of the Conservative Party and Stanley Baldwin, under whose government the country saw its general strikes. The rise of Modernism in the arts – in the work of figures such as the Sitwells, Woolf and Huxley, Jacob Epstein, and Barbara Hepworth – was accompanied by the birth of mass entertainment in the cinema and the radio, all of which contributed to the fragmentation of pre-war ideas and social structures. Many of these elements find their way into episodes of *You Rang, M'Lord?*, with Stanley Baldwin himself turning up for dinner in one episode. In 'Beg, Borrow or Steal', for example, the Meldrums play host to the 'Dadaist poet' Aubrey Wilmslow, who recites his work 'Lost souls, lost souls, wandering, wandering' through a megaphone to the accompaniment of minimalist strings – an obvious parody of the Sitwells' performances of *Façade* during the 1920s; Lady Lavender tries her hand at Cubist sculpture and Adlerian psychology; and in 'Meet the Workers', when James discovers Henry listening to the BBC on his crystal set, he expresses his culture's fear about the democritising effects of mass entertainment: 'Could give people ideas. If anyone could listen to it, it could be dangerous. What's to stop a Labour politician talking about socialism?'. *You Rang, M'Lord?*'s more overtly political discussion of class can be seen as a depiction of the period in which it is set, but it is also worth pointing to the sitcom's own historical context in the late 1980s and early 1990s at the end of Thatcherism; in *You Have Been Watching*, David Croft expresses strong opinions about what he sees as the destructive effects of Margaret Thatcher's policies on the function of the BBC.

You Rang, M'Lord? articulates some of the class conflicts of the 1920s through its visual representation as well as its dialogue. The ensemble structure of Perry and Croft's sitcoms always includes a 'common' space in which the entire troupe can interact with one another – the church hall parade in *Dad's Army*, for example, or the staff room meeting in *Hi-de-Hi!* – and *You Rang, M'Lord?* is no exception: the two spaces (one for each of the two class groupings in the series) are the Meldrums' dining room, usually at breakfast, and the kitchen, used as the dining area of the servants (and Constable Wilson). With Perry and Croft's usual emphasis on realistic representation, the two locations are starkly different, the Meldrums' dining room characterised by its dark, formal, antique opulence, and the kitchen by its simpler, more homely, and more inviting aspect (figures 16, 17). The opposition between them, however, is countered by the fact that the servants eat as well as (and in some episodes better than) their employers, as a result of Mrs Lipton's deliberate overcompensation in the quantity of food prepared, and of Alf's 'liberation' of the wine in Lord Meldrum's cellars. Both Alf and Constable Wilson become passable wine connoisseurs, in fact, able to discourse on the virtues of Château Lafite and Montrachet. Thus, even as the division between the gentry and the working class is maintained physically, Perry and Croft's script, and their development of Alf's and Wilson's characters, blur some of the cultural distinctions that traditionally serve as markers of class status.

If the hierarchy among the household's servants is represented visually by the order in which they sit around the kitchen table, then Mabel's position at the absolute bottom of the order is apparent from the fact that she is not allowed to sit with them at all. As the only member of staff not to 'live in', she is spurned by most of the Meldrums' other servants. When she arrives late, her pay is docked because, as James insists, 'You can't let a woman of her class take liberties', and he is quite taken aback at the suggestion that Mabel sit with them at table: 'What, her, the daily woman, sitting down at the table with us?'[7] Mabel's own awareness of her abject position is demonstrated by her self-effacing, sarcastic remarks. When attempting to persuade the others that she should be allowed to accompany them on the staff picnic, she offers to 'eat my food behind the bushes' so she won't be seen; on another occasion, refering to the fact that the mere sight of her is unacceptable to the Meldrums, she proposes that when she ventures upstairs 'I'll put a rug over meself and stay close to the wall'.[8] On several occasions, however, Perry and Croft deliberately overturn this hierarchy, often by means of Alf, who, for example, ensures her inclusion in the staff picnic by democratic process, and who invites her to the servants' ball. In both of these examples, Lady Lavender's interaction with Mabel disrupts further the strict division of the classes. For the picnic in 'A Day in the Country', Lord Meldrum hires a charabanc to take the whole household on the trip. During the first part of the journey, the two classes occupy separate sides of the bus, but after a brief stop Meldrum insists that they mix and interact – though with little genuine success. Lady Lavender fails to recognise Mabel as a servant, referring to her, in fact, as 'Lady Mabel'. Once the picnic gets under way, the hypocrisy (or inadequacy) of Meldrum's notion of 'All classes together, united as one happy family having a jolly good time' becomes all too obvious; the Meldrums sit apart from the servants to dine and Alf and Ivy wait upon them 'hand and foot', as Ivy says resentfully. But if the two class groups are largely segregated, one exception offers an important visual disruption – Lady Lavender and 'Lady Mabel' dine together apart from everyone else. A similar dynamic occurs in 'Come to the Ball', when Lavender again relates to 'Lady Mabel' as an equal and lends her a dress for the ball.

If these moments in *You Rang, M'Lord?* operate to undermine the class hierarchy implicit in the sitcom on a visual or symbolic level, then Perry and Croft's scripts take plenty of opportunities to enact the same sorts of disruptions through explicit dialogue, especially in Alf Stokes's resentment of the behaviour of the upper classes and in the upper-class characters' overtly fallacious assumptions about the working classes. In *You Rang, M'Lord?*'s pilot episode, we learn that Alf's investment in his failing music hall act is partly a retreat from his career as a butler – a career, moreover, in which Ivy insists that he excels. Alf's reluctance to re-enter service (which proves financially necessary for him and for Ivy) is driven by his ever-present dislike of the 'toffs', who, he insists, are 'not our betters – they've just got more money'.[9] Scarcely an episode passes without Alf expressing such sentiments in response to his treatment by the Meldrums or to remarks made by James in defense of class hierarchy; these are often accompanied by expressions of his own desire for, and predictions of, change. In 'Beg, Borrow or Steal', he hatches a plan to persuade Lady Lavender to part with her controlling share in the

Union Jack Rubber Company, and Ivy begs him not to spoil their 'lovely job' in the Meldrum household. Alf's reply here is emblematic of his class resentment:

> A lovely job? Waiting hand and foot on these parasites? For the first time in my life I've got the chance to be someone in this world. Do you know what my ambition is? I want to walk in that dining room where they're all poshed up, drinking port and cracking nuts and going on about the working class, and I want to say, 'Excuse me, m'lord, THRRRP!' [makes two-fingered gesture].

Although it ends in a characteristically comic, scatological punchline, Alf's speech is a more serious (and more hostile) statement of class conflict than we have encountered in other Perry and Croft sitcoms. In the same episode, Teddy is irritated that the staff have opinions about how the household is managed (James suggests that the staff might take offence at Teddy's bringing in one of Madge Cartwright's maids for the poetry evening) and asks 'Are the staff getting bolshy? Is there someone down there who's an agitator?' While the suggestion seems absurdly paranoid, some of Alf's pronouncements border on the subversive or revolutionary. In 'Labour or Love', for example, Alf responds to Henry's catchphrase, 'Where will it all end?', with the spectre of class conflict: 'I'll tell you where it will all end – in Revolution. If things go on as they are, the workers will be forced to take to the streets and fight for what's due to them.' Ivy and Mrs Lipton are upset by this 'bolshy' talk, but Mabel, as the representative of the down-trodden masses, concurs with Alf. Just as Alf's serious remarks about the parasitic nature of the aristocracy cited above are diffused by the raspberry and the obscene gesture, so Alf's threat in this scene is moderated by a joke: James responds to Mabel's agreement with Alf by saying 'If that's how you feel Mabel, I suggest you go and do the washing up in Russia'.

One might argue, of course, that these comic dismissals of class conflict and hostility sufficiently undermine any serious discussion of class ideology in *You Rang, M'Lord?*, or that Alf's principal motivation in wishing to overthrow the hierarchy of class is nothing more than greed, despite his claims to the contrary: 'It's not greed – it's politics. I'm talking about the redistribution of wealth'.[10] But Perry and Croft's representation of the upper classes in *You Rang, M'Lord?* is almost always unsympathetic. Two characters – Poppy and Teddy – stand well above the others in their outspoken hostility to those they see as their social inferiors. (Teddy fetishes working-class women, as I will explore in the next section of this chapter, though what is viewed by other aristocratic characters as his unnatural interest in maids and nurses is not necessarily separate from his classist contempt.) Poppy, as I demonstrated earlier, is petty and manipulative, enjoying her abuse of power over James, Ivy and the staff at large. In 'Come to the Ball', Poppy is persuaded to lend Ivy an evening dress, but she deliberately ruins it, by pouring a glass of red wine over it, minutes before the ball begins; and in 'Trouble at Mill', Perry and Croft give her a moment reminiscent of the abuses explored in J. B. Priestley's *An Inspector Calls*: as they return from a shopping expedition, Poppy complains to her sister, 'That girl at Swan and Edgar's was downright impertinent. I reported her to the manager. Hope she gets the sack.' Teddy expresses outrage throughout *You Rang, M'Lord?* at the suggestion that servants have opinions, and he is outspokenly tactless and resentful about the working classes on the rare occasions when he is compelled to mix with them. Thus, in response to Lord Meldrum's directive that he work at the Union Jack Rubber Company as a means of diverting his attention from maidservants, Teddy takes the luxury car to work, dresses in the most outrageously inappropriate clothing, and has Ivy and Henry bring his lunch to the factory (cold consommé and cold salmon hollandaise, amongst other things) – a slap in the faces of the company's employees, who have been compelled to take a pay cut. Teddy's actions, ultimately, provoke a strike that only Alf Stokes can resolve.

Lord Meldrum is, perhaps, less openly contemptuous of the lower classes, but Perry and Croft take care to point out the discriminatory nature of his assumptions, particularly in the ways he patronises or infantilises his employees. In 'Trouble at Mill' for example, he discusses the necessity of his employees' pay cut and 'tightening belts' even while he loads his breakfast plate again from the heaped buffet; and when he attempts to speak to his striking workers at the factory he insists that he considers them his 'children', a declaration met with hoots of derision. In 'Yes Sir, That's My Baby', he agrees to attend Cissy's work at the soup kitchen only so that he can enjoy a 'Chinese meal' in the neighbouring Limehouse with Lady Agatha. With the exception of Cissy, members of the Meldrum family turn up to the soup kitchen dressed elaborately for dinner and terrified of the area's supposed lawlessness. In the episode's concluding scene, Perry and Croft extend the Meldrums' assumptions about the working classes to categories of race: when Wilson reports that a group of Chinese men are heading for the kitchen, the family immediately assume that they are coming to rob them, and conceal all their wallets and jewellery. On entering the kitchen, the Chinese turn out to be singularly unthreatening: 'What? No soup? We are very poor, very hungry.' Of all the members of the Meldrum family, Cissy is the only one who takes a sympathetic position in response to the lower classes; Ivy makes the point several times that Cissy is the only member of the household who understands the needs of the servants. In many ways, she's as much a caricature as her sister, Poppy: her cross-dressing and non-normative sexuality are seen as part of a lifestyle that necessarily includes a 'masculine' investment in the public sphere of politics, through her support for the United Workers' Party and of soup kitchens. Her role in significant gatherings of the Meldrum family (such as the 'breakfast table' scenes that begin many episodes) is to point to the assumptions and discriminations that I have discussed above. In the case of the proposed soup-kitchen outing, she tells her father: 'People in the East End don't like being patronised. They may be poor, but their dignity is very important to them.'

Overall, then, Perry and Croft position the audience's sympathy in *You Rang, M'Lord?* with the household's servants, by having most members of the Meldrum family enact the types of behaviour that Alf most vocally resents. This is not to say that the upper-class characters do not have sympathetic moments: in *You Rang, M'Lord?*'s penultimate episode, Poppy realises that the games she has played with James's affections are at an end and that, in order to maintain her lifestyle after the Meldrums' financial collapse, she must marry Jerry, a man for whom she clearly has no strong feelings. Similarly, Teddy's near collapse and threats of suicide ('I can't go on ... There's only one way out') in 'Yes Sir, That's My Baby' are deadly serious. Again, however, Perry and Croft leave us with the understanding that the unpleasant and sobering predicaments in which these characters find themselves are entirely the result of their own irresponsible and class-specific behaviours.

An episode that articulates explicitly the conflicts of characterisation and theme in *You Rang, M'Lord?*, 'Meet the Workers', also demonstrates the complexities of the class dynamics that Perry and Croft are able to explore through this series' longer format. From the third series, when the characterisations of *You Rang, M'Lord?*'s personalities are firmly in place, this episode explores precisely the assumptions about class and the alliances between groups, made and broken, that I have outlined above. Perry and Croft establish in earlier episodes that Prime Minister Baldwin would like to place Lord Meldrum on the BBC's board of governors. In 'Meet the Workers', Meldrum returns from an encounter with John Reith, who has criticised his distance from the experience of the lower classes – he is not 'in touch with ordinary men in the street'. Meldrum necessarily resents this, though his defence, that 'I speak to all sorts of common – I mean ordinary – people', entirely validates Reith's argument. The solution to the problem, Meldrum decides, is to get to know some of his employees by inviting them to the house for dinner. This plot seems to turn on one of domestic sitcom's favourite narratives, 'the dinner party', in which outsiders to the domestic environment, from 'work', arrive temporarily to disrupt the stability of the domestic world's interiority. In *You Rang, M'Lord?*, however, the 'inside' in which the audience is generally imbricated is that of the staff rather than of the family, so, as viewers, we have a different relationship to the experience. The narrative provides Perry and Croft with an opportunity to represent the Meldrums, typically, as absurdly out of touch with 'ordinary men'; they stereotype their proposed guests by what they eat (and therefore what will be served) – tinned tomato soup, fish and chips and tinned peaches with condensed milk – how they might dress, even by their intellectual or social capabilities. Meldrum advises Teddy to stick to conversation about 'sport, music hall, and what sort of pubs they go to'. The two scenes in which these assumptions are held up for ridicule are intercut with a scene that takes place in the factory between the three invited guests, Mr Foster, Barnes and Jock. Suspicious of their employers, they nevertheless resolve to go to the dinner, and neatly overturn the assumptions made about them: they anticipate a 'six or seven' course meal, and all of them have their own dinner jackets. This classic 'comic reversal' approaches its denouement when the guests turn up a little early, prompting Meldrum and Teddy to change rapidly; Meldrum is wearing an 'old suit' and Teddy is outfitted in a parody of working-class clothes. But while the guests' initial reaction emphasises the conflict between the classes – the union secretary, Jock, makes hostile remarks about the Meldrum household's wealth, 'All got through the sweat of our labours' – this changes as the evening progresses. Poppy flirts with Jock, who responds to her advances, and by the episode's conclusion the family and guests are joined together in a series of parlour tricks and turns, including a verse recital by Jock and the Bishop's rendition of 'The Foggy, Foggy Dew'. If 'Meet the Workers' highlights the Meldrums' discriminatory and erroneous assumptions about the lower classes in ways that make them the butt of the joke, the factory workers themselves seem more than content to be co-opted by the seductive qualities of aristocratic culture.

It is left to the Meldrums' servants to comment on the ideological conflicts that inform the dynamics of the dinner party. Mrs Lipton, typically conservative, is appalled by the situation: 'Fancy inviting people of that class to dinner. It's against nature.' Alf, of course, articulates Perry and Croft's critique of the Meldrums' patronising behaviour as well as his own revolutionary impetus by declaring it 'An insult. One of these days them upstairs will be drinking raspberryade and we'll be drinking Château Lafite'. But by the conclusion of the episode the staff's attitudes, too, have shifted. While the guests socialise in the drawing room, the servants wait in the cleared dining room, physically separate from the cross-class interaction across the hallway. Alf resents the guests for being 'as bad as the toffs. They ignored us', and he asks why, if the Meldrums were intent on entertaining 'the workers', the staff was not included – 'we're workers'. Unusually for *You Rang, M'Lord?*, James shares Alf's antagonism. Elsewhere he is intent on maintaining, like Mrs Lipton, a naturalised division between classes: 'There's a dividing line between masters and servants' he claims in 'A Deed of Gift', for example, 'and it's up to us not to cross it'. But in a moment reminiscent of his behaviour following Poppy's cruel manipulation of his emotions in 'Love and Money' ('Why shouldn't I drink their wine?'), he takes Alf up on his offer of Meldrum's port and cigars, at once crossing the boundary between 'upstairs' and 'downstairs' and allying himself with Alf's position of resistance. Few episodes of *You Rang, M'Lord?* conclude with any sort of literal or symbolic reconciliation of James's and Alf's conflicting positions. Here, juxtaposed with the albeit temporary alliance of the family with the 'workers', it is particularly significant.

Following sitcom logic, the situational hierarchies return to their normative positions as the series itself continues. But the concluding images of 'Meet the Workers' express some of the differences between *You Rang, M'Lord?*'s representations of class and those of British sitcom's earlier traditions. If Alf begins in a position of sympathy or alliance with the 'workers' who come to dinner (in 'Trouble at Mill', for example, he describes himself as 'one of them'), he ends up in a position of antagonism because, he realises, 'they're as bad as the toffs' when given a chance to participate in the world of upper-class privilege. 'It's a topsy-turvy world', he tells James as they share Meldrum's port and cigars in an emblematic moment of 'sticking together' and class solidarity. But elsewhere in the episode, he relishes the prospect that one day the positions of the Meldrums and their staff will be reversed: 'them upstairs' condemned to raspberryade while 'we'll be drinking Château Lafite'. The presumption of class aspiration isn't the subject of mockery in *You Rang, M'Lord?* as it is, for example, in the characters of Hancock and Harold Steptoe. The class alliances made or broken in 'Meet the Workers' are used to critique the characters' sense of opportunism; thus, Jock begins his visit with open hostility to the Meldrums' aristocratic privilege, but he is ultimately seduced into ignoring his fellow workers (the Meldrums' staff) and participating in frivolous party activities. Alf and James's temporary alliance develops from their feelings of resentment about the opportunities afforded the guests – Alf complains that, after all, the staff are also workers, and James pronounces that the experience of aristocratic life is wasted on the dinner guests: 'Pearls before swine'. The fact that we don't see the restoration of the normative order at the episode's conclusion leaves these discourses of desert and opportunism in class hierarchy – discourses entirely contemporary to the political and social conflicts of the late 1980s and early 1990s – open for reflection.

'Morals like tomcats': transgressive sexuality in *You Rang, M'Lord?*

More than any other Perry and Croft sitcom, *You Rang, M'Lord?* discusses issues of sex and sexuality. Opportunities for sexual relations in the male-dominated situations of *Dad's Army* and *It Ain't Half Hot, Mum* were few and far between, of course, and with the exception of Gladys' passionate rivalry with Sylvia for Geoffrey Fairbrother, sex was not a dominant theme in *Hi-de-Hi!* – at least between the regular characters and aside from the broad 'seaside postcard' nature of its humour. *You Rang, M'Lord?* is replete with sexual relationships, however, most of which are non-normative or transgressive within the situational context of the Meldrums' 1920s household: Meldrum himself has an adulterous relationship with Lady Agatha; Teddy is erotically fixated on lower-class women in service (maids, nurses and nannies); Poppy is attracted to working-class men (James Twelvetrees particularly, a reciprocal attraction); and Cissy is identified as a lesbian in an ongoing relationship with another woman, Penelope. The majority of the normative relationships above or below stairs are seen as dysfunctional or unwanted – Madge Cartwright's futile pursuit of Teddy's affections, for example, or Henry's unreturned interest in Ivy, and Ivy's unreturned interest in James. Perhaps the only stable normative relationship in the series belongs to Mabel and her unseen husband, prompting her to observe in 'Love and Money' that 'They've got morals like tomcats, these aristocrats'. In this section I would like to focus on two characters – Cissy and Teddy – who typify Perry and Croft's characterisation of non-normative sexual relations in *You Rang, M'Lord?*, since both characters represent innovations or departures from their previous discussions of sexuality.

Homosexual stereotyping and homophobia are issues that have been among the most frequently considered by critics of Perry and Croft's sitcoms, in the characters of *It Ain't Half Hot, Mum*'s Gloria and *Hi-de-Hi!*'s Barry Stuart-Hargreaves. As I discussed in earlier chapters, David Croft is adamant that neither of these characters was scripted as homosexual (Gloria is simply a transvestite and Barry a social climber), a claim he also extends to his and Jeremy Lloyd's Mr Humphries. In the case of Cissy, however, Croft states explicitly their intention to present a homosexual character; as he remarks in *You Have Been Watching*, Cissy 'gave us a chance to touch gently on Lesbianism which was not understood by Lord Meldrum or the staff'. A little inconsistently with Croft's clear-cut distinction between Gloria's transvestism and homo-sexuality, Cissy's sexuality is often denoted precisely through her cross-dressing and the transgressive practices that it signifies. Whether dressing for riding, tennis, family outings or dinner, Cissy invariably dresses in clothes of a masculine cut, though even her most foppish outfits (like her pale pink dinner jacket in 'Meet the Workers') are outdone by the routine flamboyance of Teddy's clothes. She also, like Teddy, wears a monacle. In *You Rang, M'Lord?* cross-dressing is an indicator of sexual difference, and Meldrum makes several complaints about Cissy's clothes and the associations to which they point. In 'Love and Money', for example, he is unhappy with her male dinner dress and the impression that it will create for an important business associate attending a fancy-dress party: 'Cissy, what have you got on? You look like a damned waiter. And all your friends dressed as boys. What is Sir Jasper going to think?' He is similarly distressed about Teddy's Greek dancer costume, which has a skirt; and cross-dressing's potential to disrupt heterosexual configurations of desire is dutifully underscored at the end of the episode, when Teddy is seen dancing with a maidservant, whom he is apparently unable to identify as a man in drag despite his handsome moustache. Elsewhere, Cissy's cross-dressing is placed in direct comparison with Poppy's femininity ('Poppy, what a pretty dress' says the Bishop in 'The Phantom Signwriter', 'And Cissy, what a pretty ... erm ... pair of trousers'), or used as an associative link with same-sex relations (figure 18). In 'A Deed of Gift', Cissy claims that she's having her late mother's engagement ring 'turned into a tiepin', though Poppy remarks that 'I thought I saw your friend Penelope wearing it the other day', thus associating the traditional symbol of commitment in a relationship with both cross-dressing and lesbianism.

Perry and Croft's representation of lesbianism does, however, go beyond these suggestions and associations. In *You Rang, M'Lord?*'s first two series, Cissy is seen in several scenes with her 'friend' Penelope Barrington-Blake (Sorel Johnson) in ways that suggest they are a couple. If Cissy invariably dresses as a man, Penelope is costumed in luxurious and fashionable female clothes, and they are placed in shots composed deliberately to provoke comparison with heterosexual couples. In 'Please Help the Orphans', for example, in a scene in the drawing room,

Poppy, Cissy and their respective partners discuss whether to go out to the Boot and Britches or the Kit Kat Club. Poppy is dancing to a gramophone record as Jerry fixes cocktails, both of them attired in evening dress. Cissy and Penelope are similarly dressed – Cissy as a man, Penelope as a woman – and Penelope lounges on Cissy's knee. The scene suggests that we are in the presence of two couples through its structural composition and costuming. In other episodes Cissy and Penelope sit together with Cissy's arm across the back of Penelope's chair, and in 'Love and Money' we see Cissy and Penelope dancing a tango at the fancy-dress party, as Cissy's female friends – dressed as men – look on. The most significant moment, though, in the delineation of Cissy and Penelope as a couple occurs when they kiss – a remarkable scene in a situation comedy from the early 1990s. The scene occurs in 'Beg, Borrow or Steal', and the shot is replicated almost exactly in 'Royal Flush' (figure 19). Lord Meldrum stands in the background as Cissy greets Penelope, directly in front of him, with a kiss. 'You look divine!', Penelope says to Cissy. As the two walk away, Meldrum asks his brother, 'Do girls usually kiss each other on the lips these days?', to which Teddy responds, 'I don't know. I always kiss girls on the lips.' The behaviour of the avidly heterosexual Teddy, then, marks the kiss between Cissy and Penelope as an erotic exchange. The scene in 'Royal Flush' is similarly composed, with Meldrum flanked by Teddy and Poppy. Although Cissy's sexual difference is made clear in these scenes – in word and image – she is still contained, literally, within the same frame as the 'family', and not exiled to the fringes of the 'inside' (as in the 'gay next-door neighbour' sitcom stereotype) or constituted as an external threat to the sitcom's domestic stability.

As Mark Lewisohn points out, *You Rang, M'Lord?* is 'an unlikely groundbreaker in the recurring portrayal of a lesbian character', and Murray Healy concurs: '[t]he recent [c. 1995] media furore over lesbian characters in soaps has obscured the fact that Lloyd [sic] and Croft's *You Rang, M'Lord?*, first screened in 1988, was the first British series ever to have a regular lesbian character, Sissy [sic], and, furthermore, right at the heart of the respectable family'.[11] Neither Lewisohn nor Healy evaluates Cissy's representation beyond the mere fact of her portrayal; and another account suggests that she is a slightly less positive presence. Stephen Wagg's summary of the sexual chaos in Perry, Croft and Lloyd's sitcoms characterises Cissy as a 'young lesbian aristocrat [who] fancies her father's maid', and he includes her in a group of 'minor authority figures' whose 'self-importance ... is undone by the sexual innuendo they can't help uttering'.[12] It seems to me, however, that Cissy's character, though potentially reducible to an unpleasant stereotype, is represented in positive terms. There is not much evidence, for example, that Cissy 'fancies' Ivy, certainly not in the aggressively abusive ways that Poppy 'fancies' James. The staff warn Ivy repeatedly about spending too much time alone with Cissy in her bedroom – 'Just put the tray down and come out quickly' and 'Don't stop too long'.[13] But these prejudices held by the staff are not borne out by the series itself: in *You Rang, M'Lord?*'s opening episodes, Cissy is seen to wink at Ivy on a few occasions, but this is not followed through in later series. Cissy certainly shares intimate scenes with Ivy: in 'A Deed of Gift', Ivy attends Cissy as she dresses and ties up the laces on her tennis shoes, and Cissy compliments Ivy's looks – 'You're really quite pretty' – and shows her how to apply make-up. This scene is immediately juxtaposed with Poppy's obvious flirtation with James. There are several ways to read this juxtaposition: the pairing of the sisters' scenes might reveal, for example, the differences between the ways in which they undertake seduction; or it might distinguish between an aggressive heterosexuality and a non-invasive homosexuality; or it might distinguish between a character who abuses her position of authority and one who doesn't. In any event Ivy trusts Cissy, and this trust is never abused, despite Ivy's naivety, through *You Rang, M'Lord?*'s run.

Although Cissy's sexuality is often placed in parallel scenes with Poppy's, as I've discussed above, the more interesting comparison for Perry and Croft's treatment of sexuality in *You Rang, M'Lord?* is that of the Honourable Teddy Meldrum and his erotic fixation with working-class women, particularly those in uniform associated with domestic service. Other upper-class characters in *You Rang, M'Lord?* – most of the heterosexual female characters, in fact – are attracted to the servant James Twelvetrees, but Teddy's interest in maids, nurses and nannies is discussed by the other characters as non-normative: 'At least my taste in women is normal' retorts Meldrum when Teddy draws attention to his affair with Lady Agatha. In the nine years since Teddy returned from the War, he has put five of the Meldrums' maids in the 'family way', necessitating Lord Meldrum's paying off the women through discreet arrangements made by his solicitor. The war is blamed for Teddy's peculiarity, though it is hinted that it actually predates his shell-shock: we learn that he apparently enjoyed being spanked by his nanny. 'What is it that attracts my brother to these servant girls', Meldrum asks in 'A Deed of Gift', and he attempts to dampen Teddy's ardour by hiring Ivy, a 'plain' maidservant, in *You Rang, M'Lord?*'s pilot episode. This 'plainness' is, however, precisely the quality that Teddy fetishises in women; during the course of *You Rang, M'Lord?*, he makes countless references to 'chapped hands', 'shiny, scrubbed faces', 'frizzy hair', freckles and glasses. The pathos of Teddy's scene in 'Yes Sir, That's My Baby' in which he threatens suicide in the face of having to marry Madge Cartwright, a woman of his own class, is alleviated by his reminiscences about affairs with former maids as he sorts through his collection of lace caps and savours the odours of coal tar and carbolic soaps. Perhaps the most articulate defence he offers of his obsession occurs in a 'A Deed of Gift': 'Purity, no sham, no pretence, everything stripped off. There they are in their attic bedrooms, threadbare carpet on the bare boards, rickety chest of drawers, with a cracked mirror and the iron bedstead ...' Although Meldrum is concerned about Teddy's liaisons with maidservants because of the expense he incurs bribing them to keep quiet, his objection goes beyond Teddy's casual encounters. During the course of *You Rang, M'Lord?*, Teddy becomes particularly enamoured of Madge Cartwright's maid, Rose, and in 'Gretna Green or Bust', they elope and plan to marry. Meldrum and Madge pursue Teddy, and succeed in preventing the union; Rose is abandoned along the way and is rescued only through the generosity of Alf and Ivy: 'the likes of us have got to stick together', Alf tells her. This makes clear, I think, that the objections to Teddy's erotic impulses are not the result of conventional ideas about sex outside marriage, but express a prejudice against cross-class sexual liaisons. Meldrum seeks to intervene in Teddy's activities in ways typical of discourses about normalising sexual behaviour. 'You've got to be seen to ...' he insists. In 'Labour or Love' this intervention takes the form of a consultation with the Freudian psychoanalyst, Professor Heinrich von Mannheim (Kenneth Connor). The scene, of course, enacts a parody of psychoanalysis and ends unsuccessfully, as do Meldrum's other attempts to rein in Teddy's desires – by threatening to exile him to the family's rubber plantation, and by sending him to a work as a labourer at the Union Jack Rubber Company. The latter attempt backfires at Meldrum's expense: instead of experiencing the exhausting and distracting effects of physical labour, Teddy catches a whiff of carbolic soap on a female factory worker, and his advances precipitate a strike.

Teddy's non-normative sexual objectification of working-class women is criticised much more obviously in *You Rang, M'Lord?*, then, than the non-normative sexuality of Cissy. One might argue that the absurd caricature of sexual fetishism enacted by Teddy's character is possible because its particular circumstance – the abuse of a power relationship between a master and servant in this type of domestic environment – is far removed from the immediate experience of a 1990s audience (the recent, alleged case of sexual abuse in Prince Charles's household notwithstanding), though sexual harassment in the workplace has become an issue of increasing sensitivity in recent years. *You Rang, M'Lord?* would seem to suggest that, while it was unthinkable to represent homosexuality in the mainstream media before the 1970s, it had become unpalatable to ridicule it in the 1990s. We might ask, though, if Perry and Croft would have been able to present onscreen homoeroticism (Cissy and Penelope kissing in, for example, 'Royal Flush') had the genders of the individuals been reversed. Would the BBC have endorsed the spectacle of two homosexual men kissing as an appropriate component of a situation comedy broadcast in prime time, before the 9.00 'watershed' (after which more 'adult' material is permitted)? Within the context of *You Rang, M'Lord?* itself, frank discussion of homosexuality is relatively scarce or buried in double entendre ('I've just been practically attacked in the Turkish baths!' says Teddy; 'You have to be very careful in those places' replies Meldrum).[14] When Ivy wants to know why the other members of staff caution her not to remain too long in Cissy's room, they reply with their usual repressive sensibility: 'Least said, soonest mended'. Similarly, when Cissy responds to Meldrum's praise for Mussolini – 'But he's a dreadful fascist, Daddy. The first thing he did when he came into power was throw all the homosexuals into prison' – Meldrum tries to suppress the conversation: 'Cissy, please. Not at the breakfast table.' We might, of course, take refuge in Perry and Croft's claims to historical realism: homosexuality was hardly a suitable topic of conversation at the breakfast table of a traditional aristocratic family in the 1920s, and male homosexuality was subject to legal prosecution, which female homosexuality was not; thus to acknowledge openly the existence of same-sex relations, especially between men, would have been entirely anachronistic. But *You Rang, M'Lord?*'s representation of lesbianism to an early 1990s audience also plays a significant part in its configuration. It seems to me that *You Rang, M'Lord?* recognises that homosexuality is no longer an acceptable subject for mockery or overt abuse and, as such, presents it in its least threatening form (the relatively culturally sanctioned spectacle of two women kissing) through a character who has been constructed as one of the most sympathetic of the series. Although Cissy's non-normative sexuality places her outside the ideological centre of the 'work family' of *You Rang, M'Lord?*, in which the bourgeois family of viewers is imbricated, she is recuperated through her apparent empathy with the underclass. Ivy insists of Cissy in 'A Day in the Country', 'She seems to understand us better than the others'. Furthermore, just as the Meldrums, standing in for the authentic voices of the 1920s, displace or repress open discussion of homosexuality, so *You Rang, M'Lord?*, as a series, displaces a bourgeois, mass cultural audience's anxiety about lesbianism as a non-normative sexuality onto the representation of another non-normative sexuality – Teddy's cross-class fetishism. From this perspective, Teddy's ludicrous fascination with 'chapped hands', 'shiny, scrubbed faces' and carbolic soap functions as a carefully constructed 'safety valve' for the mockery of non-normative sexual relations.

Perry and Croft's coterie of actors

One of the most obvious hallmarks of Perry and Croft's sitcoms is their writing for a large ensemble cast rather than for the small bourgeois family unit of most domestic situation comedies. Any viewer of Perry and Croft's work will notice, furthermore, that they use many of the same actors between series. The effect of this 'coterie' of performers is, perhaps, intensified when one watches twenty-five years' worth of sitcoms in a relatively short span of time, so that an actor's performance in one series is overwritten by his or her next performance like a palimpsest. But any viewer familiar with the traditions of British sitcom could hardly fail to notice that *You Rang, M'Lord?* seems almost a 'Perry and Croft reunion' for actors from their earlier series. Many of the actors in *You Rang, M'Lord?* had significant earlier roles, such as Bill Pertwee (Constable Wilson/ARP Warden Hodges in *Dad's Army*), Donald Hewlett (Lord Meldrum/Colonel Reynolds in *It Ain't Half Hot, Mum*), and Paul Shane (Alf Stokes/Ted Bovis in *Hi-de-Hi!*), but several had appeared in cameo roles, such as Brenda Cowling (Mrs Lipton), who played Private Godfrey's girlfriend in *Dad's Army*, and Perry Benson (Henry), who played a small role in *Hi-de-Hi!* Even in their casting of *You Rang, M'Lord?*'s minor characters, Perry and Croft draw on earlier series' casts: Frank Williams (Bishop/Vicar in *Dad's Army*), Stuart McGugan (Jock/Atlas in *It Ain't Half Hot, Mum*) and Felix Bowness (Mr Pearson, the 'Teetgens Grocery Man'/Fred Quilly in *Hi-de-Hi!*).

From their perspective as writers (and, in David Croft's case, as a director/producer), working with actors from previous series makes good, practical sense. Rigelsford, Brown and Tibballs quote Croft: 'Doing a television series is no different from any other walk of life ... It's nice to work with people you know. Also, because you've worked with them in the past, you know that they are going to produce the goods. It's a feeling of mutual trust.'[15] Perry and Croft's own remarks about the mutual compatibility of their casts are certainly reinforced in the accounts of individual performers, and in texts about the series such as Graham McCann's book on *Dad's Army*. But their familiarity with performers also, Croft's autobiography suggests, influenced the process of their writing, with characters apparently conceived in response to individual actors and developed according to their abilities. In the last chapter, I discussed how 'Peggy's Big Chance' was written to allow Su Pollard an opportunity to explore new aspects of Peggy's character. In the case of *You Rang, M'Lord?*, Croft notes that as a conceptual form, the series was driven by five principal characters, each suggested by a 'Perry and Croft coterie' performer, with the other regular characters 'emerging' during the construction of the pilot script.[16] There are fine distinctions to be made here. In my interview with David Croft, he was quick to refute any possibility that the character an actor played in one series informed the actor's characterisation in a later series; he pointed out, for example, that Constable Wilson is a markedly different character from ARP Warden Hodges, and he felt that the dynamic of the relationship between Captain Ashwood and Colonel Reynolds in *It Ain't Half Hot, Mum* had little bearing on the relationship between Lord Meldrum and his brother Teddy. With *You Rang, M'Lord?*'s minor characters this seems less clear cut. Despite Frank Williams's long career of diverse performances, his two characters for Perry and Croft are both ecclesiastics: *Dad's Army*'s Reverend Timothy Farthing popularises a clerical stereotype – that of the nasal, ineffectual English vicar – that *You Rang, M'Lord?*'s Bishop slips into with ease. Perry and Croft might bridle at this suggestion, of course, but the issue raises once again the polysemous nature of televisual media – the conflict between the authors' intentions and the tendency of the audience to misread or resist them. To provide an anecdotal example: several viewers with whom I spoke, who were familiar with Perry and Croft's earlier work but not, apparently, with *You Rang, M'Lord?* in anything other than a cursory manner, assumed that it functioned as a sequel to *Hi-de-Hi!* in the same way that Croft and Lloyd's *Grace and Favour* presented *Are You Being Served?*'s afterlife at about the same time. The association of the actors Paul Shane, Jeffrey Holland and Su Pollard with the roles of Ted, Spike and Peggy, and the enduring nature of the relationship between the three of them as a televisual signifier overruled even the most obvious differences between the two series – why were characters from a series set in the 1950s working in a 1920s household?

Although the coterie of actors associated with heritage cinema, and especially with Merchant/Ivory productions (Helena Bonham-Carter, Julian Sands), suggests obvious parallels here, I think that the most convenient comparative structure for the Perry and Croft coterie is that of the *Carry On* performers, because of the similar genre and their multiple appearances across a range of historical settings. There is clearly less intention to play down or dissociate connections between roles in the case of the *Carry On* actors – while Sid James does appear as significant historical figures such as Henry VIII (*Carry On Henry*) or Mark Antony (*Carry On Cleo*), he just as often plays a character called 'Sid', whose primary character traits are suggested by his surname: Sidney Fiddler (*Carry On Girls*), or Sir Sidney Ruff-Diamond (*Carry On Up the Khyber*). Frances Gray addresses this issue with respect to female actors in her essay, 'Certain Liberties Have Been Taken with Cleopatra: Female Performance in the *Carry On* Films', in which she argues that the recurrence of actresses across the *Carry On* phenomenon 'undermined any possibility of identifying actress and stereotype'. The genre's dependence on comic stock events and routines rather than coherent characterisation, like the *lazzi* of *commedia dell'arte*, allowed actresses such as Barbara Windsor or Hattie Jacques the opportunity to showcase their individual talents, effectively 'liberating' them from otherwise stereotypical casting.[17] Gray's argument – that viewers of the *Carry On* films identify with the actresses themselves rather than the roles or stereotypes they occupy, and that '[o]ne of the pleasures of watching a *Carry On* was to see familiar faces in new roles' – is broadly applicable to *You Rang, M'Lord?*[18] Although both Perry and Croft remark on the fact that Su Pollard 'just couldn't find the right niche' before *Hi-de-Hi!*, she excels at the portrayal of what we might call the 'gormless, working-class, northern girl', though Peggy Ollerenshaw is clearly a more caricatured representation of this cultural stereotype than Ivy Teasdale.[19] There is more coherence in the construction of both of these characters than in female roles in *Carry On* films – David Croft has described his work as comedy of 'character' more than 'situation', in fact – but the two roles allow their actress to demonstrate her performance range within the limits of the 'Su Pollard' part, providing various opportunities for physical and oral comedy, as well as pathos and drama. Part of the pleasure of *You Rang, M'Lord?*, it seems to me, depends on the audience's observation of what Gray identifies as the 'familiarity' of 'old faces' in different roles, so that a significant component of our enjoyment of Ivy's character is our reflection on Su Pollard's performance within the context of our familiarity with *Hi-de-Hi!*'s Peggy. In the case of minor or non-recurring characters, the simple act of recognition is also a source of viewers' pleasure. My own experience of watching 'A Deed of Gift', for example, was unexpectedly enhanced by my recognition of John Clegg ('Mr La-di-dah Gunner Graham' from *It Ain't Half Hot, Mum*) as the Meldrums' solicitor, Franklin.

To reflect on the nature of this pleasure in recognition, or in the tacit association of actors and performances, across Perry and Croft's four sitcoms, is to explain one of the unique characteristics of *You Rang, M'Lord?*, I think, and to answer some of the charges made by Mark Lewisohn that I quoted at the beginning of this chapter. The series' principal characters, he claims, 'were not loveable; in fact, Alf was quite menacing and James was just too snobbish and unbending a character to generate a response from the audience'.[20] To some extent, this reading of *You Rang, M'Lord?* is borne out by my own analysis of the series, and corroborated by David Croft who admits that it was a 'darker' production than their previous sitcoms. If, as I have argued, the domestic unit within the sitcom – the Meldrum family – remains a largely unsympathetic group of characters, and the surrogate family of work relationships 'below stairs' is apparently composed of characters that are often not 'loveable', then where do we locate the sitcom's 'inside' in which the audience is to be imbricated? Although Lewisohn admits that *You Rang, M'Lord?* was 'far from a ratings disaster', he proposes that its failure 'to attract the level of audiences normally reached by Perry and Croft' is a result of this 'unloveability' – effectively, Perry and Croft's refusal to provide the sitcom with a comfortable 'inside'.[21] I would argue, however, that the 'family' in which the audience is imbricated is not the domestic or work units represented within the narrative of *You Rang, M'Lord?*, but rather the 'metatextual' family of Perry and Croft performers that constitutes a significant part of its cast. The pleasure experienced by the audience through its familiarity with, or recognition of, the sitcom's actors is that of its imbrication within a stable interior. This, if nothing else, testifies to Perry and Croft's achievement: to have fostered not only a distinct style of representation in sitcom that is able to survive, including, in the case of *You Rang, M'Lord?*, significant experimentation with form, but also to have created a company of performers that 'read' across their whole twenty-five-year collaborative career.

Notes

1 Author's interview with David Croft.
2 'A Deed of Gift'.
3 Personal correspondence with Rob Cope, PA to Su Pollard.
4 Vincendeau, *Encyclopedia of European Cinema*, p. 204.
5 Higson, 'The Heritage Film and British Cinema', p. 240.
6 Croft, 'You Have Been Watching', p. 202.
7 'The Phantom Signwriter' and 'A Deed of Gift'.
8 'A Day in the Country' and 'Please Help the Orphans'.
9 'Love and Money'.

10 'Labour or Love'.

11 Lewisohn, *Radio Times Guide to TV Comedy*, p. 737. Healy, 'Were We Being Served?', pp. 255–256.

12 Wagg, 'Social Class and Situation Comedy', p. 15.

13 'The Phantom Signwriter' and 'A Deed of Gift'.

14 'A Day in the Country'.

15 Rigelsford, Brown, and Tibballs, *Are You Being Served?*, p. 17.

16 Croft, 'You Have Been Watching', p. 202.

17 Gray, 'Certain Liberties Have Been Taken with Cleopatra', p. 101.

18 *Ibid.*

19 Perry, *A Stupid Boy*, p. 268.

20 Lewisohn, *Radio Times Guide to TV Comedy*, p. 737.

21 David Croft's autobiography explains *You Rang, M'Lord?*'s lower than usual ratings as a result of imprudent scheduling: 'A Saturday show it was not' (p. 204).

Afterword:
'Well there you are then ...!'

6

The title of this section corresponds to that of the last episode of *You Rang, M'Lord?*, Perry and Croft's final collaboration. It is an expression often used (in the North of England, at least) to provide closure to conversation, and this is the meaning that Perry and Croft intend. All the main characters are neatly provided for: the House of Meldrum continues to decline, with its rubber factory retooled and run as a workers' co-operative by Cissy, as Meldrum himself stands in a dining room largely bare of possessions and toasts their anticipated new prosperity in the upcoming 1930s. A bitter Poppy, in funereal black instead of her usually bright attire, is trapped in an unhappy marriage to Jerry; and Teddy, with a heavily pregnant Rose in tow, is now a successful car salesman. The servants have fared better. Mabel and Henry remain on the staff, now promoted to maid and butler; Mrs Lipton has married Constable Wilson; Alf has started a successful seaside review – the 'Jolly Follies' – and, in purely professional partnership, James and Ivy are about to open a boarding house. 'Well There You Are Then ... !' is a wistful episode, with sad farewells, hints of possible sequels, glimpses of period nostalgia, and the grimly amusing foreshadowing of even more difficult times to come – an entirely appropriate testament to Perry and Croft's work.

I intend for the title of this final section of my book to operate in another way, too; having reached the end of an investigation of Perry and Croft's four sitcoms, we might ask ourselves exactly where *we* are – in other words, what has *Jimmy Perry and David Croft* achieved? There can be little question, I think, of Perry and Croft's own achievement: a twenty-five year career together, in addition to their work apart before, during and after their collaboration; a staggering volume of co-written, directed and produced episodes; a record of strong viewing figures and lasting popular acclaim. But when we make mention of their 'significant contribution' to British televisual history, what do we mean?

As with any book that organises its material on the basis of authorship, this study has sought and found similarities between Perry and Croft's sitcoms, trademarks that establish them as a category of their own. Perry and Croft have an obvious talent for writing comedy for a large ensemble, and for particular performers whose comic strengths they understand. That both writers hail from backgrounds in which theatrical performances with large casts predominate can be no coincidence – variety theatre, pantomimes and concert parties; there are elements of all these traditions throughout Perry and Croft's work. These dynamics cannot be easily accommodated in a domestic context, and so the environment of 'work' becomes their principal territory, in which the complexities of class can be represented and explored. Although Perry and Croft's writing shows some adjustment for a changing audience during their careers, their sitcoms address an 'Everyman': a solid, middle-class amateur, a Mainwaring rather than a Wilson, someone less coarse that Ted Bovis but more down-to-earth than the Meldrums, an individual with more education than BSM Williams but less than Geoffrey Fairbrother, a recognisable 'English type' that belongs very distinctly to the last century.

If there are distinctive characteristics to Perry and Croft's sitcoms, then this book has also registered differences and developments across their writing career that are frequently tied to larger cultural change. Several critics have identified Perry and Croft's work as inherently conservative in its system of values, perhaps because they seem to be anchored in a past constructed in nostalgic terms and therefore appear isolated from contemporary politics. I think that a cultural studies approach to these sitcoms is useful in revealing that this is not necessarily true; *Dad's Army*, to be sure, is not *Till Death Us Do Part*, and *You Rang M'Lord?* is not *Absolutely Fabulous*, but Perry and Croft's sitcoms do, nevertheless, enter into dialogue with the cultural moments in which they were produced. The best example, of course, is *It Ain't Half Hot, Mum*, which has drawn criticism for its representations of race and sexuality. While certainly not a radical statement about racial or sexual politics, the series is obviously structured by the discourses about these categories as they circulated in the late 1960s and early 1970s, even as it purports to be an accurate representation of its mid-century subject. The extent to which Perry and Croft use this as a deliberate strategy is difficult to assess; when I interviewed David Croft he told me that he felt writers often retroactively claimed more credit for the sophistication of their ideas than perhaps was their due. But Perry and Croft, clearly, had a very strong sense of what their intended audiences would find funny, a territory defined largely, as many theorists and practitioners of comedy have remarked, by anxiety about cultural change. As Andy Medhurst writes:

> One of comedy's chief functions, then, is to police the ideological boundaries of a culture, to act as a border guard on the frontiers between the dominant and the subordinate, to keep the power of laughter in the hands of the powerful. Yet at the same time, because comedy is nothing if not contradictory, humour can also be disruptive to the social order, a full-blown challenge or a persistent sniping from the margins, a force for the advocacy of social change, ridiculing power rather than reinforcing it.[1]

Perry and Croft's popularity depends precisely, I think, on this dynamic. Despite the sitcoms' historical locations they deal, collectively, with the issues central to the ideological structures of British cultural identity – class, race, sexuality, gender – as the cultural boundaries between the 'dominant and the subordinate', or between the normative and non-normative, shift across decades.

One of the most unusual aspects of my research for this book was my personal involvement. My relationship to each of Perry and Croft's sitcoms is distinct: I watched both *Dad's Army* and *It Ain't Half Hot, Mum* as part of a family of viewers, though the latter was particularly meaningful to me as I grew into an awareness of its comic strategies and routines – in other words, I 'got' the jokes. My interest in *Hi-de-Hi!* was never strong as an original viewer, since my comic tastes had been otherwise dictated by new traditions appealing to youth culture (the comedy of *The Young Ones*, for example), and I had left England by the time *You Rang M'Lord?* was broadcast, only encountering it as the subject of academic research. Understandably, then, I was able to study *You Rang M'Lord?*, if not with more 'objectivity', then certainly with less personal baggage, than *It Ain't Half Hot, Mum*, which had, in addition to its own implication in the cultural contexts of its time, a further 'layer' of meaning for me. To return briefly to the terms used by Steve Neale and Frank Krutnik, I was compelled to acknowledge my own imbrication in *It Ain't Half Hot, Mum* as a member of its original, 'uncritical' audience. Chapter Three was the most difficult section of this book to write because of this tension between the 'original viewer' and the 'scholarly writer', which returns us to the concept of polysemy: texts, including situation comedies, might mean 'different things to different people', but they also shift in meaning and significance for individuals over time. This is true of any example of mainstream popular culture that we initially encounter as participants rather than as detached observers, and it presents us with richer, more complex, multilayered texts for investigation that demand an acknowledgement of the role of our own subjectivities in the critical process. The recognition of this complexity justifies (should one feel compelled to do so) the serious consideration of texts like Perry and Croft's sitcoms; simply because they are 'popular' does not mean that they are ephemeral, thirty-minute slices of disposable, forgettable mass cultural expression.

Any study has its limitations. In pursuing a cultural studies model largely derived from literary or media studies, I have not spent much time on questions of production or design. About the latter, indeed, there has been very little written; in *Reading Between Designs: Visual Imagery and the Generation of Meaning in The Avengers, The Prisoner, and Doctor Who*, Piers Britton and Simon Barker assert that, with the exception of their book, '[n]o serious, sustained examination of the role of scenic or costume design in the medium [of television] has been attempted', and even their text addresses 'design as a vehicle for ideas rather than design as a process'.[2] Britton and Barker admit the difficulties of writing about design, both in terms of the gap between designers' understanding of their own work and the process of scholarly criticism ('the nature of their art means that designers, unlike scholars, are not intellectually bound by language systems: they do not need to think in a syntactical or critical fashion'), and in terms of the polysemous nature of the visual image.[3] Their point – that '[w]hile certain associations may be well understood by members of the [design's] target audience ... the factors that condition individual viewers' sympathies, or antipathies, are not predictable' – is well demonstrated by a sustained analysis of the range of associative meanings generated by the costume design for Rupert Giles (Anthony Stewart Head) in *Buffy the Vampire Slayer*.[4] Perry and Croft's sitcoms, with their historical settings and meticulous eye for detail, are rich subjects for an analysis of scenic and costume design, especially as those designs reinforce the series' ideas, or, as in the case of *It Ain't Half Hot, Mum* cited in Chapter Three, how design constraints dictate the structures of the sitcoms themselves.

Since this book has mostly attempted to take comedy very seriously, I would like to close on a lighter note. Many writers have attempted to elucidate the process of comedy or the means by which laughter is generated, but I have never really found a convincing critical assessment of that most evanescent quality of successful comedy: good comic timing. And perhaps this is how it should be. In one of *You Rang, M'Lord?*'s episodes ('Trouble at Mill'), George Meldrum's family expresses some surprise that he knows the Prime Minister, Stanley Baldwin, well enough to invite him to dinner. 'We see a lot of each other in the Turkish baths', he replies, with Donald Hewlett's perfect, deadpan delivery. In *Hi-de-Hi!*'s 'Hey Diddle Diddle', Gladys bursts in on Geoffrey Fairbrother as he is about to pull on a pair of trousers. Simon Cadell holds them modestly in front of him, and then, after a perfectly timed pause, reaches down and slowly zips up the fly. Neither of these moments sounds like much from its description, of course. But each of them, like countless other perfectly timed comic moments, demonstrates the unique combination of an actor's performance, experienced direction, and the superlative writing that is the particular talent of Jimmy Perry and David Croft.

Notes

1 Medhurst, 'Introduction', p. 16.
2 Britton and Barker, *Reading Between Designs*, pp. 1, 3.
3 *Ibid.*, p. 7.
4 *Ibid.*, pp. 12–13.

List of television programmes

Dad's Army (BBC, 1968–77)

Writers: Jimmy Perry and David Croft; Directors: Harold Snoad (series 1–8), Bob Spiers (series 9); Producer: David Croft.

Series 1: 6 episodes

'The Man and the Hour' (31 Jul 68)
'Museum Piece' (7 Aug 68)
'Command Decision' (14 Aug 68)
'The Enemy within the Gates' (21 Aug 68)
'The Showing Up of Corporal Jones' (28 Aug 68)
'Shooting Pains' (4 Sep 68)

Series 2: 6 episodes

'Operation Kilt' (1 Mar 69)
'The Battle of Godfrey's Cottage' (8 Mar 69)
'The Loneliness of the Long Distance Walker' (15 Mar 69)
'Sergeant Wilson's Little Secret' (22 Mar 69)
'A Stripe for Frazer' (29 Mar 69)
'Under Fire' (5 Apr 69)

Series 3: 14 episodes

'The Armoured Might of Lance Corporal Jones' (11 Sep 69)
'Battle School' (18 Sep 69)
'The Lion Has 'Phones' (25 Sep 69)
'The Bullet is not for Firing' (2 Oct 69)
'Something Nasty in the Vault' (9 Oct 69)
'Room at the Bottom' (16 Oct 69)
'Big Guns' (23 Oct 69)

'The Day the Balloon Went Up' (30 Oct 69)
'War Dance' (6 Nov 69)
'Menace from the Deep' (13 Nov 69)
'Branded' (20 Nov 69)
'Man Hunt' (27 Nov 69)
'No Spring for Frazer' (4 Dec 69)
'Sons of the Sea' (11 Dec 69)

Series 4: 13 episodes

'The Big Parade' (25 Sep 70)
'Don't Forget the Diver' (2 Oct 70)
'Boots, Boots, Boots' (9 Oct 70)
'Sgt – Save My Boy!' (16 Oct 70)
'Don't Fence Me In' (23 Oct 70)
'Absent Friends' (30 Oct 70)
'Put That Light Out' (6 Nov 70)
'The Two and a Half Feathers' (13 Nov 70)
'Mum's Army' (20 Nov 70)
'The Test' (27 Nov 70)
'A. Wilson (Manager)?' (4 Dec 70)
'Uninvited Guests' (11 Dec 70)
'Fallen Idol' (18 Dec 70)
Christmas Special: 'Battle Of The Giants!' (27 Dec 71)

Series 5: 13 episodes

'Asleep in the Deep' (6 Oct 72)
'Keep Young and Beautiful' (13 Oct 72)
'A Soldier's Farewell' (20 Oct 72)
'Getting the Bird' (27 Oct 72)
'The Desperate Drive of Corporal Jones' (3 Nov 72)
'If the Cap Fits' (10 Nov 72)
'The King was in His Counting House' (17 Nov 72)
'All Is Safely Gathered In' (24 Nov 72)
'When Did You Last See Your Money?' (1 Dec 72)
'Brain Versus Brawn' (8 Dec 72)
'A Brush with the Law' (15 Dec 72)
'Round and Round went the Great Big Wheel' (22 Dec 72)
'Time On My Hands' (29 Dec 72)

Series 6: 7 episodes

'The Deadly Attachment' (31 Oct 73)
'My British Buddy' (7 Nov 73)

'The Royal Train' (14 Nov 73)
'We Know Our Onions' (21 Nov 73)
'The Honourable Man' (28 Nov 73)
'Things That Go Bump in the Night' (5 Dec 73)
'The Recruit' (12 Dec 73)

Series 7: 6 episodes

'Everybody's Trucking' (15 Nov 74)
'A Man of Action' (22 Nov 74)
'Gorilla Warfare' (29 Nov 74)
'The Godiva Affair' (6 Dec 74)
'The Captain's Car' (13 Dec 74)
'Turkey Dinner' (23 Dec 74)

Series 8: 8 episodes

'Ring Dem Bells' (5 Sep 75)
'When You've Got To Go' (12 Sep 75)
'Is There Honey Still For Tea?' (19 Sep 75)
'Come In, Your Time Is Up' (26 Sep 75)
'High Finance' (3 Oct 75)
'The Face on the Poster' (10 Oct 75)
Christmas Special: 'My Brother and I' (26 Dec 75)
Christmas Special: 'The Love of Three Oranges' (26 Dec 76)

Series 9: 6 episodes

'Wake Up Walmington' (2 Oct 77)
'The Making of Private Pike' (9 Oct 77)
'Knights of Madness' (16 Oct 77)
'The Miser's Hoard' (23 Oct 77)
'Number Engaged' (30 Oct 77)
'Never Too Old' (6 Nov 77)

It Ain't Half Hot, Mum (BBC, 1974–81)

Writers: Jimmy Perry and David Croft; Directors: Bob Spiers, Ray Butt, Paul Bishop and John Kilby; Producers: David Croft and Graeme Muir.

Series 1: 8 episodes

'Meet the Gang' (3 Jan 74)
'My Lovely Boy' (10 Jan 74)

'The Mutiny of the Punkah-Wallahs' (17 Jan 74)
'A Star Is Born' (24 Jan 74)
'The Jungle Patrol' (31 Jan 74)
'It's a Wise Child' (7 Feb 74)
'The Road to Bannu' (14 Feb 74)
'The Inspector Calls' (21 Feb 74)

Series 2: 8 episodes

'Showing the Flag' (2 Jan 75)
'Down in the Jungle' (9 Jan 75)
'The Natives are Revolting' (16 Jan 75)
'Cabaret Time' (23 Jan 75)
'The Curse of the Sadhu' (30 Jan 75)
'Forbidden Fruits' (6 Feb 75)
'Has Anyone Seen My Cobra?' (13 Feb 75)
'The Night of the Thugs' (20 Feb 75)

Series 3: 6 episodes

'The Supremo Show' (2 Jan 76)
'Mind My Maharajah' (9 Jan 76)
'Bang goes the Maharajah' (16 Jan 76)
'The Grand Illusion' (23 Jan 76)
'Pale Hands I Love' (30 Jan 76)
'Don't Take the Mickey' (6 Feb 76)

Series 4: 8 episodes

'Monsoon Madness' (2 Nov 76)
'Kidnapped in the Khyber' (9 Nov 76)
'A Fate Worse Than Death' (16 Nov 76)
'Ticket to Blighty' (23 Nov 76)
'Lofty's Little Friend' (30 Nov 76)
'Flight to Jawani' (7 Dec 76)
'We Are Not Amused' (14 Dec 76)
'Twenty-One Today' (21 Dec 76)

Series 5: 6 episodes

'Front Line Entertainers' (25 Oct 77)
'Bridge over the River Hipong' (1 Nov 77)
'The Pay-Off' (8 Nov 77)
'Puddings from Heaven' (15 Nov 77)

'The Superstar' (22 Nov 77)
'The Eternal Quadrangle' (29 Nov 77)

Series 6: 7 episodes

'The Stars Look Down' (23 Oct 78)
'The Big League' (30 Oct 78)
'The Big Payroll Snatch' (6 Nov 78)
'The Dhobi-Wallahs' (13 Nov 78)
'Lead, Kindly Light' (20 Nov 78)
'Holidays at Home' (27 Nov 78)
'Caught Short' (4 Dec 78)

Series 7: 6 episodes

'That's Entertainment?' (17 Oct 80)
'The Guinea Pigs' (24 Oct 80)
'Dog in the Manger' (31 Oct 80)
'The Great Broadcast' (7 Nov 80)
'Class of 1945' (14 Nov 80)
'Star Commandos' (21 Nov 80)

Series 8: 7 episodes

'Gloria's Finest Hour' (23 Jul 81)
'Money Talks' (30 Jul 81)
'Aquastars' (6 Aug 81)
'The Last Warrior' (13 Aug 81)
'Never the Twain Shall Meet' (20 Aug 81)
'The Long Road Home' (27 Aug 81)
'The Last Roll Call' (3 Sep 81)

Hi-de-Hi! (BBC, 1980–88)

Writers: Jimmy Perry and David Croft; Directors: John Kirby, David Croft, Robin Carr and Mike Stephens; Producers: David Croft, John Kilby and Mike Stephens.
Pilot: 'Hey Diddle Diddle' (1 Jan 80)

Series 1: 6 episodes

'Desire in the Mickey Mouse Grotto' (26 Feb 81)
'The Beauty Queen Affair' (5 Mar 81)

'The Partridge Season' (12 Mar 81)
'The Day of Reckoning' (19 Mar 81)
'Charity Begins at Home' (26 Mar 81)
'No Dogs Allowed' (2 Apr 81)

Series 2: 6 episodes

'If Wet – in the Ballroom' (29 Nov 81)
'Peggy's Big Chance' (6 Dec 81)
'Lift Up Your Minds' (13 Dec 81)
'On with the Motley' (20 Dec 81)
'A Night Not To Remember' (27 Dec 81)
'Sausages or Limelight' (3 Jan 82)

Series 3: 13 episodes

'Nice People with Nice Manners' (31 Oct 82)
'Carnival Time' (7 Nov 82)
'A Matter of Conscience' (14 Nov 82)
'The Pay-Off' (21 Nov 82)
'Trouble and Strife '(28 Nov 82)
'Stripes' (5 Dec 82)
'Co-Respondent's Course' (12 Dec 82)
'It's a Blue World' (19 Dec 82)
'Eruptions' (26 Dec 82)
'The Society Entertainer' (2 Jan 83)
'Sing You Sinners' (9 Jan 83)
'Maplin Intercontinental' (16 Jan 83)
'All Change' (23 Jan 83)

Series 4: 7 episodes

'Concessions' (27 Nov 83)
'Save Our Heritage' (4 Dec 83)
'Empty Saddles' (11 Dec 83)
'The Marriage Settlement' (18 Dec 83)
'The Graven Image' (8 Jan 84)
'Peggy's Penfriend' (15 Jan 84)
'The Epidemic' (22 Jan 84)

Series 5: 6 episodes

'Together Again' (3 Nov 84)
'Ted at the Helm' (10 Nov 84)
'Opening Day' (17 Nov 84)

'Off with the Motley' (24 Nov 84)
'Hey Diddle Diddle, Who's on the Fiddle?' (1 Dec 84)
'Raffles' (25 Dec 84)

Series 6: 7 episodes

'The Great Cat Robbery' (25 Dec 85)
'It's Murder' (5 Jan 86)
'Who Killed Mr Partridge?' (12 Jan 86)
'Spaghetti Galore' (19 Jan 86)
'A Lack of Punch' (26 Jan 86)
'Ivory Castles in the Air' (9 Feb 86)
'Man Trap' (16 Feb 86)

Series 7: 6 episodes

'Pigs Might Fly' (8 Nov 86)
'The New Broom' (15 Nov 86)
'Orphan of the Storm' (22 Nov 86)
'God Bless Our Family' (6 Dec 86)
'Only the Brave' (13 Dec 86)
'September Song' (27 Dec 86)

Series 8: 6 episodes

'Tell It to the Marines' (26 Dec 87)
'Marry Go Round' (2 Jan 88)
'The Perils of Peggy' (9 Jan 88)
'Let Them Eat Cake' (16 Jan 88)
'Wedding Bells' (23 Jan 88)
'The Wind of Change' (30 Jan 88)

You Rang, M'Lord? (BBC, 1988–93)

Writers: Jimmy Perry and David Croft; Directors: David Croft and Roy
Gould; Producer: David Croft.
Pilot: 'You Rang, M'Lord?' (29 Dec 88)

Series 1: 5 episodes

'The Phantom Sign Writer' (14 Jan 90)
'A Deed of Gift' (21 Jan 90)
'Love and Money' (28 Jan 90)

'Fair Shares' (4 Feb 90)
'Beg, Borrow or Steal' (11 Feb 90)

Series 2: 7 episodes

'Labour or Love' (11 Nov 90)
'Trouble at Mill' (18 Nov 90)
'Money Talks' (25 Nov 90)
'The Meldrum Vases' (2 Dec 90)
'The Wounds of War' (9 Dec 90)
'Stranger in the Night' (16 Dec 90)
'Royal Flush' (23 Dec 90)

Series 3: 7 episodes

'Please Help the Orphans' (10 Nov 91)
'Current Affairs' (17 Nov 91)
'Mrs Lipton's Nasty Turn' (24 Nov 91)
'Meet the Workers' (1 Dec 91)
'Gretna Green or Bust' (8 Dec 91)
'The Night of Reckoning' (15 Dec 91)
'A Day in the Country' (22 Dec 91)

Series 4: 6 episodes

'Yes Sir, That's My Baby' (20 Mar 93)
'Requiem for a Parrot' (27 Mar 93)
'Come to the Ball' (3 Apr 93)
'The Truth Revealed' (10 Apr 93)
'Fall of the House Of Meldrum' (17 Apr 93)
'Well There You Are Then ... !' (24 Apr 93)

Bibliography

Allen, Robert C. (ed). *Channels of Discourse*, Chapel Hill, NC, University of North Carolina Press, 1987.

Apter, Michael J. '*Fawlty Towers*: A Reversal Theory Analysis of a Popular Television Comedy Series', *Journal of Popular Culture*, 16.3, Winter 1982, 128–138.

Baker, Roger. *Drag: A History of Female Impersonation in the Performing Arts*, New York, New York University Press, 1994.

Bakhtin, Mikhail. *Rabelais and His World*, trans. Hélène Iswolsky, Bloomington, IN, Indiana University Press, 1984.

Berger, Arthur Asa. *Narratives in Popular Culture, Media, and Everyday Life*, London, Sage Publications, 1997.

Black, Peter. *The Biggest Aspidistra in the World*, London, BBC, 1972.

Bourne, Stephen. *Black in the British Frame: Black People in British Film and Television 1896–1996*, London, Cassell, 1998.

Boyd-Bowman, Susan. 'Back to Camp', in Jim Cook (ed), *BFI Dossier No. 17: Television Sitcom*, London, BFI, 1982, 56–65.

Briggs, Asa. *The BBC: The First Fifty Years*, Oxford, Oxford University Press, 1985.

Briggs, Asa. *A History of Broadcasting in the United Kingdom*, 5 volumes, Oxford, Oxford University Press, 1961–95.

Britton, Piers D. and Simon J. Barker. *Reading Between Designs: Visual Imagery and the Generation of Meaning in The Avengers, The Prisoner, and Doctor Who*, Austin, TX, University of Texas Press, 2003.

Buscombe, Edward (ed). *British Television: A Reader*, Oxford, Oxford University Press, 2000.

Cardwell, Sarah. *Adaptation Revisited*, Manchester, Manchester University Press, 2002.

Cook, Jim (ed). *BFI Dossier No. 17: Television Sitcom*, London, BFI, 1982.

Cook, Jim. 'Narrative Comedy, Character and Performance', in Jim Cook (ed), *BFI Dossier No. 17: Television Sitcom*, London, BFI, 1982, 13–18.

Corner, John (ed). *Popular Television in Britain: Studies in Cultural History*, London, BFI, 1991.

Crisell, Andrew. *An Introductory History of British Broadcasting*, London,

Routledge, 1997.

Crisell, Andrew. *Understanding Radio*, London, Routledge, 1994.

Croft, David. 'You Have Been Watching', unpublished manuscript.

Crowther, Bruce and Mike Pinfold. *Bring Me Laughter: Four Decades of TV Comedy*, London, Columbus Books, 1987.

Curtis, Barry. 'Aspects of Sitcom', in Jim Cook (ed), *BFI Dossier No. 17: Television Sitcom*, London, BFI, 1982, 4–12.

Curtis, Richard, Ben Elton, John Lloyd and Rowan Atkinson. *Blackadder: The Whole Damn Dynasty, 1485–1917*, London, Penguin, 1999.

Daniels, Therese and Jane Gerson (eds). *The Colour Black*, London, BFI, 1989.

Dyer, Richard (ed). *Gays and Film*, London, BFI, 1980.

Dyer, Richard, Christine Geraghty, Marion Jordan, Terry Lovell, Richard Patterson and John Stewart. *Coronation Street*, London, BFI, 1981.

Eaton, Mick. 'Television Situation Comedy', *Screen*, 19.4, Winter 1978–79, 61–89.

Ellis, John. *Visible Fictions*, London, Routledge, 1982.

Fawkes, Richard. *Fighting for a Laugh: Entertaining the British and American Armed Forces 1939–1946*, London, Macdonald and Jane's, 1978.

Feuer, Jane. 'Genre Study and Television', in Robert C. Allen (ed), *Channels of Discourse*, Chapel Hill, NC, University of North Carolina Press, 1987, 113–133.

Fiddy, Dick. *Missing Believed Wiped: Searching for the Lost Treasures of British Television*, London, BFI, 2001.

French, Philip. 'The Golden Shows of Radio Comedy', *The Listener*, 3, December 1970.

Geraghty, Christine and David Lusted (eds). *The Television Studies Handbook*, London, Arnold, 1998.

Goddard, Peter. ' "Hancock's Half-Hour": A Watershed in British Television Comedy', in John Corner (ed), *Popular Television in Britain: Studies in Cultural History*, London, BFI, 1991, 75–89.

Gray, Frances. 'Certain Liberties Have Been Taken with Cleopatra: Female Performance in the *Carry On* Films', in Stephen Wagg (ed), *Because I Tell a Joke or Two: Comedy, Politics, and Social Difference*, London: Routledge, 1998, 94–110.

Gray, Frances. *Women and Laughter*, Charlottesville, University Press of Virginia, 1994.

Grote, David. *The End of Comedy: The Sitcom and the Comedic Tradition*, Hamden, CT, Archon Books, 1983.

Hall, Stuart. 'The Whites of Their Eyes: Racist Ideologies and the Media', in Paul Marris and Sue Thornham (eds), *Media Studies: A Reader*, New York, New York University Press, 2000, 271–282.

Healy, Murray. 'Were We Being Served? Homosexual Representation in Popular British comedy', *Screen*, 36.3, Autumn 1995, 243–256.

Higson, Andrew. 'The Heritage Film and the British Cinema', in Andrew Higson (ed), *Dissolving Views: Key Writings on British Cinema*, London, Casell, 1996, 232–248.

Hill, John. *Sex, Class and Realism: British Cinema 1956–1963*, London, BFI, 1986.

Holland, Patricia. *The Television Handbook*, London, Routledge, 1997, 2000.

Hughes, John Graven. *The Greasepaint War*, London, New English Library, 1976.

Hunt, Leon. *British Low Culture: From Safari Suits to Sexploitation*, London, Routledge, 1998.

Kamm, Jürgen. ' "Oh what a Funny War": Representations of World War II in British TV Comedy', in Wolfgang Görtschacher and Holger Klein, *Modern War on Stage and Screen/Der moderne Krieg auf der Bühne*, Lewiston, NY, Edwin Mellon Press, 1997, 265–283.

Kirkham, Patricia and Beverly Skaggs. '*Absolutely Fabulous*: Absolutely Feminist?', in Christine Geraghty and David Lusted (eds), *The Television Studies Handbook*, London, Arnold, 1998, 286–298.

Koseluk, Gregory. *Great Brit-Coms: British Television Situation Comedy*, Jefferson, NC, McFarland and Company Inc., 2000.

Langdon-Davies, John (ed). *The Home Guard Training Manual*, revised by General Sir Alexander Godley, Brooklyn, NY, Chemical Publishing Company Inc., 1942.

Lewisohn, Mark, *The Radio Times Guide to TV Comedy*, London, BBC, 1998.

Lovell, Terry. 'A Genre of Social Disruption', in Jim Cook (ed), *BFI Dossier No. 17: Television Sitcom*, London, BFI, 1982, 19–31.

Mackenzie, S. P. *The Home Guard: A Military and Political History*, Oxford, Oxford University Press, 1995.

Marc, David. *Comic Visions: Television Comedy and American Culture*, Boston, Unwin Hyman, 1989.

Marc, David. *Demographic Vistas: Television in American Culture*, Philadelphia, University of Pennsylvania Press, 1984.

Marwick, Arthur. *A History of the Modern British Isles, 1914–1999*, Oxford, Blackwell Publishers, Ltd, 2000.

McCann, Graham. *Dad's Army: The Story of a Classic Television Show*, London, Fourth Estate, 2001.

Medhurst, Andy and Lucy Tuck. 'The Gender Game', in Jim Cook (ed), *BFI Dossier No. 17: Television Sitcom*, London, BFI, 1982, 43–55.

Medhurst, Andy. 'Introduction', in Therese Daniels and Jane Gerson (eds), *The Colour Black*, London, BFI, 1989, 15–21.

Neale, Steve and Frank Krutnik. *Popular Film and Television Comedy*, London, Routledge, 1990.

O'Connor, Alan (ed). *Raymond Williams on Television: Selected Writings*, London, Routledge, 1989.

Palmer, Jerry. *The Logic of the Absurd*, London, BFI, 1987.

Perry, Jimmy. *A Stupid Boy*, London, Century, 2002.

Pertwee, Bill. *Dad's Army: The Making of a Television Legend*, London, Pavilion, 1997.

Pines, Jim. *Black and White in Colour: Black People on British Television Since 1936*, London, BFI, 1992.

Potter, Dennis. 'Where Comedy is King', *Sunday Times*, 16 October 1977.

Putterman, Barry. *On Television and Comedy: Essays on Style, Theme, Performer and Writer*, Jefferson, NC, McFarland and Company, Inc., 1995.

Rigelsford, Adrian, Anthony Brown and Geoff Tibballs. *Are You Being Served?*, San Francisco, KQED Books, 1995.

Self, David (ed). *Situation Comedy*, London, Hutchison, 1980.

Shields, Rob. *Places on the Margin: Alternative Geographies of Modernity*, London, Routledge, 1991.

Stallybrass, Peter and Allon White. *The Poetics and Politics of Transgression*, Ithaca, NY, Cornell University Press, 1986.

Stam, Robert. *Subversive Pleasures: Bakhtin, Cultural Criticism, and Film*, London and Baltimore, Johns Hopkins University Press, 1989.

Taflinger, Richard Francis. 'Sitcom: A Survey and Findings of Analysis of the Television Situation Comedy', unpublished PhD dissertation, Washington State University, 1980.

Taylor, Eric. *Showbiz Goes to War*, London, Robert Hale, 1992.

Taylor, Paul Alan. 'Theories of Laughter and the Production of Television Comedy', unpublished PhD thesis, Centre for Mass Communications Research, University of Leicester, 1985.

Took, Barry. *Laughter in the Air*, London, Robson Books, 1981.

Turner, Graeme. *British Cultural Studies: An Introduction*, London, Routledge, 1996.

Vincendeau, Ginette. *Encyclopedia of European Cinema*, London, BFI, 1995.

Wagg, Stephen (ed). *Because I Tell a Joke or Two: Comedy, Politics and Social Difference*, London, Routledge, 1998.

Wagg, Stephen. 'Social Class and Situation Comedy in British Television', in Stephen Wagg (ed), *Because I Tell a Joke or Two: Comedy, Politics and Social Difference*, London, Routledge, 1998.

Webber, Richard. *Dad's Army: A Celebration*, London, Virgin, 1997.

Wells, Catharine. *East with ENSA*, London and New York, The Radcliffe Press, 2001.

Wheen, Francis. *Television*, London, Century, 1985.

Wheldon, Huw. *The Achievement of Television*, London, BBC, 1975.

Williams, Raymond. *Television: Technology and Cultural Form*, New York, Schoken Books, 1975.

Wilmut, Roger (ed). *Monty Python's Flying Circus: Just the Words*, 2 volumes, London, Methuen, 1989.

Wilmut, Roger. *Kindly Leave the Stage: The Stage History of Variety, 1910–1960*, London, Methuen, 1985.

Wilmut, Roger. *Tony Hancock – Artiste*, London, Methuen, 1978.

Wilson, Tony. *Watching Television: Hermeneutics, Reception and Popular Culture*, Cambridge, Polity Press, 1993.

Young, Lola. *Fear of the Dark: 'Race', Gender and Sexuality in the Cinema*, London, Routledge, 1996.

Index